M000308575

KATHLEEN FERRELL

FEAR NOT! WALK-IN-JOY

Stepping Through Your Obstacles to Joyous Living

The World Ignites 3

The Body Grows 2 4

Paul's Conversion
Acts 22:3-16

Conversion of Lydia and
the Jailer   Acts 16:11-34

The Magic Yearning

The Plague from Within 6

The Prodigal Son
Luke 15:11-32

5 FEAR

7 FEAR   FEAR

The Pharisee and the Tax Collector
Luke 18:9-14

13

The Heroine's Rescue

Frozen to this World by Fear

All the World is a 12 Stage for Fear

Paul's Final Letter Before Dying
2 Timothy 1:3-14

The Rich Young Man
Mark 10:17-31

Ananias and Sapphira
Acts 4:32-5:11

Heavenly Treasure

KATHLEEN FERRELL

FEAR NOT!
WALK-IN-JOY

Stepping Through Your Obstacles to Joyous Living

Fear not! Walk in Joy

For information about this title or to order other books and/or electronic media, contact
the publisher:

Pure Joy

Pure Joy Publishing
P.O. Box 1706
Stockton, CA 95201

Fearnotwalkinjoy.com
Fearnotwalkinjoy@gmail.com

Library of Congress Control Number: 2012935348
ISBN: 978-0-9852845-0-3
Printed in the United States of America
Cover photo: David Ferrell/Bethany Bender

With Gratitude

To Renee, Cathy, Sally, Dave, Dan, Amy, Richard, Dee Ann, and all the many who have strengthened me and prayed for this work

To Bethany for translating my sketches into beautiful illustrations and Emily Epperson for her cheerful tutoring

To Wayne and Jason Jackson, for their patient and scholarly Bible teaching over these many years

To Teresa Hampton, who encouraged me at a moment that I needed it most

To my wonderful Dad, whose love and devotion gives me courage

To my God-given sons, Ethan and Jordan

To my husband, David, who stepped out thirty-two years ago and shared with me the gospel of Jesus Christ

Table of Contents

1   *A Heroine's Journey through Fear* – *Joy amidst the Fear of the unknown*   1
    The shepherds who came to worship Jesus (Luke 2:1-16)

2   *The Perfect Fear Storm* – *A windstorm of thought*   21
    Jesus calms a storm (Mark 4:35-41)

3   *The World Ignites* – *Pushing through Fear to embrace a new life*   41
    Paul's conversion (Acts 22:3-16)

4   *The Body Grows* – *Following the Bible Map through Fear*   59
    Conversion of Lydia and the jailer (Acts 16:11-34)

5   *The Magic Yearning* – *Satan and the power of suggestion*   79
    The prodigal son (Luke 15:11-32)

6   *The Plague from Within* – *Fearful insecurity that sickens*   99
    The Pharisee and the tax collector (Luke 18:9-14)

7   *Predators on the Savanna* – *Fears from the sensual world*   119
    Simon and the woman in repentance (Luke 7:36-50)

8   *Frightened Little Women* – *Fear-driven decision making*   141
    Lot's daughters (Genesis 18:22–19:29)

9   *The Long-Abandoned Garden* – *Fear of rejection that paralyzes*   167
    Parable of the talents (Matthew 25:14-30)

10 *The Desert Crossing of Life* – *Fears about our health*   187
     A woman with an issue of blood (Mark 5:25-34)

11 *Frozen to this World by Fear* – *Fearful attachment to things*   209
     The rich young man (Mark 10:17-31)

12 *All the World is a Stage for Fear* – *Fear that pushes us to lie*   231
     Ananias and Sapphira (Acts 4:32-5:11)

13 *The Heroine's Rescue* – *The Fear of death*   253
     Paul's last words to Timothy (2 Timothy 1:3-14)

Notes   273

Bibliography   279

Foreword

 ust as the very air we breathe goes frequently unnoticed until we are
forced to come to grips with its importance and power, so FEAR is an
incredibly powerful and invasive force whose damaging tentacles have affected
us all. Kathleen has, in great boldness and honesty, undertaken to reveal its
real influence and destructive nature in such a way to help us all control this
beast. May we all benefit from this journey.

— Dan Jensen

Preface

*I*f Jesus' earthly Journey had been filmed, we would be able to see His expressions and hear His tone of voice as He painted truths inside the hearts of those He touched. The camera would have zoomed in on His face as He felt compassion for the woman with the issue of blood, or pulled back to a wide angle to watch that rich young man turn his back and walk away from Him. How blessed we are that Jesus' interactions with the Fearful are recorded for us in Technicolor word pictures in the Bible! As He embodied the Love of the Father in His every gentle word and gesture, He changed the course of our Fear-driven world.

Overwhelming Fear thunders beneath our behavior when we are unaware of its power. In our haste to prove that we trust in God—we often plug our ears to what that Fear can teach us, and do not stop to admit, "I am afraid." "When I am afraid, I put my trust in you" (Psalm 56:3).

As you grow to see Fear as incredible information about yourself and others, you open a marvelous gift to be used in your life. When you choose to look at a Fearful experience as a learning gift, you add new insights to your knapsack of wisdom as you walk your life Journey.

Fear not! Walk in Joy contains research and stories to help you see your life Journey, and the Journeys of others, as glorious opportunities to Joyfully hold the Lord's hand while stepping through earthly troubles and hardships. Unless specified, all names and stories are fiction, and are included in this study for purposes of illustration.

Some chapters bring you God's comforting arms wrapped around you when you are deeply frightened (Chapters 2, 4, 5, 8, 13). Other chapters may challenge you to face your personal responsibility when you feel Fear (Chapters 3, 6, 7, 9–12). Within that comfort and challenge, please know that I wrestle with living this same balance every day. My daily Journey is flawed and struggling, and I often land in the mud asking the Lord's forgiveness for my hasty words and actions.

A fictional Heroine's story is written alongside this study in hopes that by watching her survive the labyrinth of choices, you might remember that we all walk a Journey through terrifying obstacles. The immensely powerful forces of Joy, Love, Integrity, and Gratitude are capitalized as these ideals provide the illumination energy for deciphering the gifts beneath your Fear. More than 300 years ago, John Bunyan personified these powers with capital letters in *Pilgrim's Progress*. And while it may take some adjustment for you to read them capitalized, hopefully your awareness will be raised concerning the force of these virtues.

As someone who dearly loves you gives you the exact gift you wanted or needed, God provides help when you are learning from Fear growth experiences. He studies and knows you and tutors you in the skills you need to thrive—just where you are. He Loves you so much that He will keep gifting you over and over . . . until your last breath.

~ 1 ~
A Heroine's Journey Through Fear
Joy amidst the Fear of the unknown
The shepherds who came to worship Jesus (Luke 2:1-16)

*O*nce upon a time, a child drew her first breath of air on this planet, and everything changed. Her uniqueness was established the moment the one sperm and one egg united to create her, and that same combination will never occur again. Just as the first man was given life by God's breath, the exact soul the Lord breathed into her will never be given to another. She is perfectly designed for her one-way Journey, and is not here by chance.

The Journey of her life is a story of Heroism, Cowardice, Fear and Joy. Rising up against monumental adversity, she becomes a Heroine by serving her Divine purpose—glorifying the King. There is no royal blood in a Heroine's veins, for the courageous are born in hospitals, huts, and back rooms. Greatness is never thrust upon her, but adversity is. Her title is only bestowed by her King, who has watched her meet with danger and overcome it.

Telling a Heroine's story is really telling your story, for the obstacles and choices that she endures will also be presented to you on your life Journey. If you choose a Heroine's pathway in the labyrinth of your life, you will need to make daily choices of valor. The deepest desire to be useful to the King brings the insight that your Divine purpose is greater than your fleshly life. No sacrifice on your part can touch the sacrifice that the King himself has given. Serving the

1

King means working to overcome adversity and battling through hardship—to glorify His Cause. Surmounting dangers and fighting through misfortunes creates your triumph and victory. Without hardships, you have no pathway to be crowned a Heroine.

Great crusades are not accomplished in failure. Crippling Fear of the unknown stands as a wall of foes in the pathway of anyone seeking to serve the King. Challenges may entice you to drop your banner in the dirt, turn and retreat, but your story is not a story of survival, it is a story of great Love. At each challenge, as you work through your Fear and wear the armor of His Love, the King blesses your Journey with boundless Joy!

In those days a decree went out from Caesar Augustus that all the world should be registered. This was the first registration when Quirinius was governor of Syria. And all went to be registered, each to his own town. And Joseph also went up from Galilee, from the town of Nazareth, to Judea, to the city of David, which is called Bethlehem, because he was of the house and lineage of David, to be registered with Mary, his betrothed, who was with child. And while they were there, the time came for her to give birth. And she gave birth to her firstborn son and wrapped him in swaddling cloths and laid him in a manger, because there was no place for them in the inn. And in the same region there were shepherds out in the field, keeping watch over their flock by night. And an angel of the Lord appeared to them, and the glory of the Lord shone around them, and they were filled with fear. And the angel said to them, "Fear not, for behold, I bring you good news of great joy that will be for all the people. For unto you is born this day in the city of David a Savior, who is Christ the Lord. And this will be a sign for you: you will find a baby wrapped in swaddling cloths and lying in a manger." And suddenly there was with the angel a multitude of the heavenly host praising God and saying, "Glory to God in the highest, and on earth peace among those with whom he is pleased!"

When the angels went away from them into heaven, the shepherds said to one another, "Let us go over to Bethlehem and see this thing that has happened, which the Lord has made known to us." And they went with haste and found Mary and Joseph, and the baby lying in a manger (Luke 2:1-16).

Perhaps it was extraordinarily still on that special night. Maybe the shepherds were gazing at the astonishing star above, as they leaned on their staffs and watched over their woolly charges. Without warning, the quiet predictability of their lives was pierced open by the angel of the Lord and **His glory**. For thousands of years the world waited to hear that the Son of God, the Messiah, the Deliverer was among us. "Fear not, for behold, I bring you good news of great joy that will be for all people." The Saviour of the world has come! The heavenly messenger reassured the shepherds: "Do not be afraid! This is great news!" *God knew that their human anxiety would be overwhelming and did not want this glorious moment diminished by Fear.*

The shepherds thoughts may have swirled with Fear—"What is happening? An angel is telling *us* that the Messiah is here?" Shepherds were considered lowly and "contaminated" people by the orthodox Jews, for they lived with their lice and tick infested sheep. Yet, the glory of God shone around *them!* Those "unclean," yet pure-hearted men who cared for the littlest of lambs served a Divine purpose as the first to bow and worship Jesus, the Lamb of God.

When God says, "Don't be afraid," He gives a reason! Trust in Him is not a blind loyalty oath. Hundreds of times throughout the Bible, God says, "Fear not! Do not be afraid!" and shares *the reason to trust Him and not be frightened.* The angel proclaimed the magnificent reason to those humble shepherds, "I bring you good news of great joy. Jesus Christ is born!"

The shepherds could now testify and carry the message that changed the history of the world. So often, God uses those who are willing, but unlikely, to serve His Cause. Months earlier, when the angel appeared to the virgin Mary and told her that she would bear the Christ child, he said, "Do not be afraid, Mary, for you have found favor with God" (Luke 1:26-37). Her godly character was evidenced in her response, "Behold, I am the servant of the Lord, let it be to me according to your word" (Luke 1:38). Joseph was told in a dream, "[D]o not fear to take Mary as your wife, for that which is conceived in her is from the Holy Spirit" (Matt. 1:20). Mary and Joseph had been selected to nurture the son of God, who would bring salvation to the world. What exceptional qualities this young woman and man displayed by dealing with their Fear of the unknown, and embracing their new life with trusting Joy.

As you read this book in the 21st century, remember that just like those shepherds and Mary and Joseph, God Loves *you* and does not want *you* crippled by a life of Fear. The King did *not* want His beloved children to be Fearful when he announced the birth of Jesus Christ! As He *knew* them and guided them through their Fear, so He will guide you, if you will believe that life's one-way Journey is about serving Him (Eph. 6:10-20). *The King whom you serve has no equal* and cannot be conquered, for He is Master of the Universe. *He has no Fear* and cannot be defeated. A true Heroine thrives under the King's protection, for His Love helps her grow through Fear and walk in Joy! "For our heart is glad in him, because we trust in his holy name" (Psalm 33:21).

WHAT IS FEAR?

If a loud noise startles an infant, he lets out an ear-piercing cry and flails his arms. His Fear of the unknown is displayed instantly! If a child is picked on or scolded for being afraid, he learns to hide his Fears in order to gain acceptance. The Fears are still there; they just lie deep inside, surfacing in motives and behaviors. These inner Fear-filled motives cause him to react, panic and become paralyzed.

Fear is your reaction to threat—real or imagined. Fear is a survival reaction that focuses inward to protect when you feel—"I am scared. I am in danger." Fear is information—information about the surrounding world and information about *you*.

The two facets of Fear are best expressed in the wonderful song "Amazing Grace." "Twas grace that taught my heart to Fear (respect) and grace my Fears (terrors/anxieties) relieved."[1] *Fear* is used throughout the Bible to mean:

- Respect—a deep reverence for God's Love and power. "Fear God and keep his commandments for this is the whole duty of man" (Ecc. 12:13).

- Anxiety—worry over the future and our frailty. "[T]he sword that you fear shall overtake you" (Jer. 42:16).

The sword of Fear can be used skillfully, as a great knight defending the gospel and living a life of courage. *Increasing* our respectful Fear of God actually *decreases* our Fear-filled anxiety for living! "And those who know your name put their trust in you, for you, O LORD, have not forsaken those who seek you" (Psalm 9:10).

The word *Fear* used for anxiety has its roots in the Greek word phobeo (phobia), meaning "to be afraid, flee, be struck with Fear, be seized with alarm or amazement."[2] It is this anxiety that powers the Fear of the unknown, which is really Fear for the *future*. Anxiety within asks the question, "What is going to happen to me?" Your Fear-filled anxieties fall into two categories:

Physical Fears: Cancer, tornados, snakes, autism, joblessness, Alzheimer's disease, war, and crime top the list. Physical pain, suffering, or death will come upon you or those you Love—from these concerns.

Spiritual Fears: You are feeling, "I am not worthy of God's Love." Or you are frightened because your daughter is marrying a non-Christian. These are spiritual Fears for your soul, or the souls of others, and inside them is your Fear of the future.

What is your Fear for the future?
- Terrorists have taken over my plane, shot the pilot and the man next to me.
- I watch helplessly as men grab my daughter and force her into a car.
- The doctor just said, "The tumor in your brain is cancer."
- I will spend my life caring for this bipolar child.

Every type of Fear-extinguishing therapy has as its first step: *Name the Fear.* Stop right now and write down your Fear list.

_____

_____

_____

_____

_____

What is your worst nightmare? Somehow, when Fear controls your life, your worst nightmare comes true. *Your Fear list is an exceptional diagnostic tool about the most intimate you.* Your Fear list is also your Love list. What you Love the most, you will Fear losing the most.

Anger, jealousy, sorrow, revenge, despair, depression, and control often have their roots in Fear. Fear results in paralyzing thoughts such as, "I can't handle this." Fear can move within you quietly as a stealthy opponent, or sound like a war trumpet in full panic. Remember, *Fear is threat.* You may react using anger, control, insensitivity, but the underlying feeling is still Fear. You must look beneath these symptoms and *recognize Fear as your obstacle* before you can deal with it. As you look deeper into your Fears, think about what frightened you as a child.

Up a long, steep staircase were three large bedrooms, one each for my teen-age brother, sister, and me. I was only four years old when we moved into this big house in Oregon, and every night I was sure there was a nest of snakes hiding in the sheets at the foot of my bed. I would curl up near the headboard, surrounded by my stuffed animals and pillow, which served as a barrier against the reptile menace. My heart would pound with terror imagining what lurked in the dark abyss at the footboard. I thought surely the serpents would bite off my toes if I dared extend my feet into their domain.

As best as I can figure, my childish mind had merged the Fear of my sister's pet snake with an experience swimming in a lake where tiny sunfish swirled around my feet. This Fear continued for years. The winter that I was seven, we moved to a compact Washington, D.C. townhouse, and I now shared a room with my teen sister. On a family trip to Florida, she acquired a young alligator that lived in a cooler between our beds. That real alligator sleeping two feet from me never gave me the torment that I had suffered from the imaginary snakes under the covers.

Monsters live in the dark. When you cannot face your Fears, they control you. When you decide to shine a light on your Fears, look them in the eye and speak their names, you can deal with them squarely. In growing through Fear-powered anxiety, you must be willing to *challenge* Fearful thoughts.

Learning from Fear:
* brings immense information about your deepest needs
* takes inner courage
* powers great personal change
* unlocks deep mysteries about your actions
* also means learning about Love

When you disregard your Fears, they operate as a cruise-control reactor throughout your life Journey. If you constantly felt ignored as a child, your cruise-control says, "You are not important. No one cares about you." If you desire to live the full life God has opened for you, you must come off of cruise control and stop your "life car" from just *reacting* to changes in the road. You know how it works. Any incline in the road just brings acceleration. Imagine staying on cruise control when the traffic gets tight. Terrifying! You keep steering and reacting, but you constantly have near misses. Uncontrolled Fear is like *living on cruise control* and falling asleep at the wheel. *It will take you places you do not want to go, and eventually you will crash.* A traveler on blind cruise control will bump wildly into the walls of life's labyrinth and careen down into chasms below, guarding his face at every curve. This is the navigation of overwhelming Fear. *When you do not recognize Fear, you have something else steering you—always.* Fear is my greatest spiritual weakness.

If you wonder, "Why can't I make any lasting change in my life?" *peek through the keyhole of your heart and look at your Fears.* When you do not identify Fear, you cannot conquer Fear. You cannot fight something that you do not name. Sensing, "I don't feel good," could mean you have a cold or lung cancer. You must diagnose the problem to find the remedy. If it is a Fear problem, there is a remedy. "For I, the LORD your God, hold your right hand; it is I who say to you, 'Fear not I am the one who helps you'" (Isaiah 41:13).

YOUR BRAIN ON FEAR

When your brain perceives a physical or emotional threat, your pupils dilate, you sweat and you get ready to run. Your biological reaction is the same whether you are watching a horror movie or a man is holding a knife to your throat. Real or imaginary, your brain says that something is happening to *you*.

In 1995, I read Daniel Goleman's groundbreaking book, *Emotional Intelligence,* and became fascinated with the thrilling scientific evidence for God's creative design in our brains. The Lord's blueprint is seen in the design of our brain's reaction to Fear. Two tiny amygdalae serve as rapid reactors on each side of the brain. They help us respond to danger quickly—even before the neocortex (the analytical and thinking part of the brain) gets a chance to mull over a response. "This puts the amygdala in a powerful pose in mental life, something like a psychological sentinel, challenging every situation, every perception, with but one question in mind . . . 'Is this something that hurts me? Something I should fear?'"[3]

The amygdala is the first-responder sentry sounding the trumpet at any immediate sense of danger. The nerve signal of any sound-sight-touch shoots right to the amygdala and it tells your body to react. When a car comes screeching toward your child, you instantly reach out and grab him, thanks to your amygdala.

This wonderful fight-or-flight reaction was designed by God for our protection. But if someone had a severely distressing childhood or has lived a very stressful daily life, the constant state of alert may have damaged the brain and worn out the protection circuitry. A stressful life can keep the amygdala primed to sense danger and react based on past experiences—not Reality. *Traumatic emotional experiences get deeply engraved into our brain's wiring.*

Violence and mayhem sell. Scary movies tantalize us to step into Fear, deal with it, survive, and walk away. The nightly news gives us up-to-the-minute Fear and anxiety to add to our cart of worries such as, "China pulls out and destroys the U.S. economy. Details at 11." But we must realize that much of what we worry about will *never happen*. And when we constantly listen to negative commentary detailing all that is wrong with the world, our brains become bathed in a *chemical soup of anxiety*. Negativity breeds Fear in our brains and actually *alters our neurocircuitry*—transforming our outlook on the world.

Think of your brain as a moist, green meadow that beckons you and your horse to cross it one morning. If you daily use that same pathway, you will gradually wear down a trail that becomes mud. This is how your brain grabs hold of *negative thinking*. When you practice negative thinking (Fearful thinking) your brain actually strengthens the neural connections to PERCEIVE LIFE NEGATIVELY.[4]

The brain actually has a negativity *bias* as it reacts *more strongly to bad news* than to good. As the brain surges with electrical activity, *it retains details of negative experiences over positive*. When researchers studied this in relationship interactions, they found it took *five* positive interactions to counteract *one* negative interaction within the brain.[5] Be careful. Developing a "negative" brain takes no work at all!

FEAR MANAGEMENT and AVOIDANCE TRAINING

> Sheila's parents were both killed in a car accident when she was nine years old. She and her sister grew up as orphans. As a forty-year-old woman she was obsessively safety conscious, pausing longer than needed at every stop sign and double-checking during street crossings. She and her husband chose not to have children. Clearly, she sought to avoid the Fears that she had lived. *When you grow up feeling threatened by Fear, your brain constantly perceives danger.*

Fear of the unknown powers a craving to *control* the unknown. It compels you to covet the predictability of life's outcomes. You may feel, "If I can predict what comes next, I can prevent pain." But the craving for control is never satisfied, because the volatility of life among humans means—arrows will pierce you from out of the darkness.

Walled in by their Fear, some Americans responded to 9/11 by refusing to fly or leave home. Randomness terrifies us. When the innocent are drawn out into the sea by a tsunami, we grasp that this can happen to *us,* and we search for ways to defend against the worry. Much of our avoidance of planes, bugs, and even forming friendships is to prevent the greatest of sacrifices: giving up control. Fear's instruments—*control and anguish*—stretch out, trying to command the feelings and choices of others in an effort to protect us from being hurt.

Our son, Jordan, was bitten badly by a dog as a young boy and began to ask regularly, "Do they have a dog?" every time we would get in the car to go somewhere. His "checking" procedures only gave temporary relief for his anxiety and soon stuffed dogs and pictures of dogs were causing him strain as well. His brain was making neural connections between the terrifying experience and any canine. Becoming hypervigilant and installing "procedures" was his way of controlling exposure to more pain. It took months and years of talking through the scenario, and teaching him a procedure for greeting friendly dogs for Jordan to grow through this residual Fear.

Tightening all variables and seeking to control every detail only provides temporary comfort to the Fearful, and is not a realistic response to living. When we narrow our world, our lives become smaller, more self-centered, and disillusioned. We choke ourselves as we tighten the drawstring that might protect us from hurtful variables. We may believe that:

- Adversity should be avoided at all costs.
- Technology solves all our problems.
- Popping a pill changes a bad day into a great one.
- Difficulties should be eliminated.
- Replacing our house/car/spouse will bring happiness.
- "It's just too hard," is the catch-all excuse to justify anything.

Seeking to avoid any painful experience, we live in the constant Fear that at any moment the rug can be pulled out from under our feet. And deep inside we believe, "If I am hypervigilant and control every choice, I will never be hurt." In actuality, the power in the Lord's providing arms and guiding wisdom from His Word for this life Journey are the security you long for. Deepening your understanding of who God is, and His overwhelming tender Love for you is *the* way to grow through Fear and Walk in Joy! "But the righteous shall be glad; they shall exult before God; they shall be jubilant with joy!" (Psalm 68:3).

COPING WITH FEAR – *Adaptive vs. Maladaptive Behavior*

Patty expresses Fears about problems such as national debt, global warming, and crime. Her friend Anne is Fearful of spiders, snakes, and tornados. As we catalog our Fears of the future, we problem-solve, avoid, and make choices around those Fears. Fear powers two types of coping behaviors: adaptive and maladaptive. (The prefix of "mal" means bad.)

Adaptive Behaviors of Fear include: Bible study, exercise, spending time with friends, examining your personal health status, prayer and meditation, volunteering, and the practice of Gratitude. My choice to write this book is an adaptive behavior to help me deal with my Fears.

Maladaptive Behaviors of Fear include: hypervigilance, hoarding, overeating, overworking, smoking, overshopping, super-optimism, phobias, alcohol and drug use.

We use maladaptive behaviors, such as overspending, as consolers to calm the feeling of Fear. We see the maladaptive behaviors, but usually do not connect them with being afraid. When it is too frightening to look at the Fear inside us, *we soothe our stress with something comforting.* But as we cling to those substitutes, we end up *increasing the exact Fearful emotion* the maladaptive activities were supposed to quiet because we have added a *new* dependence. (More on this in Ch. 11.) How quickly can you list the Fears and associate the maladaptive behaviors of your friends and family? You can see clearly, "He does this because of that—it is so-o obvious." What do you see in yourself?

Denise was pouring her heart out about her teenage daughter's alcohol use to her friend Sharon. Sharon also had a troubled child. Her son was using marijuana and sexually involved with his girlfriend. Sharon picked up a cookie and said, "But I just trust in the Lord," and ate it in two bites. Denise shared again how sad she was about her daughter's behavior, and Sharon responded with another cookie in her mouth and one in her hand, "Well, you just need to trust in the Lord and not worry." Sharon was *saying* that she trusted in the Lord with her Fears, but was momentarily filling her anxiety with cookies. You can recite Bible truths, but still *act* Fearfully.

Remember, Fear-driven anxiety is the watchman in the tower sounding the trumpet. You must *identify the threat* and deal with it. Maladaptive behaviors try to transfer your *focus* onto some *thing* and away from the Fear. If I can:

- focus on some *thing,* there is less focus on my Fear inside"
- pre-worry all variables, I can prevent misery"
- make a lot of money, I will have friends"
- numb my feelings with food or shopping, I will be okay"

Think of the profound information you can acquire by opening up your Fears! Begin by asking the deep questions: "What am I feeling?" "What is this Fear's name?" "How am I coping with my Fear?" The greatest adaptive strategy you will ever learn, as you deal with your Fears is to: STOP—FEEL—NAME THE FEAR YOU ARE FEELING—ASK GOD FOR HELP WITH YOUR NEXT WORD OR ACTION—THEN RESPOND. Now you can see if you are delivering a chosen *response* or just an amygdala *reaction*. Perhaps God measures your spiritual growth by how you respond to Fear in the midst of life's difficulties and sorrows.

REALITY VS. ILLUSION

One uncomfortable certainty of your earthly labyrinth is that there will be obstacles at every turn. If you are unwilling to learn from your Journey, you may pretend that life should be tidy and predictable and those obstacles are unfair. You may soothe your Fears by fixating on an illusion of life like Cinderella, but the truth is—*pretending is a reaction of Fear.*

Illusion is a way of trying to shape a future that fits our fantasy of happiness. Many girls spend their entire lives in their tiara, waiting for Prince Charming to come and make *their* dreams come true. Their expectations of dream fulfillment are unreasonable and cause them (and others) deep pain. The Lord's ideal plan for family life is a devoted husband and wife *working* to glorify Him hand in hand. Men and women who put their hopes in their spouse to bring them all of life's Joy are living a fantasy-movie of Fear masked in delusion, not a life based in Reality. They are seeking fantasy answers for Reality problems. Heroes and Heroines face the truth of their lives, *exactly as they exist* with all stresses and strains (1 Peter 4:12).

Heroines know that Satan is a Traitor who turned away from the King of his own free will and offers you the same temptation to join him—in the misery of separation. Heroine-servants learn that the Traitor:

- must be studied in order to battle him with success
- wants to frighten you into following him
- is capable of unspeakable evil
- will lie, cheat, steal, deceive, and kill you to keep you from glorifying the King
- will fill your labyrinth with blockades and pursue you, but cannot take your soul without *your* consent (Matthew 13:49)

The King makes no deals with the Traitor or his followers. Engrave in your mind, that the King of the universe cannot be conquered or dominated. He sacrificed His only Son to bring *you* abundant life (John 10:10). If you are a servant of the King, you *get* to live under the King's shelter and serve Him of your free will. *If you exit His service, you depart from His protection* (Psalm 91). The Realities of service to the King are adversity and Joy.

> [B]ut as servants of God we commend ourselves in every way: by great endurance, afflictions, hardships, calamities, beatings, imprisonments, riots, labors, sleepless nights, hunger; by purity, knowledge, patience, kindness, the Holy Spirit, genuine love; by truthful speech, and the power of God; with the weapons of righteousness for the right hand and for the left; through honor and dishonor, through slander and praise. We are treated as impostors, and yet are true; as unknown, and yet well known; as dying, and behold, we live; as punished, and yet not killed; as sorrowful, yet always rejoicing; as poor, yet making many rich; as having nothing, yet possessing everything (2 Cor. 6:4-10).

It is an illusion that there is a perfect Heroine. Some of the most powerful Heroines of history have worked quietly with the highest level of Integrity. A Heroine has no great beauty, talent, or skill dwelling inside her, but there is a depth of character that powers her Integrity. Most Heroines are unlikely, struggle

with their flaws and weaknesses, and persevere because they believe to the core in their true Cause. It is in the strain and valor of that inner and outer conflict that they earn their title (Psalm 26:1).

When you embrace the Reality that there is both a Hero and coward living within you, you may see that growing through your Fears is *fundamental* to a valiant life Journey. *In any moment that you obey your King, your Heroine overcomes your coward and the purity of your whole self, acting in faithful unison, exudes Joy. This unison of obedience is a Heroine's quest.* As you continually work to conquer yourself, God Loves you as all one piece (John 14). Paul understood this Hero-coward struggle within himself.

> For I do not understand my own actions. For I do not do what I want, but I do the very thing I hate . . . For I have the desire to do what is right, but not the ability to carry it out. For I do not do the good I want, but the evil I do not want is what I keep on doing. Now if I do what I do not want, it is no longer I who do it, but sin that dwells within me (Romans 7:15-20).

Accepting the Hero and coward in all of us can *lower our harsh judgment* of others and increase our Joy. As we begin to see ourselves and *other* servants as each struggling along our own Journeys, every experience becomes an opportunity for growth. If you are seeking to be a Heroine in the service of your King, you must exit the fantasy-theme park of Fear-driven illusion and make the decision to *take up a service Journey in Reality. All true-life Heroine-servants—embrace Reality* (Psalm 119:175).

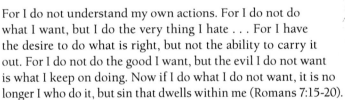

A HEROINE'S LIFE
A real life Heroine may at some critical moment ask, "Is this Cause worth dying for?" And in answering bring forth the questions, "How shall I then live for this Cause? If my existence changes the course of civilization, and every moment of my life matters, what do the years in between my dash (birth-death 1980–2020) really stand for?"

At some point in her Journey, a Heroine makes a commitment. She says, "There is no turning back; I have left everything else behind," and she vows to risk all for her Cause. A wanderer who pledges devotion to nothing, Fears losing nothing, for he has neither ties nor Joys. It is in the celebration of the milestones of a committed Journey that delights are felt.

As a Heroine decides what Cause she would give her life for, that which brings her Joy becomes clear. Insignificant trivialities of life vaporize. Withholding nothing, she now says, "I serve Him out of the deepest commitment of Love." Her openness to surmount whatever lies ahead, allows God to use her, for she is wide open to serving Him. A Heroine-servant is created at the moment a willing daughter of the Lord surrenders her spirit in complete openness to her Divine purpose—to live each breath to the glory of God.

She now accepts that she must be skilled in order to be useful in the battle against the Traitor. Without expertise in dealing with the sword of Fear, it can fall back and maim her, becoming a deadly hindrance versus a powerful weapon. Alertness, timing, speed, and endurance under pressure are techniques that a Heroine must seek to master. One underlying certainty remains: there will not be only one obstruction in life, but rather, constant burdens, hazards, and dangers. Surmounting multiple handicaps and disasters writes the resume of the victorious. Skill training is rigorous, and constant devotion to the Divine purpose is the only antidote for disenchantment on this Journey. The more accomplished she is in training, the more abundant life she will enjoy.

Your one-way Journey is perilous and unpredictable, and there is little choice over which adversities you will battle. While a Heroine's crown at the final breath is the ultimate goal, the sides of the labyrinth contain heavily secured vaults of golden wisdom. The intricately locked doors open for anyone who has learned the combinations through skill and expertise. In the midst of the most Fear-filled moment, the vaults can be opened to obtain courage that you did not know you possessed and honor which the King bestows to His Heroine-servants as they pass through the labyrinth of challenge.

Choosing the life of a Heroine-servant means that the glorious King never tires in loving and lifting you up when you fall, and grants endless hope chests of blessings for you to unlock. His steadfast Love constantly reminds His Heroine-servants to stay the course as they hold His banner up throughout their battles and press on to the Treasure at life's end. A Joyful Journey is always a challenge course, for a truly obedient Heroine knows that the Lord is in charge of all of life's outcomes.

YOUR LIFE MOVIE

Imagine that your life story is being documented on film moment by moment and titled, *This is your life!* While it can be rewound and watched at any time, each day's disc is finalized at midnight and cannot be recorded over or rewritten. You cannot record over the past.

While your childhood was filled with many events and decisions outside of your control, the Lord offers you great possibilities to use every episode of your life by asking, "What can I learn from this?" As you make sense of, fantasize, or criminalize the movie scenes of your past, you provide the voice-over commentary of the film. "This is the time that I . . ." is your voice, narrating and explaining the story of your life.

What genre is your life movie? Mystery, drama, comedy? What would the best title be? *The Greatest Whiner Ever, Always Afraid of Living* or *Me, First, Biggest, Best?* Can you title the movie of Jesus' Life? *The Great Celebration of Love, The Reason for all Existence* or *For God so Loved You.* In Jerry Jampolsky's book, *Love is Letting Go of Fear,* he writes, "The mind can be thought of as containing reels and reels of motion picture film about our past experiences. These images are superimposed not only on each other, but also on the lens through which we experience the present."[6]

We compare every *new* interaction on a parallel screen with the movies playing from our past experiences. Fear's influential effect on our body produces powerful movie memories with vivid pictures and colors. Please understand: our brains naturally *practice*—not *process*—the memories of *negative experiences.* When our Fear movies play, our bodies react the same way they reacted to the actual event, even though we are just reminiscing. Without learning to *process* negativity, we take on narrator roles of "sufferers" or "costumers" as we view our memories.

"Sufferers" enjoy protecting the past. Sufferers want to keep playing their *Wounded Forever* movie over and over and cry at the same part every time. Sufferers want to play their inner movies for *you* also—for example, *The Worst Job in the World* movie followed by *My Mother Never Met My Needs.* When sufferers gather with their friends, they play all of their movies simultaneously and argue about why "My movie is worse than your movie." There is no interest in finding their courage, or what they learned from a

painful incident. They watch for validation of
their victim-status credentials. (More in Ch. 8)

"Costumers" pretend that their old movies are all happy—*Happy Day in Every Way.*
They want a happy ending to every scene!
Costumers want all your old movies to be
happy ones too, and they think that you should
rewrite old scripts to make merry memories.
(More in Ch. 12)

"Realists" learn amazing lessons from their
life movies. *This is the Moment,* and *I Learned
so Much,* are some of their favorites. They feel
sadness at the parts of their lives that were
hurt through Fear-driven decisions, abuse,
neglect, and sin. But Realists want to *discover*
the intimate messages only *they* can glean
from their life movies (Ch. 3). Realists ask
these questions:

- "What am I feeling?"
- "What can I learn from this?"

Realists comprehend that they are powerless to alter the inner movies playing in *other* people. They learn that boundaries, inspiration, and influence are
their only implements when their lives intersect with the lives of others (Ch. 5).

All great movies have strong motivation in the plot. The Hero falls and
rises up again because he wants to save the people. What is the motive in
the plot of *your* life movie? What are your particular strengths that you can
use to glorify God? All Heroes and Heroines have one thing in common:
they overcome their Fear to accomplish a greater purpose. Yours is a Divine
purpose (Chs. 3 and 4).

Your life movie can change in an instant. A car runs the light and hits
you leaving you paralyzed. Or, you find out that your husband has committed
adultery. The plot of your life story changes course, but your *Divine purpose
to glorify God remains.* So I invite you to watch a cinema festival of Bible
Fear movies, and become a Fear detective in the stories of others (Chs. 2–13).

A great detective analyzes evidence, takes notes, and picks up on clues to benefit the case. You have the opportunity to learn from the lives of others, and write a life movie for yourself that is boring and confined or—adventurous and meaningful (Chs. 3 and 8) (Psalm 42:8).

Let's be honest. If you were to go to the TRUE LIFE BIOGRAPHY DVD section and search for a movie of someone who had a perfect life, you would return empty handed. Every human raised by humans experiences pain and disappointment. You can watch the movies of others and:

- learn to recognize your own Fearful feelings and actions (Chs. 2 and 11).
- embark on a life quest motivated by Joy and Love (Chs. 3 and 4).
- see their Fear and Fear-driven decisions (Chs. 5 and 8).
- empathize with the feelings under their choices (Ch. 7).
- feel compassionate Love for yourself and others (Ch. 10).
- drop your Fear level as you embrace your Divine purpose (Ch. 9).

Depend on the fact that life is a labyrinth Journey filled with choices, monsters, ice storms, and plague. Fear will pressure a Heroine-servant to lash out in sabotage or retreat from conflict—rather than advance to meet her problems. You only shift a Fear-filled life to forge a Joyful Journey by *changing your inner character* and expanding your *confidence* in God (Psalm 32:10).

You deal with your Fear of the unknown in serving the King—by whom you are fully known.

As you change your attitude toward Fear, you may realize that *there is no piece of your life that God is not seeking to fill with His Love*! Embracing a Journey in the Lord's service means you realize that *one of the most difficult things you will conquer is yourself.* Being passionate and synergistic with the gifts you have been given becomes triumph when you hold high the banner, *I will serve and praise You no matter what lies ahead.* "In God whose word I praise, in God I trust; I shall not be afraid. What can flesh do to me?" (Psalm 56:4).

FEARBREAKER-JOYMAKER JOURNEY

Only twice in the New Testament are Fear and Joy found in the same verse:

- "And the angel said to them, '*Fear* not! For behold I bring you good tidings of great *Joy* which shall be to all people'" (Luke 2:10).
- "But the angel said to the women, 'Do not be afraid, for I know that you seek Jesus who was crucified. . . So they departed quickly from the tomb with *Fear* and great *Joy* and ran to tell his disciples" (Matt. 28:5, 8). [*Emphases added*]

In both cases, a heavenly messenger had told some faith-filled, but unlikely Heroes—shepherds (Luke 2:10); and women (Matt. 28:8)—about the two events the world had waited for since creation: Jesus' birth and resurrection. The angel also told them, "Do not be afraid!" so that the Joy of the moment would not be overshadowed by their human anxiety.

As the One who created you knows just how Fear works within you, He also offers you *Joy-filled Divine purpose as your battle strategy*! By seeing your vital Divine purpose—to glorify the Lord, your perspective changes to be *less reactive to Fear* (Chs. 3 and 11). Your confidence will soar as you deepen your commitment to living life God's way as a Heroine-servant (Ch. 4). No person's Journey is more vital to the Cause than yours (Psalm 86:12).

Deep inside you may be asking, "But, isn't there any easier way?" Since your Fear resides within you, it is only growing *through* the Fear and *into* God's steadfast Love, that your anxieties are calmed. If you are failing at spiritual growth and personal change—*deal with your innermost Fears* (Ch. 6–12). If you never feel your Fear in the present moment and Journey through it, you will never *know the astonishing Joy that is on the other side of Fear* (Ch. 5). How would your life change if you stopped being afraid of everything, except disappointing the Lord? I would _____

_____

_____

Life is a labyrinth Journey with many decisions:

1. Storms—How do I focus on the goal as I navigate life? (Ch. 2)

2. Reflection moments—How have others handled this? (Ch. 3)

3. Comprehension—How do I read this Map I have been given? (Ch. 4)

4. Direction choices—Do I take this path or that path? (Ch. 5)

5. Defense choices—How do I fight off the predators? (Ch. 6)

"Be strong and courageous. Do not be frightened, and do not be dismayed, for the LORD your God is with you wherever you go" (Joshua 1:9).

If your life expedition seeks to glorify God, you can walk the labyrinth of life with Joy! The Lord will help you, not only to endure it—but to *thrive* in it!

GROWING THROUGH FEAR

1. Reflect on a time when you came face to face with Fear. Did you meet Fear bravely or wilt and lose courage. What did you learn?

2. What Cause would you *give* your life for? What Cause would you *live* your life for?

3. As God knew Mary and Joseph and used them to raise the Lord Christ, how did He use your parents to inspire *you* to glorify Him? Were they great examples to emulate or poor examples to inspire you to make different choices?

4. Right now, at this time in your life, what Fears are you getting the opportunity to grow through? Ask the Lord today to help you recognize and grow through your Fears. Pray with someone else about facing your Fear.

5. Mary submitted Joyfully to the life purpose the *Lord chose* for her. Name some other unlikely biblical Heroines who submitted.

~ 2 ~
The Perfect Fear Storm
A windstorm of thought
Jesus calms a storm (Mark 4:35-41)

One evening, the Heroine's labyrinth opens on to a foggy harbor. Nightfall is approaching and the wind is just beginning to stir as the different ship captains call out, inviting her, "Come aboard!" As she walks the wharf, she asks them if they sail beneath the flag of the King and if they can carry her safely on her Journey toward the Treasure. She boards a small sturdy vessel and they set sail immediately as the rain begins to fall.

As she watches each raindrop make its impact on the sea, the boat heads into deep waters. Within minutes, the waves grow to the size of a rich man's house and the wind begins to swirl as if it was fighting itself in a mixing bowl. Lightning strikes the mast just as the sky opens up in a down pouring sheet of rain. Holding tight to the railing, she tries to inch her way toward the hatch leading below. From out of nowhere, a rogue wave taller than a castle wall, rises at the bow and begins to crest and envelope the helpless craft. The Heroine can only pray and cling fast to the banister as the wave takes her and the ship in its spin.

Her suffocating and helpless body plunges deeper and deeper down into the fathoms of the sea and she feels no direction of earth or sky. She waits, as gradually the air trapped in her cloak helps her rise to the surface. Gasping for air, she reaches out to rest on a plank from the ship.

As quickly as the storm had risen, it begins to calm as she alone clings to a piece of wood. Then, as if she has never heard a sound before, a voice penetrates the darkness: "This is my beloved son, in whom I am well-pleased." She raises her eyes to the heavens to see a light outshining all other stars where the darkness once was. The North Star is descending toward her and shining out of the open-armed man—Jesus.

On that day, when evening had come, he said to them, "Let us go across to the other side." And leaving the crowd, they took him with them in the boat, just as he was. And other boats were with him and a great windstorm arose, and the waves were breaking into the boat, so that the boat was already filling. But he was in the stern, asleep on the cushion. And they woke him and said to him, "Teacher, do you not care that we are perishing?" And he awoke and rebuked the wind and said to the sea, "Peace! Be still!" And the wind ceased, and there was a great calm. He said to them, "Why are you so afraid? Have you still no faith?" And they were filled with great fear and said to one another, "Who then is this, that even the wind and the sea obey him?" (Mark 4:35-41).

WHO ARE YOU?

Earthquakes, storm waves, and hurricanes awaken Fear in anyone who has experienced them. The anxious pleas of the disciples awakened Jesus and with mere words He put the earth back to rights. With every sign and wonder, they were learning the magnitude of this God-in-human-form's power, but were finding it hard to comprehend. Read that verse again, "And they were filled with great fear and said to one another, 'Who then is this, that even the wind and the sea obey him?'" (Mark 4:41).

The great Teacher asked the questions, "Why are you so afraid? Have you still no faith?" for He wanted them to have a faith deeper than any Fear-driven anxiety. A faith that said, "I believe you are the God-man, the only Jesus Christ. You are completely in charge of everything!" That was the purpose of miracles: to confirm His authority and Lordship. *Jesus was the son of God* (Matt. 16:16).

The storm at sea let the disciples visualize this lesson: *Jesus is the calm in the storms of life*. A calm that shows He is the Divine Power. Staying in the boat with Him is the goal. A squall in life offers a great opportunity to grown through Fear. "All authority in heaven and on earth has been given to me" (Matt. 28:18).

This most unlikely Hero, this Jesus, was born in a stable to a virgin mother and He had a lot of convincing to do. Most people were not like Simeon and Anna (Luke 2:25-38) who readily bowed down to the Messiah. Most people were like Nathanael, asking the question: "Can anything good come out of Nazareth?" (John 1:46). Every day of His life, with His teaching and miracles, He was showing them, "I am the one Messiah. I have power over the earth, over death, and over life." They drew their own conclusions, "You are the Christ." (Matt. 14:33; 16:16; Mark 3:11; 8:29, 15:39; Luke 9:20; John 1:34, 49; 20:31).

Every doubt and inquiry the disciples had, parallels what *we* experience when we are learning who He is. As if they were asking the question for you and me: "Who are *you* that we should drop our lives and follow you?" And with every lesson and every miracle He answers, "Don't be afraid; you can trust me; I am *the* Lord Christ." With the death of the apostles, the need for miracles was gone. His Word was written down for us to learn from, and we THRIVE on it. The Bible is a navigation chart for the Journey of every ocean and sea and a journal of His holiness. It is the Map to pilot you through the labyrinth of life (Psalm 66:5-6).

Within weeks of calming the storm, Jesus showed his power:
- to cast out demons that plagued a man's spirit (Mark 5:1-21).
- to heal and raise from the dead a precious daughter (Mark 5:21-43).
- to meet physical needs by feeding the five thousand (Mark 6:30).
- to be in command of and to walk on the wind and waves (Mark 6:45-52).

Jesus kept answering the question—Why should we Fear and respect you?
- I know the hairs on your head (Matt. 6:25-34).
- I know how much temptation you can take (Matt. 26:41).
- I control the wind and the sea (Mark 4:35-41).
- I was there the moment you were conceived and will be with you the moment you die (Gen. 2:7; Job 33:4; Luke 16:22; Acts 17:25).
- In me is eternal joy, when you are translated (John 11:25).
- I am the only son of God (Matt. 27:43; John 1:14; John 10:36; John 11:4).

Jesus told the disciples, "[E]verything written about me in the Law of Moses and the Prophets and the Psalms must be fulfilled" (Luke 24:44).

The Godhead: Father, Son, and Holy Spirit, planned the voyage of the world since creation and their timing is perfect. Jesus volunteered to be the human servant-sacrifice and North Star. His earthly life is the shining example of how we should navigate the course of our lives and await our reward in the glorious heavenly Treasure (Matt. 5:17-20). He is the co-writer of the plan with the Father and Spirit and knows the plot, the rising action, and the phenomenal ending to the story, which began with the creation and ended with the most incredible miracle of Jesus' life—his own resurrection. This is *The Epic Movie of the World – Part I.*

The overflowing, abundantly Joyful life that you are seeking comes from the Love and sacrifice of Jesus. Every apostle lived and died testifying of the life of Jesus that he "had seen and heard" (Acts 4:20; John 1:7). He is not just a man from history. He is alive and working to help you navigate your life-voyage toward the Treasure. He is "the bright morning star" (Rev. 22:16).

GOD IS WORKING!

When sin came into the world through Adam, the garden's gates were sealed and the real life of work, weather, pests, enemies, disease, and death was now Reality. While supernatural means powered miracles, God designed laws of nature, like gravity, to cause the physical world to work in harmony and be logical. Only for the purpose of demonstrating God's power, Love, and supremacy were miracles performed. The Bible tells the whole true story and we *get* to study God's Word and learn His ways. But since we do not live in the garden of Eden, we suffer disease and pain because of human free choice in this fallen world. This is Reality (Rom. 5:12).

In my college years, I spent a wonderful summer singing opera at a large music festival in the South. After rehearsal one evening, a group of us decided to go out for some dinner and were piling into my VW Bug for the trip into town. The fireflies were lit and I was dressed in my cute blue skirt as I approached the window of the tenors' cabin atop the hill. Girls were not allowed in, so I thought that I would walk across the dark front porch and knock on their window to let them know that we were there. In the dark and in my youthful exuberance, I had not seen a recessed staircase in the porch floor and in a split-second I fell fifteen feet below to the bottom. I landed on my head and was too embarrassed and too badly hurt to cry. Thirty-four years later, I still have a dent in the right side of my skull and pay for regular physical therapy on my neck.

What if the Lord had suspended gravity just for me? Or made miraculous exceptions anytime a faithful Christian was threatened? The recessed staircase in that dark porch had no railing around it to distinguish it in the dark. I did not "deserve" to fall. What would the world be like if I could receive a miracle anytime I asked? How would I ever have learned caution, empathy, and patience from my neck-damaging accident if He had suspended gravity just for me?

Our Fears of disease and disaster are learned from living in a world of natural cause-and-effect consequences. Hurricanes, floods, and earthquakes are going to happen. Innocent people are going to die tragically. Natural disasters have occurred since we left the paradise of Eden, and they are Fear-making events. *Just because storm fronts collide does not mean that God is not completely in charge of this world that He created!*[1] (Isaiah 66:1; Rev. 4:11).

God intricately designed this natural world to make sense. "In the beginning, God created the heavens and the earth" (Genesis 1:1). He designed the precision of the stars and the rotation of the planets all for our benefit.[2] "For his invisible attributes, namely, his eternal power and divine nature, have been clearly perceived, ever since the creation of the world, in the things that have been made. So they are without excuse" (Romans 1:20).

"Blessed is he whose help is the God of Jacob, whose hope is in the LORD his God, who made heaven and earth, the sea, and all that is in them" (Psalm 146:5).

"By faith we understand that the universe was created by the word of God, so that what is seen was not made out of things that are visible" (Hebrews 11:3).

Often we react to things out of our control as the disciples did by saying, "Do you not care that we are perishing?" (Mark 4:38). When we are scared, hurting, and just cannot see His workings, we are tempted to lash out at God. Our Creator and sustainer supplies His children every moment with His providing hand, but often we can only see in hindsight how the Lord guided and protected us.[3] "And we know that for those who love God all things work together for good, for those who are called according to his purpose" (Rom. 8:28).

Paul describes God's providing hand working in our lives as doors being opened.

- "And when they arrived and gathered the church together, they declared all that God had done with them, and how he had opened a *door* of faith to the Gentiles" (Acts 14:27).
- "[F]or a wide *door* for effective work has opened to me, and there are many adversaries" (1 Cor. 16:9).
- "[A] *door* was opened for me in the Lord" (2 Cor. 2:12).
- "At the same time, pray also for us, that God may open to us a *door* for the word, to declare the mystery of Christ, on account of which I am in prison" (Col. 4:3). *[Emphases added]*

Here in the western states, our rainy season begins when the meteorologists announce, the "storm door is opening." Low pressure systems swirl down from the Arctic and Pacific oceans and blow massive, wet, cold fronts into our lives. These rain and snowstorms sometimes cause accidents and flooding but also bring the life-giving moisture we need to sustain us through the seven warm months when we receive no rain. God's omniscience of where you are, what you need, and which "storm doors" are opening (or closing) ahead of you far exceeds any weather-tracking Doppler radar!

Right now, as you sit peacefully and read this book, there may be a massive Category 5 hurricane brewing that will impact your life. It may be far offshore and your inner forecaster has not begun a storm watch for it. It may blow onto your life's coastline when you least expect it and decimate your banks. A storm of the century may be a health crisis, or trauma of gale-force winds that will take your body wherever they wish. Wind gusts may push you overboard, but remember one thing: *Jesus is the calm in the storm of your life.* He will not just throw you a life preserver, but will jump in the water with you, cradle you in His arms as you tread water, and carry you to shore. He will never, ever, let go (Matt. 28:20). Even if in Fear and panic you drift away from Him, He will use searchlights, grappling hooks, and ropes to reach out until—you push away from His Loving arms.

- You must recognize the rescue mission that He is sending for you.
- You must do the work, paddle hard and bail the water from your craft.

- You must put on storm gear and boots and learn how to sail.
- You must respect the weather reports and the *limits of your power.*

His natural laws and workings are set for your preservation. In a time of miracles, God told Noah to build an ark because it was going to rain for forty days and nights, but *Noah chose to listen.* "By faith Noah, being warned by God concerning events as yet unseen, in reverent fear constructed an ark for the saving of his household" (Heb. 11:7).

Before you lived through the tropical storm of your life, you could not imagine that a human could endure such suffering. But Jesus says, "I am the Son of God. I Love you and I care for you" (Matt. 27:43; John 10:36). *He is in charge of the waters, the storm, the boat, and you.* His powerful and Love-guided Providence is working in ways that you cannot comprehend, pouring out goodness that you can only see at the end of the voyage (Romans 11:33).

Sometimes you will need to wait out a storm in surrender and other times you must tighten down your sail, point your bow straight into the wave, and ride the crest to the other side. At the serene moment when you feel the storm is over, you are actually in the eye of the hurricane. When the prediction of what might happen next is terrifying and your *death is imminent, Jesus is still the calm in your storm and will cradle you over to the heavenly Treasure.* The point of Jesus' coming is to guide you through life's tempests, not to keep you from the downpours that come with living. His Loving arms are right in the middle of the typhoons of life, caring for your Fears and offering you lessons to learn (Psalm 121).

"'For the mountains may depart and the hills be removed, but my steadfast love shall not depart from you and my covenant of peace shall not be removed,' says the Lord, who has compassion on you" (Isaiah 54:10).

"God is our refuge and strength, a very present help in trouble. Therefore we will not fear though the earth gives way, though the mountains be moved into the heart of the sea. . . . 'Be still and know, that I am God'" (Psalm 46:1-2,10).

GODLY RESPECT VS. FEARFUL ANXIETY

My husband and two small sons were asleep in the car as I cruised down the country highway. I was thoroughly enjoying watching the newborn lambs snuggling close to their mothers, and every field was lush and green. I don't know how long the policeman's lights had been flashing before I finally noticed them. "Ma'am, you were speeding at 75 mph in a 60 zone," he said firmly, with his ticket book in hand.

"You are absolutely right, officer," I said. "I was speeding, and I'm very sorry."

A bit shocked by my honesty, the police officer swallowed hard and said, "I am sure that you won't do that again, will you?"

"Oh no sir, I apologize," I said respectfully.

"Well, have a nice day." He tipped his hat and left.

I spoke to the officer with respect because 1) He was the law and I was the offender 2) I understood that I was wrong.

When I want someone's favor, I am careful and respectful. No one in their right mind would speak to a judge disrespectfully. But in what ways do we respect/disrespect the Lord? How many mercy-warnings does the Lord give us before we receive severe consequences? I have been driving for thirty-seven years and have not yet had a speeding ticket—not that I have not deserved one (Psalm 86:11).

The Lord shows compassionate Love as we seek to obey Him during stormy challenges. Godly Fear gives us freedom to relax inside His safe limits. "The Fear of the Lord is the beginning of wisdom" (Psalm 111:10; Proverbs 1:7 and 9:10). I may ask myself this question a dozen times every day, but I strive for it to be the compass for my behavior: *"Is this pleasing to the Lord?"* (Ephesians 5:10).

Believing that the Lord knows and sees all, I had to tell the truth to that officer. My godly Fear pushed me to be truthful and respectful. With road rage on the upswing, how often did that officer who was "just doing his job" receive respect from offenders? Respect is fundamental to every healthy relationship. Respect says, "I understand your authority," and its resulting healthy Fear can prompt us to action. Obeying the Lord's teachings shows we understand that *He is the Creator and rule maker* and we must live as *He* would want, with *reverence for Him and respect for others* (Ephesians 3:9).

If value and respect were a universal goal of interaction, our world would be turned upside down. The glass that now separates me from my bank teller would be removed. In respect, anxiety dissipates and godly Fear reigns (Ecc. 12:13; Job 21:22).

- Godly Fear brings *freedom*.
- Godly Fear says, "I am going to behave within these certain confines because I want to walk in His ways."
- Godly Fear means holding God in awe for his great goodness, and desiring to please HIM with every facet of life.

"Let all the earth fear the LORD; let all the inhabitants of the world stand in awe of him!" (Psalm 33:8)

"So that those who dwell at the ends of the earth are in awe at your signs. You make the going out of the morning and the evening to shout for you" (Psalm 65:8).

No person is always respectful or disrespectful, for we choose our behavior every moment. When you come to grips with the fact that within *you* there lives respect and disrespect, you will be open to seeing *weakness* in Reality. Rodney Dangerfield use to decry that he "got no respect." From gang leaders to spouses, the same phrase is heard today. "She does not respect me!" Whether it is in a high school, retirement home, or at your dinner table, I offer you my saying: "Want respect? Be respectable."

That does not mean that people will fall down to worship you, or step aside as you pass. People will still be mean to you and hurt you, and you will still have the same struggles and trials. But as you strengthen your heart of respect within, you will live in the peace of your Integrity, be regarded as a Christian, and *honored by the Lord*. Fear multiplies within you when you obsess over the opinions that other's have of you (Matt. 10:19; Mark 13:11; Luke 10:41, 12:11). When you look at everyone as sailing their own life voyage filled with choices, you see *your* life in perspective. When your Integrity is in place, the opinions of other people matter less. Raging, lying, and evasive behavior will not bring you respect. Honest, forthright, and *God-fearing behavior—will bring you respect.* "Be angry and *do not sin*; do not let the sun go down on your anger" (Ephesians 4:26). *[Emphasis added]*

DO NOT SIN is the boundary limit of respect and disrespect specified in Ephesians 4:26. There is buried fortune to be found as you look deep inside to ask *why you feel anger and Fear.* But, "Sin not" (KJV) is the moment where you keep your inner Fear thoughts from powering your *actions.* I may

feel jealous—the DO NOT SIN line—but I am not going to *say* something mean. *I am going to examine the root of my Fear-driven jealousy and wait to act.* Disrespectful words and actions *cross* the DO NOT SIN boundary (Psalm 59:12; Isaiah 59:13).

If your teenage daughter spills your purse in the driveway, leaves everything there, and gets in the car, you can say, "What are you doing? Come clean this up." That corrects her and requires her to respect your property. But if you say, "You stupid girl, how could you treat my purse (me) this way? You are such an idiot!"

- You have crossed the line of DO NOT SIN.
- Your words have *acted out* your Fear.
- You mixed the way she treated your *things* for how *you* feel disrespected.
- You feel she does not see you with the honor you deserve.
- You feel unvalued and *unloved.*

Now the young lady definitely needs correcting, but *removing your Fearful feeling of being dishonored makes the level of discipline appropriate.* Even in a turbulent or stormy moment, respect must be the guide. The DO NOT SIN boundary means we accept the Lord's boundary of respect in our human relationships.

- We do not rage or scream at people when we are angry with them.
- We do not abuse people, lie, or cheat in our marriages.
- We do not say hurtful, mean things, with or without a smile.

Fear-motivated respect compels us to learn to *listen* to our Fear-driven anxiety when we interact. Do you recall the Fear sword from Chapter 1? *When you Fear the consequences of your mistakes*, then you seek to make good choices; that is good Fear and godly respect! It motivates you to walk obediently in His ways. "There is no fear of God before their eyes" (Rom. 3:18). If you want respect, honor, and clarity without Fear-filled anxiety, study the perfectly honorable life of Jesus and align your life and actions up with Him. Respect will flow from His life into yours as you continually ask the question, *"Is this pleasing to the Lord?"* (Eph. 5:10).

THOUGHT STORM

The greatest tempest that humans survive every day is the Thought storm taking place inside their brains. Thought storms plague us mortals. Like the first tiny raindrops on the windshield of our mind, they begin softly with thoughts, such as, "Maybe Jesus was a fake. Maybe He does not care about me at all." The drops of thought come harder and faster as the wind begins blowing, and soon a squall-level hailstorm, increasing in speed and intensity, demolishes all in its path. Left alone for an hour, this hailstorm will dent your car and destroy every flower in your garden! Thought storms are produced by—written by—directed by—*your insecurities and Fears.* NOW PLAYING ON SCREEN 2: *FEAR STORM IN YOUR MIND!*

Fearful Thought storms are upsetting. Our hearts pound and our minds race and we accelerate to problem-solving speed. Our bodies do not know if the feeling of Fear is real or imagined. Just driving along on a normal day, your mind can wander to a co-worker's attitude. One thought follows another and . . . you know the rest of the story. By the time you get to your destination, you have had an internal typhoon because of this Thought storm playing in your head! We all do this every day. As you call to mind that Fears can be—real or imagined, realize that your *Thought storms are a big part of those imagined Fears.* Like storm waters draining down to the lowest point, your *brain will grab hold of "negative" thoughts, flow downstream with them, and land in a reservoir.* If you learn to recognize negative thoughts like the first drizzle of an approaching storm, you will begin to make new plot choices as you write your life script.

Soap opera plots are based on Thought storms that infect the characters' minds and prevent the truthful communication that would help people grow. *Thought storms are great in producing the tensions that power dramatic movies, but they are disastrous to those who want to live a truthful and Joyful existence.* Gathering information and asking questions reveals Reality (Rom. 12:17). You can learn to shelter yourself from Fearful Thought storms as you:

- Watch the Thought storm as it *begins* in your mind.
- Find your *Fear at the heart of the storm:* "Do I feel disrespected or unloved?"
- Pray for help with the *Fearful feeling under the storm.*
- Replace the Thought storm with the WORD of the Lord. "[T]ake every thought captive to obey Christ" (2 Cor. 10:5b).
- Do something adaptive: drink a glass of water and take a walk!
- Clap your hands loudly to bring your mind to Reality and away from the whirlpool of Fear-driven anxiety.
- Consciously choose how you are spending your mental time.

I have learned to say, *"Wow, I am having a Thought storm, where did that come from?"* I then ask myself to make a conscious choice, "Ok, you have another hour to drive here, and you can spend your thought time any way you want. Do you *want* to spend it this way?" *Obsessive thinking can ruin your life! Unattended, your Thought storm Fears will power you to maladaptive behaviors and, if left on cruise control, will drive you off a bridge to drown at the bottom of the sea* (Psalm 139:2).

An experienced sailor learns to harness the wind's energy in his ship's sails and use it! He finds a way to make a forceful challenge—useful to him. Developing internal radar to detect your Fear-driven Thought storms and motives and channel them is a vital skill in learning to sail with Joy (Proverbs 12:20).

THE TEMPEST-MAKER – Satan the Pirate

Satan is the Pirate of life's epic voyage (2 Cor. 11:14-15). The Pirate terrorizes us with the Thought storm of, "If God really loved you, He would not let this happen to you." In the 31,536,000 seconds that comprise a year, the Pirate and his crew are blowing Thought storm clouds toward YOU and will use them to create openings to board your vessel and take you captive (Jude v.6). Until the moment you depart to the next world, he will use gale-force winds of hardship and illusion to make you surrender. The Pirate knows your Fear lists and your Love lists (1 Peter 5:8-9; Job 1:6-12). Because of your Fears and Loves, this Pirate and tempest-maker will entice you on voyages that look easy. *He* wants to be your guide on the Journey (James 4:7). Satan wants you to focus on:

- all of the negative and bad things that "ruin your life"
- the offenses and failings of other people

- God letting you down because bad things happen to you
- how tough it is to live right

   If you have not learned to sail when storm waves are rattling you, he will take advantage of your weakness and look for ways to gain a deeper foothold into your Thoughts—robbing you of a Joy-filled crossing. Jesus verbally told Satan to get away from Him when the Pirate was preying on His Fears. Do you? Jesus knew the power in the Word and quoted the Holy Scriptures (Matt. 4; Mark 1; Luke 4).

   Like a four year-old against an Extreme Games swimmer and mariner, your abilities are not in his league and you will fail in every event/situation against the Pirate. He is a masterful seaman and his skilled expertise is inexhaustible. But, with *Jesus as your captain, you can navigate through storms and beat him in every event/temptation.* Since Satan knows *he cannot keep you* from the eternal reward in Heaven, his cunning intelligence is constantly looking for new ways to make you *slip, fall,* and *blow off course and away from the Treasure.* When you hold the hand of Jesus, He brings you favorable currents from above and cradles you when you are in the deep. *Grasp the truth tightly that—only your choices keep you from the Treasure.* "No temptation has overtaken you that is not common to man. God is faithful, and he will not let you be tempted beyond your ability, but with the temptation he will also provide the way of escape, that you may be able to endure it" (1 Corinthians 10:13).

FEAR DETECTOR

   As I played in the surf of Virginia Beach, I saw a man sweep his metal detector back and forth methodically. He walked down the beach slowly and then turned back at the buoy and advanced his grid as if he were using mental graph paper and did not want to miss scanning any square inch. He was looking for buried treasure. My nine-year-old mind envisioned silver goblets and gold coins from buccaneers' treasure buried deep below.

   Training your inner Fear detector gives you access to great riches. A wealth of insight is available to you when you learn to detect Fear in yourself and in others. When you see Fear, you see *hurt* and *motive* and gain understanding.

   Metal detectors are one of the most useful tools in minefields and airports. Sweeping an area with detecting technology will unearth hidden and

underground bombs that kill and maim. As you
learn to detect those Fear–bombs lying beneath
the surface of your actions, you will acquire
the preliminary knowledge that you need to
diffuse those bombs (Proverbs 24:4-5). Thomas
Jefferson once wrote, "Knowledge is power."[4]

In order to grow through your Fear, you
must decide that you are not afraid of detecting your **underlying insecurities** that drive your
maladaptive behaviors. Like finding the bombs
in underground mine fields before they explode, you can learn to detect and
diffuse the Fears under your behaviors. "My heart became hot within me. As
I mused, the fire burned; then I spoke with my tongue" (Psalm 39:3).

CLUB MEMBERSHIP

Throughout my life, I have belonged to many different groups. I have been
a Girl Scout, a mom, a music teacher—a member of these groups or clubs.
If I feed my Fears continually, Fearful living becomes my occupation and
hobby, and I strengthen my membership in the "Fear Club." A "Fear Club"
gathers its members for a Cinema Festival for sufferers and costumers. This
week is Angie's turn and her Fear movie is: *I Get No Respect So I Am Angry*!
Infomercials advertise books on *How to Blame Others Better: Refining your
Technique* and an award-winning favorite, *Dominating the Conversation with
your Victim Story*.

Can you list other club memberships for your social network? "Whiners'
Anonymous Club" and "You-Can-Go-To-Heaven-Doing-Anything-You-Want
Club" have huge memberships. The minutes of the "Crime-Is-Everywhere
Club" rehearse all the offenses committed in their town. They join together
to watch endless news reports and share techniques of how to worry over
global, political, and local issues.

The "Walk in Joy Club" is taking new members. Anyone can join. You
must *want* to learn *who Jesus is* and *want* to live a life of less Fear and more
Joy in order to join.

JESUS VS. INVENTED gods

Idol worship powered the economies of the ancient world and rules the
world that we live in today in the form of materialism. The reason for inventing a "god" for idol worship was:

- to be able to design something and pretend it had power
- to make money off those you convince to believe in it
- to set the rules for what pleases this "god"
- to design the rewards given for pleasing this "god"
- to manipulate others by Fear and revenge

Fear causes men and women to build an imaginary god in their minds—*so they can live however they want.* The Pirate tells you that *inventing* your own idea of god will comfort your Fears and lessen your pain. A 21st century "Invented god" is designed to make you feel good. Your "Invented god" can always be *pleased* with you—*if you plan it right!* Since you set the standards used to judge your behavior, you always have his favor and approval. If you ask someone who is inventing an idea of god this question, "Are you your highest law?" The answer would be: "Yes."

Your "Invented god" might give you salvation by caring for orphans. You give money and run charity drives and this is a great use of your daily time and energy. All good works are admirable! However, *a noble cause will do nothing to save your soul.* This is a false promise from a "do-gooder Invented god." *Jesus, blood sacrifice is the only Cause that saves souls.* I can donate my heart, lungs, and kidneys to save you physically, but it will do nothing to save your soul. "In him we have redemption through his blood, the forgiveness of our trespasses, according to the riches of his grace" (Eph. 1:7).

Since you make up the rules, you get to write a salvation plan that allows you to fulfill your pleasures *and* please your "Invented god." At a funeral, a friend of the deceased said, "Rick is up in Heaven with a beer in one hand and laying down today's bet on horse #9 with the other." The deceased had been an avid drinker and gambler, and he had "invented a god" who allowed that: Heaven was all about satisfying worldly pleasures (2 Thess. 2:11).

"Invented gods" operate by manipulation and exchange. "If you do this for me, then I will give you this." The followers of the "Invented god," in turn, treat each other with the same manipulation and exploitation. "What is in it for me?" replaces "Is this pleasing to *the* Lord?" as their daily question. When you are tempted to "invent" an idea of God, ask this question, "What am I trying to justify within myself?"

- An it's-ok-to-drink-alcohol Invented god says, "Just don't hurt anyone else and it's ok" (Ch. 8).
- A costumer's Invented god wants you to be perfect and happy! (Ch. 12).

- An indulger's Invented god says, you get it all—"You are worth it" (Ch. 11).
- A sufferer's Invented god keeps her victim status on display for all (Ch. 6).

Once I had a straight A, eighth-grade public school student ask me, "Who was the first person to think up the idea of God anyway?" When I paused to gather my thoughts before answering, he said, "I mean, who thought up the concept?" As if the Creator of the world was an advertising campaign of the ancient idol makers! (Isaiah 44:8).

The God who we cannot see is actually bigger than this world and is THE power of the universe, while the fake gods that men build in their minds are powerless—except that men *serve* them (1 Thess. 1:9). *We are constantly disappointed, angry, and Fearful because our "Invented god" does not bring us the peace and Joy that our spirits long for.* It is an impatience that says,

"I WANT TO BE PERFECTLY HAPPY RIGHT NOW.
I DO NOT WANT TO WAIT FOR A HEAVENLY REWARD" (Matt. 5:12).

At Jesus' baptism (Matt. 3:17; Mark 1:11; Luke 3:22), the adoring Father spoke from Heaven: "This is my beloved son, in whom I am well-pleased." In Jesus, the plans of the True Loving God are fulfilled. Their tender Father-Son Love only deepens the precious sacrifice given, so that we can have spiritual oneness with Him (John 17:11; Eph. 4:4).

> Long ago, at many times and in many ways, God spoke to our fathers by the prophets, but in these last days he has spoken to us by his Son, whom he appointed the heir of all things, through whom also he created the world. He is the radiance of the glory of God and the exact imprint of his nature, and he upholds the universe by the word of his power. After making purification for sins, he sat down at the right hand of the Majesty on high, having become as much superior to angels as the name he has inherited is more excellent than theirs. For to which of the angels did God ever say, "You are my Son, today I have begotten you."? Or again, "I will be to him a father, and he shall be to me a son"? (Heb. 1:1-5).

At the Transfiguration (Mark 9:1-13), Jesus glows with the glory of Heaven and is endorsed by not only Moses and Elijah, but the Father himself, who speaks again saying, "This is my beloved Son; listen to Him." Jesus was the perfect and sinless essence of God and the only God-in-human-form ever to exist.

He is the perfect balance of Love in all its forms: in kindness, in hope and comfort, and in obedient Reality. He is the God-man to pattern our lives after. Our Fear lessens as we study who He is, in contrast to who we *pretend* that He is. How can we live for Him if we do not know Him? Studying the revealed nature of God in every *Bible* example *keeps us from inventing a god that does not exist,* and reveals the abundant Joy we can have in Him.

Jesus Loves you, cares about your Fear storms, and does not want you overtaken by them. The Pirate wants you to invent gods to distract you from the real Love and power of the true and living God.

- The true and living God is fixed and unchanging.
- He created and sustains every molecule of the world.
- His sacrificial Love is seen in the surrendered life of Jesus.
- *He does not morph with your feelings.*
- His Love is an active verb seen in the Bible and in your life.

Even in the midst of a Category 5 life storm, you can see how He cared for the disciples and cares for you—if you will look with a thankful heart. Don't trust in "pretend" gods from fantasy movies. Trust the real Loving God that you know from His Word, who has the power to *take care of you* right there in the midst of every storm!! If His steadfast Love cared for Christians in the past, will He not do it in the future? Let His perfect Love cast out and give your Fears perspective. "There is no fear in love, but perfect love casts out fear. For fear has to do with punishment, and whoever fears has not been perfected in love" (1 John 4:18).

"He [Jesus] is the image of the invisible God, the first born of all creation for by him all things were created, in heaven and on earth, visible and invisible, whether thrones or dominions or rulers or authorities—all things were created through him and for him" (Colossians 1:16).

In Jesus, the Creator extends His Loving hand and says, "I Love you so much, my Son comes to teach and bring you close to Me." Jesus' life and death was the ultimate gift to *you.* Your gift is Joyful life now, and unspeakable Treasure at life's end.

FEARBREAKER-JOYMAKER JOURNEY

"Wondrously show your steadfast love, O Savior of those who seek refuge from their adversaries at your right hand" (Psalm 17:7).

What Heroine ever Journeyed without surviving a squall in her life? Navigating the storms of hardship composes the plot of a Heroine's story. In one moment her sails are set as she basks in the sunlit breeze, and the next she is dashed upon the rocks. A Heroine-servant's *response to Fear* and her *deeds* pilot her destiny (Ruth 3:11).

Storms of adversity will blow on your Journey, but if you sail under the Lord's flag of protection, you will be blessed by God's perfect balance of allowing *your* free will while exercising *His* providential control. *He makes no mistakes.* Your friends may abandon you, your spouse may cheat on you, your preacher may let you down, but THE God is ever-faithful. As the waters pour over the bow of your life's boat, your distress call is heard loud and clear by the "master of ocean and earth and skies"[5] (Psalm 146:6). You *get* to take cover in His arms. *Life without Him is the worst thing that can happen to you.* Remember:

- Joy will power your Journey as you deepen your Love for *Him*.
- Detecting Fear beneath Thought storms is the voyage of growth.

Growing through Fear has little to do with the tempest around you, and everything to do with what is changing *inside*. Thunderstorms can help you realize the preciousness of life and inspire you to look in *Gratitude* at all the blessings that have been showered upon you. Whether you can see a storm coming on radar or the waters are splashing across your bow and you are dangling over the side of the boat with a life preserver in your hand, *thank God* for helping you. In every "near miss" storm in life—*thank God* and ask, "What can I learn from this, Lord?" When you receive a "direct hit" storm front in your life, *thank God* and ask again, "What can I learn from this Lord?" (1 Thess. 5:18; Psalm 56). Within all the unpredictability of life on earth, you can hold on to the truth that: "NOTHING CAN KEEP ME FROM THE GLORIES OF ETERNAL BLISS WITH THE LORD—BUT ME." No storm of life can take your soul (Psalm 103:11).

"For God so loved the world _____ [you] that he gave his only begotten son, that whosoever believeth on him should not perish, but have everlasting life" (John 3:16 KJV). Read it again and put *your* name, all of it, in the blank. If you were the only human on this planet, He would have come and taught and died just for *you*. That is how great His Love is for you. If you live a Fear-filled life, you will miss your Divine purpose to Walk in Joy through this life and receive eternal Joy in the next life.

With Jesus as your Lord, you can evict the power Fear has over your choices and yield to Joy. Design a life without space between you and Him.

When my alarm rings in the morning, I whisper out loud, "Good morning, Lord, thank you." It reminds me that whatever storm rages in my life, He is ever-present, ever-powerful, and ever-faithful and I should begin the day by being ever-grateful (Psalm 32:10-11).

GROWING THROUGH FEAR

1. Think of the unlikely Heroine-servants Ruth and Esther. Can you see ways that the Lord opened and closed doors in their lives?

2. What are some goals of Satan, the Pirate?

3. When have you seen God's providing Love in the middle of a life storm?

4. How can you better prepare yourself for the inevitable storm clouds of life? What overcast skies are in your life right now that may bring storms ahead?

5. In your past, what were some ideas that you "invented" about God? Do you think www.buildyourowngod.com would be popular? How do Invented gods keep us from a walk of Joy?

6. Discuss this: If He really is the *only* God-in-human-form ever to exist, then I am going to trust Him with *everything*.

7. Challenge: Read Psalm 91.

~ 3 ~
The World Ignites
Pushing through Fear to embrace a new life
Paul's conversion (Acts 22:3-16)

A long her Journey, the Heroine chooses a familiar labyrinth passageway. She thinks, "Oh, I know this way . . ." trying to reassure herself, as the corridor begins to grow darker. This is the pathway that her friends and family have all followed, but as the shadows grow stronger, she pauses, realizing this is not the way of the Cause. As she begins to turn, the voices of her family ring out loudly in that familiar passage. They replay the moments of her life and her commitments. "Are you really going to leave the security of your family for some Cause?" they beckon, as they rehearse the memories and tokens of her childhood. "I remember how He came for me, and I want to serve Him," she says. "Why are you being rebellious?" they call out. "It is impossible to change the world!" her old friends shout at her. "Then I shall help do the impossible!" she responds, and turns to follow the passageway lit by the North Star.

I am a Jew, born in Tarsus in Cilicia, but brought up in this city, educated at the feet of Gamaliel according to the strict manner of the law of our fathers, being zealous for God as all of you are this day. I persecuted this Way to the death,

41

finding and delivering to prison both men and women, as the high priest and the whole council of elders can bear me witness. From them I received letters to the brothers, and I journeyed toward Damascus to take those also who were there and bring them in bonds to Jerusalem to be punished.

As I was on my way and drew near to Damascus, about noon a great light from heaven suddenly shone around me. And I fell to the ground and heard a voice saying to me, "Saul, Saul, why are you persecuting me?" And I answered, "Who are you, Lord?" And he said to me, "I am Jesus of Nazareth, who you are persecuting." Now those who were with me saw the light but did not understand the voice of the one who was speaking to me. And I said, "What shall I do, Lord?" And the Lord said to me, "Rise, and go into Damascus, and there you will be told all that is appointed for you to do." And since I could not see because of the brightness of that light, I was led by the hand by those who were with me, and came into Damascus.

And one Ananias, a devout man according to the law, well spoken of by all the Jews who lived there, came to me, and standing by me said to me, "Brother Saul, receive your sight." And at that very hour I received my sight and saw him. And he said, "The God of our fathers appointed you to know his will, to see the Righteous One and to hear a voice from his mouth; for you will be a witness for him to everyone of what you have seen and heard. And now why do you wait? Rise and be baptized and wash away your sins, calling on his name" (Acts 22:3-16) (Acts 9:1-19).

Within one of the most devoted lives of all history beat a heart full of Fear and hatred. Saul was "breathing threats and murder against the disciples of the Lord" (Acts 9:1). His life ambition was to rid the world of these followers of Jesus. Saul was a Jewish Pharisee and a Fearmaker.

Holy Crusades and religious wars begin in the anger of men who Fear that *their* god has been treated with contempt. ***Being afraid produces the hottest burning anger possible***. If we believe that someone/thing is threatening our god, we will battle to the death to defend him. Saul **hated** Christian people whom he had never known. He hated them enough to murder them. Saul and the Pharisees "*invented a god*" who wanted them to kill Christians. Their god said that:

- Jesus of Nazareth is a fake Messiah—we reject him.
- Jesus was poor and humble—we want royalty.
- His followers must be eliminated—they are a threat.
- A real military king/savior is coming—he will save us from the Romans.

Saul breathed out Fear. He wore the armor of his "Invented god" brightly, and carried the banner before him with the Invented god's creed displayed proudly. Saul believed with all of his heart that what he was doing was the ultimate devotion (Acts 23:1).

Before the blinding light at Damascus, Saul believed he had the autobiographical movie of his life under control. He had carefully written the "plot" of his script and it was being filmed daily. Violently ridding the world of Christian blasphemers was his mission. Now playing: **Spent his Life Killing Enemies of God—The Christians**. Saul knew what he was doing today, tomorrow, and the day after that, and the year after that, and during retirement . . . he thought.

What a contrast Saul's "light from Heaven" experience was, compared to the shepherds in Luke 2. While God did *not* want the shepherds to feel afraid (for they were being honored with good news), God shines light on Saul and says, "You are persecuting *me*, you *need to be afraid*" (Acts 9:4). Only one divine light shines from Heaven, but certainly the recipients were given different messages, depending on their relationship with the Lord!

Saul's response to the Lord's presence unveils his sincere heart. As he lay on the ground, blinded by the light of the risen Lord, he offered no lies or arguments, but said, "What would you have me to do?" (Acts 22:10). As if he was saying, "I get it. I need to change. I must turn myself around and *do* something different." Saul took the *humbling* and was as *authentic* as a human being can be. Deep inside, he had a tender, *compass heart* that pointed him to God. But he had been living on the cruise control of what he *thought* was right, instead of stopping and listening to the teachings of Jesus. *The true God slammed him to the ground with a plot change to Reality* (Rom. 1:16).

William Barclay writes about Saul, "The one who had intended to enter Damascus like an avenging fury was led by the hand, blind and helpless."[1] What was Saul thinking in the three long days of blindness and fasting, before his visit from Ananias and baptism? "And for three days he was without sight, and neither ate nor drank" (Acts 9:9). Saul's Fear-filled Thought storm must have been massive. . . . "The Messiah came and I missed him! I supervised the stoning of Stephen and have tortured and killed countless Christians! The focus of my career has been a lie!" While Fear and hate had been the guiding force of Saul's past life, he arose from the waters of baptism on *fire* for Jesus Christ; the true North Star. He even took a new name to express his new life—Paul. His new direction had no prestige or monetary rewards, but at the end, a Treasure of unspeakable glory awaited (Rom. 6:4; 1 Pet. 3:21-22). In striking the match of Jesus' Love within him, he gave up his:

- prestige as the chief prosecutor of the Jerusalem synagogue
- identity at the highest level of Jewish authority
- career pathway and aspirations of honor and reward

In becoming a devoted Christian, he received:
- immediate death threats from his Jewish colleagues (Acts 9:23)
- suspicion from all the followers of The Way of Jesus (Acts 9:26-30)
- torture, beatings, stoning, ridicule and rejection (2 Cor. 11:23-2)
- beheading for the crime of being a Christian[2]

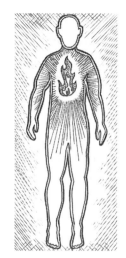

Stripped of everything he once thought important, his only connection was with Jesus Christ. No one else mattered (1 Cor. 1:30). *A pure burning flame of Divine purpose was ignited within Paul's spirit, and he began to preach boldly in the name of the Lord.* "So the church throughout all Judea and Galilee and Samaria had peace and was being built up. And walking in the fear of the Lord and in the comfort of the Holy Spirit, it multiplied" (Acts 9:31; Galatians 1:16).

RELIGIONS OF THE WORLD
Three main religions were practiced in the ancient world:

- Judaism – Jews were looking for a conquering Messiah to establish a political kingdom and maintain their identity as the chosen people.
- Paganism – Pagans worshipped many Invented gods in idols, animals, and natural phenomenon.
- Christianity – Christians followed the Way of Jesus and believed that He was the Son of the one true God, who gave Himself as one sacrifice, for one people, to be one church, which bore His name.

After Pentecost, the newly-born church of the Lord Jesus had grown like a wildfire. *The burning passion of these new Christians now set ablaze the old ways of Judaism and idolatry. The Epic Movie of the World-Part II* had begun (Gal. 3:26-27; Rom. 6:3-4). The church of Christ was Reality (Romans 16:16).

The New Testament is the account of: The way of the Jews, the way of the idolaters/pagans and the Way of Jesus. The believers of the early church of Christ Jesus taught people—in THE WAY of the Lord.

- John 14:6 – Jesus said to him, "*I am the way,* the truth and the life. No one comes to the Father except through me."
- Acts 9: 2 – "[I]f he found any belonging to *the Way,* men or women, he might bring them bound to Jerusalem."
- Acts 19:9 – "[S]ome became stubborn and continued in unbelief, speaking evil of *the Way.*"
- Acts 22:4 – [Paul said] "I persecuted *this Way* to the death."
- Acts 24:14 – "[T]hat according to *the Way* . . . I worship the God of our Fathers." *[Emphases added]*

Paul did not emerge from the waters of baptism and ask, "Which church shall I join?"—for there was only one (Eph. 1:22; 3:10; 3:21). There was only one church in the first-century and ONLY ONE WAY TO FOLLOW JESUS—*THE WAY* (Acts 20:28).

Paul had committed the highest treason against the Jews by becoming a Christian, and was now their #1 most wanted traitor. He had been a Pharisee of Pharisees (Acts 23:6) and chairman of the "We don't want Jesus—We want a better Messiah Club." They had evaluated Jesus, voted and decided that he was *not* the son of God. But in rejecting Jesus, the Jews had rejected the true God, for the fullness of God dwelled in Him (Col. 1:15-23). Paul's "best friends" from his former life, were now his lifetime persecutors. *It was as if every day of his new Christian Journey he traversed a river filled with Jewish piranhas.* Any Fear Paul had of the Jews, was scorched by the blaze of Love he had within him for his Saviour—Christ Jesus. Paul used to persecute Christians of the Way and now the Jews persecuted him. His life changed forever (Acts 14:19).

PAUL'S MISSION

Paul played no games with the Lord. When he gave himself to the Lord, it was with a pure, whole heart and no reservations. He was not thinking, "I will work this Christian thing for awhile and see what I can get out of it. If it does not go well, I will do something else." The Lord told Paul directly that his Divine purpose was to teach the gospel to the Gentiles. "I am sending you to open their eyes that they might turn from darkness to light, and from the power of Satan to God" (Acts 26:15-18). God assured Paul that:

1. He would be with him always (Acts 23:11).

2. Paul would receive a crown of life for his faithfulness (2 Timothy 4:8).

There was no contract with salary, retirement, and benefits negotiated. Paul would need to support himself. He was charged with bringing the glad tidings of a new life of Joy to those who only knew a life of Fear. Yet the Christian man Paul was asked to serve, and he accepted.

Paul accepted the cloak of responsibility and wore it so *respectfully.* As the worst criminal redeemed to serve as the kingdom's ambassador, he wore the cloak of his mission over his rough servant's tunic. Humbled and awed by the King's entrusting him with such a mission, Paul *truly believed his Joyful reward* for this work would come in *Heaven.* His *mission* was his Divine purpose: *to serve and glorify God* (Romans 1:9).

180 DEGREE TURN

> Jana and Gavin had married young and enjoyed a partying lifestyle. After the birth of their daughter, Jana was invited to church and began to wonder if there might be more to living than the lifestyle she and Gavin maintained. She was quickly converted to Christ and enjoyed learning the Bible and spending time with Christians. Even though she worked hard to be a loving wife, when she would not party, curse, or hang out with the old friends, Gavin rebelled. "Who stole my wife! Oh, that's right . . . Jesus did," he would say snottily. Jana's 180 degree turn saved her soul, but created a lifetime of frustration, anger, and persecution from her husband. Turning to follow Jesus as your guide will bring Divine purpose and meaning to *your* life. But any *shift* in one person's pathway, creates *change* for all those around, *and those direction changes will bring collisions.*

Paul had not just been wrong about Jesus, he had murdered and led the movement to *kill* the very people who were now his own brethren (Acts 22:4).

While the Lord's forgiveness encompasses every crime possible, can you imagine that a day ever passed, that Paul did not struggle with the memory of the blood on his hands or recall Stephen's face as he was being stoned to death? (Acts 26:11; 1 Cor. 15:9; Gal. 1:13).

He grew through his Fears after coming face to face with the risen Lord. Unlike many of us, Paul made no excuses for his past, but allowed it to school him and train his Fear-filled ego to submit to the Lord. As a lightning strike ignites a dead tree and burns it to ashes, Paul's old life was gone forever. When his inner flame was ignited by the light of the Lord, he saw his old direction was 180 degrees the wrong way (Gal. 1:22-24).

A FEARFUL EGO – The Smokescreen

When a human's spirit is lit with the burning flame of sacred Love for God, it must continually feed pure fuel to this flame or the smoke of the Fear-filled ego will choke it out. A Fear-filled ego is terrified of exposure and produces a large smokescreen to hide from being vulnerable. *If your Fear-filled ego goes unchecked, it will prevent you from humbling yourself in service to the Lord.* The thicker your ego-smokescreen, the harder you are trying to *convince yourself that your old way of life is right.* Fear-filled ego says, "I just can't be wrong. I have based my whole life on my Invented god and taught others to believe the same thing!"

Some religious people today are frightened, as were the Jews, that the *true* way of Jesus will cremate their well-supported house. Never mistake the *smoke of Fear-driven ego* for a pure passionate flame of Love for the Lord. The flame of Jesus' Love is devoted to *obedience*, but the smoke of Fear-driven ego is—burning trash.

Fear-driven ego will:

- prevent you from opening your heart and changing
- never allow you to say "I'm sorry," or be vulnerable
- stick you to old beliefs—regardless of what the Bible teaches
- push you to cross the DO NOT SIN line
- block your ability to look inside at the root of your Fears and heal

The smoke of your Fear does permanent damage as it billows through you, and is absorbed into your decision-making. If you decide to ignore your inner smoke alarm, Satan, the master Thief, seizes the chance to sneak into your heart amidst the pollution, leaving no trace fingerprints. Satan wants you to conceal your frightened soul within by creating the smokiest fires possible, burning old tires and rags instead of a pure propane flow. He will teach you how to make it *look* like you are a "devoted Christian," and *hide* behind the haze of ego—for covering up crime is his specialty. The larger the Fear-driven ego within, the more elaborate the cover-up deception (Job 13:9).

Fear-driven ego flashes up elaborate smoke rings to cover its hurt and keep from being exposed. The smoke must be fed by slow-burning garbage constantly, or it will die out. Acceptable fuel for an ego smokescreen is prestige, flattery, manipulation, and self-centeredness. While you are busy producing smoke, the master Thief is secretly robbing you of a life of Joy! (John 3:20).

Perhaps you do not see yourself as a Fearful person. *Notice when you feel the need to talk about yourself.* As you put yourself forth and tell of your accomplishments and importance, your Fear-driven ego is saying, "I am *not valuable* just as I am, I must promote myself, so that I will have worth."

There are two death threats to the Fear-driven ego:

1. Truth/Reality = no more smoke

2. Pure flame of *purpose* lighting your *direction* and not focused on self

Fear-driven ego's survival causes us to posture and push forward and smash the alarm monitor grid that might detect its smokescreen. Because we do not want to be exposed as Fearful and scared, we live in full defensive mode.

Fearful ego says:

- That preacher's lesson isn't going to tell me what to do!
- If I have to give up _____ to be a Christian, it's not worth it.
- I will assemble with the church when I feel like it.
- I don't need to give my WHOLE life to the Lord.

The Fearful ego refuses to say, "I have been wrong and I need to change my life direction" (Psalm 15:2). Accepting Jesus as your life guide is an *act of humility. Jesus took the form of a servant.* He had no ego involvement for his equality with God but because of a greater goal, to save you and me, *He gave up everything to serve* (Phil. 2:5-11).

If you ignore your Fearful ego smoke alarm, you will sleep through the greatest invasion robbery you will ever experience: *the loss of a life that could have known the Joy of intimacy with the Lord.* His goal is to *steal* that from you. The master Thief wants to convince you that, "If you give up your ego and your identity, you will be no one, and you will die" (Mark 4:15).

IDENTITY

Viktor Frankl, MD, PhD worked as a respected psychiatrist in Vienna, Austria before being taken to Auschwitz. He was happily married and conducting his lifetime scientific research, before the Nazis turned the lives of millions inside out. In Nazi prison camps, he dug ditches from morning darkness until evening darkness, starved and slept next to men who had been attorneys and shopkeepers. One of the Nazis' goals was to choke out every bit of dignity and identity, and to dehumanize. It did not matter who you were in the past, you now had no name or position. Reality was tattooed in your arm. Frankl was now number 119,104.[3]

Had his internal identity been sewn into the clothes that were stripped from him, he could not have endured three years of torture. He beat the 1:7 odds and dug deep within himself, to survive. While Frankl's *external identity* changed from psychiatric researcher to #119,104 to holocaust survivor, the core person who chose not to become an animal in the depths of a Nazi death camp—was still there.

If your identity *is* that you are a tennis player, a great cook, a good wife, and an ICU nurse, when that is *gone*, you may feel you have no identity and are worthless. Equating our jobs/careers with ourselves can leave us despondent at retirement asking, "Who am I?" and "Why am I here?" Without your external identities, you may be filled with Fear. *If your identity is as a devoted Christian, then it would only be through your choice to turn your back on the*

Lord, that your identity leaves you. In Reality, your priorities and choices *show* your *true identity.*

> So have no fear of them, for nothing is covered that will not be revealed, or hidden that will not be known. What I tell you in the *dark*, say in the *light*, and what you hear whispered, proclaim on the housetops. And do not fear those who kill the body but cannot kill the soul. Rather fear him who can destroy both soul and body in hell. Are not two sparrows sold for a penny? And not one of them will fall to the ground apart from your Father. *But even the hairs of your head are all numbered. Fear not, therefore; you are of more value than many sparrows.* So everyone who acknowledges me before men, I also will acknowledge before my Father who is in heaven, but whoever denies me before men, I also will deny before my Father who is in heaven (Matt. 10:26-33). *[Emphases added]*

REALITY VS. INVENTED GODS

As Paul was preparing to preach the gospel to the Gentile world, perhaps he looked back at his life and saw how God's providing hand had nurtured him since childhood with his studies of the Old Testament (Acts 22:3; Gal. 1:11-24). While the new fire-driven adventures of his life were not yet written, he was told that "imprisonment and afflictions await" (Acts 20:23). But Paul responded as he lived, "For I am ready not only to be imprisoned, but even to die in Jerusalem for the name of the Lord Jesus" (Acts 21:13). Paul turned his newly-lit inner lantern toward Jesus, *the Son of God,* and kept Him in sight. His Divine purpose was not marriage, or career, or fortune; it was obedience to the true God, not a past "Invented god."

Leaving the security of an "Invented god" is scary. Invented gods blow smoke storms that make you wander other paths and get lost from the Way. Have you heard people say, "Well, *MY god* would never ask me to do that!" As if *they* have outlined who god is—in accordance with *their* ideas, and he obeys them. An "Invented god" may blow exhaust that says:

- Everybody is a Christian and gets to go to Heaven.
- Whatever you believe is fine.
- Smokescreens are the way to happiness.

Any time you turn from the true God of the Bible, you are enveloped in an ash-filled smokescreen. A huge shift in your Fear life occurs when you *illuminate your heart* with God's truth, and banish secrecy. As you expose the *smoldering* of your Fears and breathe the fresh experience of true freedom, remember that your monsters live in the *dark.* "Live as people who are free, not using your freedom as a cover-up for evil, but living as servants of God" (1 Peter 2:16).

In Acts 26, Paul publicly *tells* how he persecuted Christians. His openness and honesty is a sign of a truly changed man! He spoke truthfully about his past life on this one-way Journey—in essence saying, "I bare my soul to you, as I have nothing to hide." Paul emulated the true God who is *straightforward* and revealed in his nature. He *plays no games* and puffs no dirty soot from smoke. A person growing through Fear to Joy will do this also.

> When Claudia was introduced to the church, she quickly began reading Bible study books around the house, and attending services on the Lord's day. Her husband had some extramarital affairs in the past, and she thought by changing her life and becoming a godly example, that he would follow the Lord also. He attended with her the evening that she decided to put on Christ in baptism, and was befriended by the congregation, but did not return. She read and studied at home and sought to be a loving wife, but months later, he announced to her that he had a new "love" and wanted a divorce. Claudia received deep compassion and support from her Christian friends, but after about six months, fell away from the Lord's church saying, "I need to do something just for me."

Claudia thought that obeying the gospel would produce a magical healing in the heart of a husband, whom she Loved very much. She saw her faithfulness as a type of "karma-payment" for changing this man. The true God gives everyone free will to obey or disobey Him. *God's Love does not work on an exchange/barter/manipulation schedule.*

Devoting your life to the Lord God means that He gives *you* the opportunity to serve *Him NO MATTER WHAT is happening around you*: no matter if your own family becomes faithful or not. Jesus' own brothers did not believe in Him until after the resurrection (Acts 1:14). God has Lovingly given you a hope for an abundant and eternal life in the Treasure. You *get* to serve Him during your Journey here, just because you *Love* Him so much. *God does not make trades* (Psalm 2:11).

LIGHT/DARK

"The Lord is my light and my salvation; whom shall I fear? The LORD is the stronghold of my life; of whom shall I be afraid?" (Psalm 27:1).

In dark, walled, medieval cities, the lamplighter began before dusk, lighting the oil lamps stationed high above the walkways. With one stroke of his torch, murky passageways began to flicker and glow. The light of salvation entered the world once at the birth of Jesus, and that light will remain here until the earth is destroyed. Jesus said, "I am the light of the world" (John 8:12; 9:5; 11:9; Phil. 2:15).

Paul understood that he was to be a lamplighter and carry the light of Christ to the Gentile world (Acts 13:47; Rom. 13:12; 1 Pet. 2:9). He knew that within God—there is no darkness. But Paul understood the struggle of light and dark within all humans, and in himself (Romans 7:15-20) and constantly encouraged Christians to battle the darkness (Rom. 2:19-22; Eph. 6:12). It is daily work to walk in the Journey of light, and ask forgiveness, whenever we pause in the shadows (Col. 1:12; 1 Jn. 2:16).

> Therefore do not become partners with them; for at one time you were darkness, but now you are light in the Lord. Walk as children of light (for the fruit of light is found in all that is good and right and true), and try to discern what is pleasing to the Lord. Take no part in the unfruitful works of darkness, but instead expose them. For it is shameful even to speak of the things that they do in secret. But when anything is exposed by the light, it becomes visible, for anything that becomes visible is light (Eph. 5:7-11).

When striking a match in the pitch-black of a cave, we instantly reveal the Reality inside. But we must continually nourish our flame with pure fuel, in order to illumine our most obscure corners. "The light shines in the darkness and the darkness has not overcome it" (John 1:5).

Growing up near Washington D.C., our family attended many ceremonies at the "eternal flame" in Arlington cemetery. This flame is fed by an underground gas pipeline and symbolizes someone's idea of eternal influence. The true eternal flame was lit when Jesus' pure blood was spilled and resurrected, to pay my penalty. We *get* to oxygenate the flame within us when we live close to the heart of God, learn His ways and His Love. The brightest flame and most intense heat are right at the source of the combustion. *Moments of purest thought and*

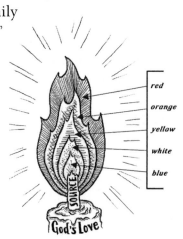

red
orange
yellow
white
blue

SOURCE

God's Love

deepest Joy are found in that hottest blue flame. "But if we walk in the light, as he is in the light, we have fellowship with one another, and the blood of Jesus his Son cleanses us from all sin" (1 John 1:7).

Without Jesus' light, you will wander your life labyrinth in pitch darkness. *If you say, "There is no corner inside me that I will hide from the radiance," your Fears release.* As you grow through your Fears, you will have illumination in this life and reward in the next! (2 Cor. 4:4-6). The light of His Love changes everything (1 John 4:9; John 1:1-18).

"The people who walked in darkness have seen a great light" (Isaiah 9:2a).

As she follows the light of the North Star, the voices of her family fade in the distance. Tears fill her eyes as she sees her name written on the wall of this new passageway next to others who have chosen to serve the Cause. With Joy welling up inside her she says, "I will serve Him no matter what lies ahead. I will talk about Him, write about Him, and sing about Him to everyone who will listen because—I fan the embers in my memory of how He rescued me. I cannot return to the darkness."

MISSION – Courage

"Courage is not the absence of fear, but rather the judgment that something else is more important than fear." —Ambrose Redmoon

Courage says, "Something must change and I must take responsibility for my part." You lack courage for life change when you are not thoroughly convinced that the *reward will equal the effort.* How quickly could you overcome your Fear of fire if your child were in a burning building? Undoubtedly you would sacrifice yourself to save her.

Most people living today would like to receive blessings from God. They see the value in some "religious training" for their children.[4] Prayer is a good idea when they need something, and hospital mammogram waiting rooms are filled with people begging the Lord's favor. Of course, a minister is always hired to "say a few words of assurance" at funerals. But the majority of people who live in the 21st century, are just not interested in *committing* to anything that would disrupt their Sunday brunch and bike ride, let alone the *courage* for a complete life course change. "[P]resent your bodies as a living sacrifice, holy and acceptable to God, which is your spiritual worship" (Rom 12:1).

If you choose to be a devoted Christian, the Lord promises:

1. He will be with you always (Matt. 28:20).

2. You will receive a crown of eternal life at the Treasure (Matt. 19:29; Mark 10:30).

"And walk in love, as Christ loved us and gave himself up for us, a fragrant offering and sacrifice to God" (Ephesians 5:2).

Ask yourself these questions:

*   Am I willing to obey Him without reservation?
*   Can I make a life course change without knowing the plot of my Journey?
*   Do I realize that my new life in Jesus may create conflict in my old relationships?
*   Do I want to cross a life-altering threshold and change my Fear-driven behavior?

Paul was willing to step through the smoke of his Fears into the light of Jesus Christ because he *knew* the Lord's goodness. *His desire to serve, please and show his Love for the Lord, became more important than his Fear*! Did Paul ever dream that his glowing life of courage would be the historical "visual aid" of a Christian servant? It is only the courageous who step out and *obey-surrender-burn through their Fears* to serve the Son of God. The idea of surrender to the Lord sounds like:

*   what weaklings and losers do
*   giving up *our* "heart's desires"
*   "I will be a nobody"

My surrender to the Lord actually means:

*   access to God's wisdom and schooling (Hebrews 5:8).
*   admitting, "I need help, I am scared, but I want to change" (Psalm 63:8).

- *He knows* every twist and turn of the labyrinth—I do not (Job 28:23-28).
- peace of mind and sanity (Isaiah 41:13; Psalm 69:13).
- I understand that He is in charge and I am not (Psalm 71:6).

Surrender is actually a trust-filled passion that can fuel your inner fire to its zenith. Do you ever pray with total surrender? "Let the will of the Lord be done" (Acts 21:14). "Lord, show me what you want me to do and I will do it without reservation." *Your desire to please Him is the kindling of courage* (James 4:15).

FEARBREAKER-JOYMAKER – *Serve Him*

As an expectant mother, I was plagued by dreams of having my baby switched with another baby in the hospital. After delivering, I asked my husband to follow our newborn to the nursery to make sure his wristband bore our names. I did not realize before giving birth, that after only seeing him for one minute, I would have known that baby anywhere. I could have picked him out of 100 babies in the nursery. He was my son, my Ethan. No one can ever replace him. That is how the Lord looks at *you*. *You are His child. Your life and presence has great Divine purpose* (Job 42:2).

It is not that you are specifically pre-destined with a stamp on your foot, but your unique skills, talents, and spirit combine, to make *you* a rare gift— useful to the Lord. Paul's conception and upbringing created a man with a *distinctive* set of abilities. Your Divine purpose in glorifying God is different from Paul's, but no less vital. While Paul's purpose was told to him, you get to *discover yours* with your brain, heart, and study of Jesus' life through the Word. *Every human soul has a Divine purpose to glorify and serve God* (Proverbs 19:21; Romans 8:28).

The passage of years will do nothing to soothe your Fears or anxieties. *Wishful thinking will never bring you to a high level of Joyful living.* Fear keeps you from a walk of Joy if you believe serving the Lord:

- is just too hard
- will not really bring rewards that are all that great
- would make you give up your identity
- would not be any fun
- does not really depend on *you,* someone else will do it

If there is Fear smoke in your life, vent the room and purify the *source* of the flame, don't tighten the room around you. Plug in your smoke alarm and keep the battery checked! *Deep Love for Jesus will dissipate the smokescreen that your Fears produce.*

Do you ever feel like a child—impatient for your reward? How difficult it is to wait to open your presents! At times after opening gifts, instead of responding with Gratitude, you think, "What else have you got?" This impatience feeds the Fears that you are "missing out," by choosing to live life the Lord's way. You want your reward *now*. *A Heroine-servant walks with patience, knowing that her reward is a crown in Heaven.* "[W]hen the chief Shepherd appears, you will receive the unfading crown of glory" (1 Peter 5:4).

If you are wide open to His providing hand, the possibilities of a Joyful Journey and meaningful life are limitless. Jesus chose the Journey to the cross for His direction. Paul served his Divine purpose as a missionary to the Gentiles on his one-way life Journey. What will your choice be? In preparing yourself you will need to:

- Study the Bible with a wide-open servant's heart.
- Look for what your experiences are here to teach you.
- Face your Fears and listen to their information.
- Believe that your life has a Divine purpose.
- Wear *your* cloak of responsibility.
- Know the *intensity* of your importance.

If you were the only human on this planet, Jesus would have come and taught and suffered and died just to save *you*. That is how important *you* are and that is why your precious life has Divine purpose. The stronger your sense of **Divine purpose** for your life and the greater your faith in the true God, the *weaker* your Fears. Will you serve Him sharing the gospel with co-workers, raising a grandchild to serve the Lord, or teaching generations of children in your Bible classes? In the movie of your life, is your faithful service the plot? (James 1:12).

The Heroine accepts her cloak of responsibility with grace for its value, but without ego. It is a cloak of honor and Divine purpose that reminds her sense of duty that her crown of glory—lies ahead. She asks not, "What comes tomorrow, my Lord?" but rather, "How can I serve you tomorrow, my Lord?"

When your one-way Journey leads you from this world, your work and influence in your congregation and family will all be finalized. The only enduring legacy is the unique footprint that your earthly steps leave behind, when your spirit is lifted up to the Lord. For *what* will you be missed? Will you be missed for you spiritual leadership? *Will you be missed for a life filled with Gratitude and good works?* You choose. You can begin today.

God asks for your devotion because He knows that following Him as a guide will bring you a life of true Joy. *Increasing your devoted service is not a selfish act, but a Loving choice of a child responding to the abundant Love of her Father* (1 John 4:19).

The deepest Love for God is motivated—*not by Fear of what God will do to me*, but by the deepest *Gratitude for what He has done for me*. Within your Gratitude for His steadfast Love, you may need to turn and make new friends, learn new habits, and clean away every distraction except that which supports your Joy-filled Journey—and keep doing that daily. "I love you, O LORD, my strength" (Psalm 18:1).

GROWING THROUGH FEAR

1. How does increasing your Love for Jesus by studying His Words dissipate the smokescreen of Fear and ego?

2. Anita Roddick wrote, "Be courageous, it's one of the only places left uncrowded." What does this quote mean? How will you grow in courage?

3. Even inside a smokestorm, a compass will still point to the North Star. What are some ways we can nurture a God-seeking, tender, compass heart within ourselves and our children?

4. What does it say about Paul's character that when he was humbled—he made no excuses?

5. Think of someone that you know who has changed their life to be completely focused on the Lord. Does the living flame within you burn brightly for the Way?

6. An area of my life where I need to change direction is:_____

_____

7. How can you pray "wide open" to serve the Lord in your life?

~ 4 ~
The Body Grows
Following the Bible Map through Fear
Conversion of Lydia and the jailer (Acts 16:11-34)

*A s she walks along the meadow pathway, the Heroine gently brushes her
fingers across the delicate wildflowers. The sun shines and a mild breeze
blows her cloak around her. Inside the billowing cape pocket, she sees the Map.
It is a Treasure Map that gives every direction needed to complete the Journey
and navigate the challenges ahead. The lives and stories of Heroes, Heroines, and
wanderers are contained in its journals. As she opens the Map, it comes alive and
interacts, demonstrating the expedition ahead. Making her way into the hills
and under the forest canopy, she reads new messages in the Map's topography,
and listens as it tells the glories of those who have walked the labyrinth in Joy.*

So, setting sail from Troas, we made a direct voyage to Samothrace, and the following day to Neapolis, and from there to Philippi, which is a leading city of the
district of Macedonia and a Roman colony. We remained in this city some days.
And on the Sabbath day we went outside the gate to the riverside, where we
supposed there was a place of prayer, and we sat down and spoke to the women
who had come together. One who heard us was a woman named Lydia, from the
city of Thyatira, a seller of purple goods, who was a worshiper of God. The Lord
opened her heart to pay attention to what was said by Paul. And after she was

baptized, and her household as well, she urged us, saying, "If you have judged me to be faithful to the Lord, come to my house and stay." And she prevailed upon us (Acts 16:11-15).

Imagine the delight to Paul, Silas, Luke, and Timothy that Lydia so readily embraced the truth about Jesus. This "seller of purple" and her friends were the first to be baptized into Christ on the continent of Europe. Lydia knew that there was more to life than being a wealthy businesswoman. She was searching for a life inside the True God. From paganism to Judaism, she had listened and learned, and then threw her tender heart open to the sacrificial Love of the Lord. The truth about Jesus the Messiah touched her sweet soul, and she wanted the life and salvation that His arms provided.

The moment Lydia was conceived—God knew her (Luke 1:13-17,44; Jeremiah 1:5). Her creator knew her DNA capabilities and family background; He also knew her *potential*. God knew what He crafted when He fashioned her, but she made the choice to use her life—for Him. She was a woman of substance.

As Lydia walked her life labyrinth, there was a door. She examined it carefully, pondering how it could take her life in a completely different direction. Then this incredible woman set her Fears aside and opened the door to a Joyful Christian life. The self-esteem of Lydia is remarkable! She not only stepped out and became a Christian, but Fearlessly opened her home to her new brothers-in-Christ—Paul and his companions.

Paul and Silas set about Philippi with the work of spreading the good news of Christ. But after healing a slave girl, trouble soon followed, and they were dragged off to jail.

The crowd joined in attacking them, and the magistrates tore the garments off them and gave orders to beat them with rods. And when they had inflicted many blows upon them, they threw them into prison, ordering the jailer to keep them safely. Having received this order, he put them into the inner prison and fastened their feet in the stocks. About midnight, Paul and Silas were praying and singing hymns to God, and the prisoners were listening to them, and suddenly there was a great earthquake, so that the foundations of the prison were shaken. And immediately all the doors were opened, and everyone's bonds were unfastened. When the jailer woke and saw that the prison doors were open, he drew his sword and was about to kill himself, supposing that the prisoners had escaped. But Paul cried with a loud voice, "Do not harm yourself, for we are all here." And the jailer called for lights and rushed in, and trembling with fear he fell down before Paul and Silas. Then he brought them out and said, "Sirs, what must I do to be saved?" And they said, "Believe in the Lord Jesus, and you will be saved, you and your household." And they spoke the word of the Lord to him and to all who were in his house. And he took them the same hour of the night and washed their wounds; and he was baptized at once, he and all his family. Then he brought them up into his house and set food before them. And he rejoiced along with his entire household that he had believed in God (Acts 16:22-34).

Paul and Silas were arrested, beaten, and painfully chained in the inner prison stocks. With open wounds from the blows, they responded to their situation by singing prayers of their Joy and confidence in the Lord! We can only wonder if this post-torture rejoicing irritated the jailer who could not escape listening to it. These servants of the Lord knew there was no depth of prison that God's Love and care for them—was not deeper still. *God's Word was on their lips, and the Holy Spirit filled their hearts, for Jesus' blood had purchased them a home in Heaven.* They expressed their Love to God in song! (Psalm 111:10).

As they sang, a very special earthquake unbolted the doors and freed the chained. Frightened that the prisoners had escaped, the jailer drew his sword to commit suicide. Paul intervened quickly, knowing that God alone gives life. "[S]ince he [God] himself gives to all mankind life and breath and everything" (Acts 17:25b). The terrified jailer fell down before them and asked the life-changing question, "Sirs, what must I do to be saved?" In the darkness of midnight, how his torch must have burst open the darkness of that windowless inner cell! *How much more the interest in becoming a child of God set fire in this man's heart.*

From pagan tormentor to innocent heart filled with Joy, the next few hours would change the jailer's life forever! His encounter with the power of God pushed him through his Fears to the other side, where the possibility of a Joyful life in God's service awaited him. Can you picture Paul and Silas explaining the death and resurrection of the Lord to the jailer and walking to share that good news with his family? *Imagine the rejoicing as they were all immersed into Christ that same night!*

The jailer looked inside himself and stepped through the:

- Fear that he had hurt the Lord's servants.
- Fear of the future—what will happen with my job?
- Fear that he might miss out on the Joy of being *saved*.

Lydia's tender heart had unfolded to the gospel with such serenity that the greatest contrast is seen when an earthquake is given *to get the jailer's attention*. At times, the Lord uses our worst nightmares to *wake us up* to the truth of Reality.

A YOUNG PART OF THE BODY

"And he [Jesus] is the head of the *body*, the *church*. He is the beginning, the firstborn from the dead, that in everything he might be preeminent. For in *him* all the fullness of God was pleased to dwell, and through him to reconcile to himself all things, whether on earth or in heaven, making peace by the blood of his cross" (Col. 1:18-20).

"[F]or the sake of his *body*, that is, the *church*" (Col. 1:24b).

"And he put all things under his feet and gave him as head over all things to the *church*, which is his *body*, the fullness of him who fills all in all" (Eph. 1:22-23). *[Emphases added]*

Lydia, the jailer, and their families now formed a congregation of the Lord's church at Philippi. They were now part of *His* body and would need to *grow to Love each other* as they Loved Jesus—their head. As the Lord gathered them together on the first day of every week (Sunday) to worship and break the bread (Acts 20:6-7; Matt. 26:26-29), they would have:

- been taught from a gospel account of the life of Jesus (2 Tim. 1:10)
- shared the inspired letters of the apostles (Phil. 1:1-2)
- reasoned how to apply apostolic teachings to their lives (Titus 2:11-14)
- read from the Old Testament—how all history pointed to Jesus (Heb. 11:1-3)
- celebrated the Lord's supper (Acts 20:7)
- sung songs of praise to God together (Matt. 26:30)
- given their money to help with the work of the church (1 Cor. 16:1-2)
- encouraged each other to grow in Love (Phil. 2:1-2)
- learned to deal with their Fears about the future by trusting in God's steadfast Love (Psalm 25:10)

With all reverence, these Christians came together in simplicity, humility, and Joy—to praise the Lord! How *different* some church assemblies look today than the early church! Can we wonder if the brethren at Philippi came together at Lydia's house? The worship gatherings of the Lord's day lasted many hours (Acts 20:7-12). It was a *precious opportunity* to gather together in the Lord's presence—every week—on His day! *Believer's hearts and voices joined in harmony on this special day and sought to honor the blood sacrifice of Jesus.* Studying the Word together was their greatest Joy and the *highlight* of their week! Can you imagine that these new Christians ever *chose to miss* assembling and worshipping the Lord? Would they have ever ignored the Lord and "made plans" for Sunday?

THE MAP
"For the word of God is living and active, sharper than any two-edged sword, piercing to the division of soul and of spirit, of joints and marrow, and discerning the thoughts and intentions of the heart" (Hebrews 4:12).

I leaned over to get as close as possible to the glass museum case. I had just flown across the ocean, and my first stop was to see the Codex Sinaiticus. Dating from c. 350 A.D., this Bible contains the earliest copy of the Greek New Testament. The amazing accuracy and sideline corrections show the care that was used in bringing down to *us,* these exact words and their meaning. When the Lord was asked: "Are you the Christ, the Son of the Blessed?" Jesus said, "I am, and you will see the Son of Man seated at the right hand of Power and coming with the clouds of heaven" (Mark 14:61-62). The men who witnessed His life wrote it down for you and me, so that *we may believe* (John 13:19). The accounts of the Bible are genuine and authentic because:

1. The writers wrote down, "That which was from the beginning, which we have heard, which we have seen with our eyes, which we looked upon and have touched with our hands, concerning the word of life" (1 John 1:1).

2. When Peter and John were threatened with punishment if they did not stop teaching about Jesus, they said, "Whether it is right in the sight of God to listen to you rather than to God, you must judge, for we cannot but speak of *what we have seen and heard*" (Acts 4:19-20). *[Emphases added]*

3. All of the Apostles died as martyrs except John. They were tortured, crucified and beheaded. No one sacrifices their life that way for a "fake" Jesus.[1]

4. The harmony of the 66 books written by 40 different writers over 16 centuries is startling.[2]

5. While the diverse writers came from different backgrounds, they chart the history of the world, from creation through the birth/growth of the church, in one cohesive Journey.

6. "Lord" and "said" occur together thousands of times in the Bible. God speaks with the authority of the Creator/sustainer and fulfills His words of promise.

7. It shows the lives of those who obeyed and disobeyed. It records the stories of those who were close to God, but made mistakes, like king David and the apostle Peter. Any book that was contrived in order to prove something, would record only the good, not Reality.

"All Scripture is breathed out by God and profitable for teaching, for reproof, for correction, and for training in righteousness" (2 Timothy 3:16).

One of my greatest delights is sharing my small collection of Bible antiquities in public school settings. From a beautifully illuminated page of 1 Corinthians painted in the year 1275 to a page of a 1612 King James Bible, I describe to students how carefully the translators worked to bring us the exact meaning of God's Word. I watch their eyes get big as I describe William Tyndale's 1536 entrapment and burning at the stake for the crime of translating the Bible into English. It is a joy to share with students the passion that has driven Lovers of God's Word to guard and protect it with their lives.

Since the first Gutenberg Bible came off the printing press in 1455, the Bible has sold more books that any other volume in history. Six billion Bibles, printed in 2,572+ languages are read and studied by people on every continent.[3] The Bible is the revealed will of God and people want to read it! As the printed Bible came into the hands of every man, hearts that had been told what the Bible said could now open this Treasure Map and *read the Word* for themselves.

Psalm 119 contains 176 verses about the treasure in the Word of God:
"I have stored up your *word* in my heart, that I might not sin against you" (Psalm 119:11).

"You are my hiding place and my shield; I hope in your *word*" (Psalm 119: 114).

"The sum of your *word* is truth, and every one of your righteous rules endures forever" (Psalm 119:160). *[Emphases added]*

Our lives as Christians and reason *not* to live in Fear rely on the *fact* that His Word is truth! The New Testament books were written down "within seventy years of the death of Christ, and by the men whose names they bear!"[4] Luke, the physician, accompanied Paul on many of his journeys. He not only wrote the book that bears his name, but with scientific precision recorded the details of the book of Acts. One-quarter of the New Testament was written by this one man who witnessed the new birth of the Lord's body/church at Philippi.[5]

So why do we reject the Bible as our life Map and use our wayward internal GPS system for guiding us on this life Journey? Many look to TV or movies for spiritual guidance and think, "A 'television morals' GPS is easy and Map reading is way too hard!" God wants you to *learn* His Word and His ways. *You must exert the energy to reap the benefit*. If you could download the mind of Christ into your own spirit, you could be guided by His thoughts, desires, and wisdom. The Bible Map *shares with you* the life, teachings, and motivations of the Lord Christ. God opens His hand and says, "Don't be afraid of what is ahead, I have drawn a Map for you since the creation and I will guide you through it."

"Your Word is a lamp to my feet and a light to my path" (Psalm 119:105).

My Dad served as a navigator for flight missions between China, Burma, and India during WWII. He still owns the maps he used for radar navigation through the Himalayan mountains as he guided their plane to land on makeshift jungle airstrips. He had to constantly focus on the map grid, tune the radar set to pick up different frequencies, and compare his position with the topography below. It was a skill that required training and diligence to accomplish the work and stay alive. To be guided by the Bible Treasure Map you must:

- believe that the Map coordinates are fixed and documented by history
- study and learn to use the Map correctly

- look at Map reading as a skill that must be learned and not downloaded
- submit to what you discover as the truth
- know that everything recorded is because of the great Love for you

Many guides will offer you their hand in the labyrinth, *but only One drew The Map.* God Loves you too much to leave you sitting in the darkness with your head in your hands. With the Map in hand  and the compass of a tender heart, you can step through Fear. You may still trip and land in the mud at times, but He will raise you up and clean you off and help you back on the pathway again. God gave *you* the Bible Treasure Map as an ever-present way of *guiding* you through this one-way Journey. And as you ask for help to deal with your Fear, accept that part of the answer is in *learning the wisdom* He has given you in His *Word*.

CODEX AMIATINUS

As the Medici family had already sealed their dominance in business, banking, and every fine art, they sought to share their wealth of accumulated knowledge with the Renaissance world. In 1525, they commissioned Michelangelo to design a beautiful Scholars' library, so that men could come from all over the world to study from their collection of thousands of ancient manuscripts. Ascending Michelangelo's marble staircase into the reading room, you can see the same benches where the giant books were chained by section. On display under glass, you can view beautifully illuminated medical books from the year 950, or illustrated herbal encyclopedias from 1127. The wealth of information contained here is astounding.

Underneath the large public Scholar's Library is a little known inner sanctum. Professors and scholars today can come and research from original, ancient Greek and Latin texts as they write academic dissertations and textbooks. I had read that the library held the earliest copy of the Latin Vulgate Bible, the Codex Amiatinus dating to the 8th century, and I had hoped to see it. I ventured beneath the library down a long passageway where an armed guard stood at the door. In broken Italian, I asked if it was possible to see the Codex Amiatinus. He took me inside to another guard who explained to me in Italian that "You would have to be a very important person or a professor with papers in order to study here." As I pivoted to leave, I stopped and said, "Oh, 'profesora,' I do teach a post-graduate music class for teachers!" He smiled, and started to find the paperwork. After filling out seven forms and surrendering my passport, camera, wallet, and hotel keys, I was escorted down a winding medieval passageway to a study room deep beneath the library. The dark ancient passage was barely wide enough for a man's shoulders and every few feet I could see into shelved rooms filled with priceless medieval books and ancient manuscripts. My heart was pounding with excitement! As we entered the inner cloister, I saw three older professors (two with beards) seated around the one table in the room. They worked on their laptops as they studied from large archaic Greek and Latin texts. The books still bore the heavy iron shackles on their bindings from when they once were chained to the study benches in the Scholars' Library above. I felt like jumping up and down! It was so exciting just to *be* there with all of that ancient knowledge! After the librarian had me fill out three *more* forms, they brought out a blue velvet cloth on which to lay this later copy of the original Codex. I caught myself cooing, "Oh this is s-o-o amazing!" over and over, under my breath. I then decided I had better play it cool and "act" like I belonged there. Even with my weak Latin skills, I could find the book headings and read John 1, "In the beginning was the Word, and the Word was with God, and the Word was God." Enraptured with passage after passage, I ended by reading Philippians 2:2, "[C]omplete my joy by being of the same mind, having the same love, being in full accord and of one mind." It was the thrill of a lifetime.

Those animal-skin vellum pages, so precisely written with the ink of insect juices 12 centuries ago, contain the essence of the same words that you and I are studying today. Even in the Dark Ages of mankind, if you wanted to know the truth about the light of Jesus Christ—it was there.

"Let the word of Christ dwell in you richly, teaching and admonishing one another in all wisdom, singing psalms and hymns and spiritual songs, with thankfulness in your hearts to God" (Colossians 3:16).

TENDER HEART AND STIFF NECK

When we see ourselves resisting the power of the Word of God in our lives, we must remember that even after we are saved, the Fear struggle between light and dark exists inside everyone of us. These qualities manifest themselves in us as:

Light		Dark
Tender-hearted		Stiff-necked
Love		Fear
Kindness		Hatred
Good		Evil
God-centered		Self-centered
Valued		Unimportant
Reality		Fantasy

Human nature indwells all these feelings and characteristics. After becoming a Christian, we spend our lives nurturing our *tender compass heart,* while training and "rehabilitating" our *stiff neck* (Ex. 34:9). It is a lifetime exploration to recognize the Fear-driven stiffness inside us and embrace the Joy of strengthening our spirits with God's Love. Knowing all things, God sees the tender and stiff-necked in each of us and by the Holy Spirit's incredible providing hand, offers us experiences by which we can grow (2 Cor. 1:9-10).

> Do nothing from selfish ambition or conceit, but in humility count others more significant than yourselves. Let each of you look not only to his own interests, but also to the interests of others. Have this mind among yourselves, which is yours in Christ Jesus, who, though he was in the form of God, did not count equality with God a thing to be grasped, but emptied himself, by taking the form of a servant, being born in the likeness of men. And being found in human form, he humbled himself by becoming obedient to the point of death, even death on a cross. Therefore God has highly exalted him and bestowed on him the name that is above every name, so that at the name of Jesus every knee should bow, in heaven and on earth and under the earth, and every tongue confess that Jesus Christ is Lord, to the glory of God the Father (Phil. 2:1-11).

Your tender heart grows strong as it pumps the blood of godliness throughout you. A stiff neck is softened through exercise and feeling the Love of the truth! How exciting that you are absolutely *in sync with the Lord's will when you are praying for strength to be a light-filled and tender-hearted Christian.* Long after the first conversions, Paul wrote to remind these brothers and sisters at Philippi:

> Do all things without grumbling or disputing, that you may be blameless and innocent, children of God without blemish in the midst of a crooked and twisted generation, among whom you *shine as lights in the world,* holding fast to the word

of life, so that in the day of Christ I may be proud that I did not run in vain or labor in vain (Phil. 2:14-16). *[Emphases added]*

What if Paul had harshly judged the jailer to be a completely stiff-necked man and said, "He is one mean, rotten guy; there is no way *he* will ever become a Christian." What if when the jailer was about to take his precious life, Paul and Silas just let it happen—I mean, he was a bad guy, right? Paul knew his job was to **share the Word of salvation. *God was in charge of the outcome.***

No human can be all good or all bad; not even you . . . and certainly not me. The jailer did not see his Divine purpose until Paul and Silas reached out to show him that his soul was *Loved*! As a pagan, he only knew about vicious, hostile, "Invented gods" whose followers lived in terror of offending them. Paul got to tell this tender-hearted man: "God Loves you! Don't be afraid of Him! If you will open your heart to Him, your life will change forever and you can walk in Joy" (1 Tim. 1:5).

THE BODY

In the late 18th century, abolitionists began talking to people of conscience about ending the British slave trade from Africa to the Americas. They showed people the actual heavy iron shackles that gouged into men's ankles, wrists, and necks on the sea voyage to slavery. They built boxes to demonstrate the tiny 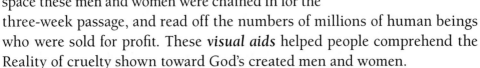 space these men and women were chained in for the three-week passage, and read off the numbers of millions of human beings who were sold for profit. These **visual aids** helped people comprehend the Reality of cruelty shown toward God's created men and women.

The newborn body of Christ at Philippi was a visual aid to the Roman world. Their neighbors, co-workers, and masters saw these new Christians *changing* as they were liberated from idol worship and set free from the *slavery of sin,* and began to grow in Love (John 8:32-34). These new Christians had to step out everyday into a heathen world that knew nothing of Jesus, except what it saw in *them*. The Roman world was powered by Fear and:

- The lust for power and wealth was unquenchable.
- Domination by Fearful ego was the ultimate control.
- Business operated by cheating, bribery, and intimidation.
- Patrician, plebian, slave, and ethnic groups sharply divided people.

- Roman soldiers took what they wanted and ruled by Fear.
- No one had security/safety or protection—except for the wealthy.
- Human life was cheap—slavery and prostitution were ways of life.

Hatred was everywhere, and the feeling beneath all hatred is Fear. What a challenge for these slaves, soldiers, business people, and jailers to now knit together as the body of Christ Jesus congregation at Philippi. The morning after a slave had come up from the saving waters of baptism in 1st c. Philippi, he woke up and *he was still a slave.* He had to *want* to learn how to live the Christian life, *right there in his Reality.* Even in their scrubbing, trading, and serving, these new Christians courageously showed they wanted more in their life than the darkness of Fear. Christian slaves risked being beaten if they were caught for slipping away from their duties and gathering on the Lord's day. But, in the Lord's body, slaves and masters, poor and rich, men and women, worshipped side by side, with full equality in the Lord (Gal. 3:26-28). People who had been raised in the strict Roman "classes" and taught to *hate* each other were now asked to deal with their Fear of being rejected and *Love each other as brothers and sisters—as Jesus Loved them* (John 15:12).

In Philippians 1:3-14, the word "adelphoi" meaning "brothers" is used interchangeably for DNA siblings, and sisters and brothers of God's family—*His body—the church.*[6] "I want you to know, *brothers*, that what has happened to me has really served to advance the gospel," (v. 12) "And most of the *brothers*, having become confident in the Lord by my imprisonment, are much more bold to speak the word without *fear.*" (v. 14) *[Emphases added]*

Paul knew the Philippians suffered in daily life, but he also commended them for sticking together and facing the enemy as *one body* with one truth. "[T]hat I may hear of you that you are standing firm in one spirit, with one mind striving side by side for the faith of the gospel, and not frightened in anything by your opponents" (Phil. 1:27-30). *Paul wrote them this letter from his prison cell in Rome!* Visualize them gathering around when that letter arrived, telling their grandchildren the stories of their conversion, and what their lives were like before they knew God's Love.

Many Christians met together daily! (Acts 2:42-47; 5:42; 12:12). Imagine a young devoted slave sneaking away after his master fell asleep, to go and be embraced and encouraged for a few hours in the home of Christian brethren (Acts 12:12). Perhaps they held hands and prayed for strength to deal with hardships or read precious words of comfort and Love from a gospel. Can you imagine that they would have fed their physical bodies each day and not fed themselves from the Bible Treasure Map? This young Christian body knew it needed constant Love and nourishing vitamins to survive daily living in a world of idol worship (Proverbs 17:17).

> For just as the body is one and has many members, and all the members of the body, though many, are one body, so it is with Christ. For in one Spirit we were all baptized into one body—Jews or Greeks, slaves or free-and all were made to drink of one Spirit. For the body does not consist of one member but of many. If the foot should say, "Because I am not a hand, I do not belong to the body," that would not make it any less a part of the body. And if the ear should say, "Because I am not an eye, I do not belong to the body," that would not make it any less a part of the body. If the whole body were an eye, where would be the sense of hearing? If the whole body were an ear, where would be the sense of smell? But as it is, God arranged the members in the body, each one of them, as he chose. If all were a single member, where would the body be? As it is, there are many parts, yet one body. The eye cannot say to the hand, "I have no need of you," nor again the head to the feet, "I have no need of you." On the contrary, the parts of the body that seem to be weaker are indispensable, and on those parts of the body that we think less honorable we bestow the greater honor, and our unpresentable parts are treated with greater modesty, which our more presentable parts do not require. But God has so composed the body, giving greater honor to the part that lacked it, that there may be no division in the body, but that the members may have the same care for one another. If one member suffers, all suffer together; if one member is honored, all rejoice together (1 Cor. 12:12-26).

A body works together effortlessly, as the internal organs each do their jobs. The liver does not resent the kidneys, nor the pancreas fight with the lungs! No part of the body would sabotage another part. All parts are directed by the "head" and have a common purpose. *As each organ supports the health of the other, they meet their goal—to thrive!* "[H]olding fast to the Head, from whom the whole body, nourished and knit together through its joints and ligaments, grows with a growth that is from God" (Col. 2:19).

The tender Love with which Paul wrote to Lydia, the jailer and their families, decades later in this letter to the Philippians, shows that they were not living lives of "negativity," but were fulfilling their Divine purpose: were faithful and abounding with Joy. "Therefore, my brothers, whom I love and long for, my joy and crown, stand firm thus in the Lord, my beloved" (Phil. 4:1). This is the most Loving and Joyful book of the New Testament; 18 times Paul uses the words for Joy or Rejoice. If you could take the blood pressure of this part of the body of Christ, the numbers would have been great!

These new Christians must have overcome their Fear of rejection and grown in spiritual maturity as they bonded *together* as a spiritual family.

Even today, any congregation that is abounding in Love as the Philippians has set aside personal desires and differences and focused on working together *Joyfully* as one body in the Lord.

> Let your reasonableness be known to everyone. The Lord is at hand; do not be anxious about anything, but in everything by prayer and supplication with thanksgiving let your requests be made known to God. And the peace of God, which surpasses all understanding, will guard your hearts and your mind in Christ Jesus (Philippians 4:5-7).

The Philippian brothers and sisters were encouraged to:
- face life without anxiety (Phil. 1:20-21)
- submit their worries to the Lord (Phil. 4:6)
- meet adversity and grow (Phil. 3:12-21)
- put into their eyes, ears and heart what is honorable (Phil. 4:8-9)
- be faithful in assembling together (Heb. 10:25; Phil. 1:3-11)
- strive to be one body with the same mind and Love (Phil. 2:1-11)
- live humbly and shun the darkness of rivalry (Phil. 2:3)
- grow a heart/mind of gratitude (Phil. 2:1-11)
- live with JOY (Phil. 2:18)

Do you picture this congregation having a lot of cliques? Imagine if they had looked at their new brethren and said, "But there isn't anyone here that I can relate to!" *The Philippians thrived as the body of Christ because they looked at each other as souls, not as "matching buddies."* What a blessing that God designed the church to be inter-generational and inter-cultural!

> [S]peaking the truth in love, we are to grow up in every way into him who is the head, into Christ, from whom the whole body, joined and held together by every joint with which it is equipped, when each part is working properly, makes the body grow so that it builds itself up in love (Eph. 4:15-16).

Paul Loved the Philippians because they Loved the **Lord** and Loved *each other*. "I hold you in my heart" (Phil. 1:7). They knew God had blessed them with release from the slavery of sin and their Joy was complete! God withheld nothing from them and withholds no Joy from you! Think of how the faithfulness of these simple people inspires *you*, long after their physical bodies have turned to dust? Answer this question—"What was *their* Divine purpose?"

A wanderer strolls along the labyrinth and pulls out the Map to glance occasionally saying, "I know the basics, I don't need to study this Map." Folding it up to put it back in the pocket, the Map drops in the dirt unnoticed, as she walks away.

As the sun rises each morning, the Heroine awakens to give thanks to the Creator and spend time with the Map. She has fallen in Love with His Words and must pull herself away from it each day to complete her tasks. She reads that a faithful Journey through adversity is the only way to partake of the Treasure. As she discovers the deep truths in the Map, they invite her to study deeper and hear the Love underlying each message:

"You are not your slave branding, or your family background. You are not a throw away. . . . You are Loved. . . . You are my precious child and I gave my life just for you." The Heroine-servant closes her eyes, and is strengthened to live this day, as a tribute to her Lord and King.

NAVIGATING THE MAP OR WANDERING

The wicked queen of the Snow White fantasy story asked the mirror every day, "Mirror, mirror, on the wall, whose the fairest of them all?" The day came when the mirror did not tell her what she wanted to hear—and she shattered it. We treat the Bible Map in the very same manner if we say, "Map, map, I love you so, tell me that I'm fine and I don't have to grow." When your Fantasy movie ends and the DVD pops out, *you are sitting in a room of Reality.* A Fearful stiff-neck will tell you to put in another movie and keep pretending that the "movie morals GPS" will be your guide through the labyrinth of life. **When you read the Bible Map about how Christians should live and worship, and you ignore it, you are saying to God**:

"YOU ARE NOT GOING TO TELL ME WHAT TO DO.
I DON'T CARE WHAT YOU SAY."

Maps lead us forward toward a goal. The real Bible Treasure map will guide you to the real riches—Heaven. "But one thing I do: forgetting what lies behind and straining forward to what lies ahead. I press on toward the goal of the prize of the upward call of God in Christ Jesus" (Philippians 3:13b-14).

A Heroine-servant grows through Fear by passionate Bible study and prayer. The flag of her life expedition displays: "I am prepared and will not be deterred." It is her greatest Joy to grow in the skill of Map reading. What if my Dad had cheated his way through navigator's school and had not learned the intricacies of radar navigation? He learned the complexities of map reading to *keep their bodies alive in wartime*. The two most powerful motivators in all humans are *Love* and *Fear*:

- I *Love* God so I want to know Him through His Word.
- I *Fear* being left behind in the darkness of separation from Him.

You are living in wartime. Satan is the Dark Enemy who wants to kill your body and have your spirit dwell in torment with Him. Your only defensive *weapon* is the sword of the Spirit, which is the *Word of God* (Eph. 6:17). Stiff-necked *Fear* wants you to:

- be constantly confused about your life direction and follow the GPS learned from the movies and your parents
- believe you can live and worship however you want
- think the best congregation of the Lord's body is the most entertaining
- wear the name Christian, but spend no time in the Word daily. "Popping open" your Bible when you "can" usually means that you dust it off before services
- spend the moments of your life in front of the television
- criticize the Bible's truth to rationalize disobeying
- judge that the heavenly Treasure *will not be that great*
- stop talking to God and pouring your Fears and Joys out to Him
- disbelieve that there is one God, one Jesus, one Spirit, one church

A preacher-friend of mine, George Jensen, said once, "We may as well have little cubbies built in the foyer for everyone to keep their Bibles safe as they won't be using them during the week." Self-sabotage because of lack of devotion to God's hand-written Map is the unfortunate norm among Christians (Phil. 3:18). As the expedition of life takes explorers into difficult places, they lay the Map down and make the choice to go it alone. Just as human bodies starve without nutritious food, explorers quickly become wanderers and are lost without following *the* Map's direction inch by inch. Accept the Reality that your Christian-life Journey is:

- always tilted at an incline to provide muscle-building exercise
- designed for you to grow to be a light in a dark world
- always in view of the Lord—24/7
- filled with guides who will reward your stiff neck
- an expedition requiring constant reflection and courage
- meant to be walked within the Body (1 Cor. 12:27)

Reverencing that you breathe, study, and worship in *God's presence* helps build spiritual vigor along this one-way Journey of life. As your Fears are submitted to God, you read His answers in the pages and characters within His Word. If you want to know about God, you must spend time listening to Him (Phil. 3:17). Train for your life expedition by studying the Bible:

- with a reading schedule, daily email, or one-year Bible
- at a regular time and place—*when you are not sleepy*
- applying it to daily life: "How would Paul have handled this?"
- by meditating on a truth for the day (Proverbs 25)

Keep Bibles everywhere to remind you to read before eating and before recreation. Write down Bible verses and memorize them: on breaks at work, at stop lights, while doing dishes, and on the treadmill. If you want less Fear, increase your Faith in *who* your amazing God is. His Loving hand is seen in every page of His Word and when He tells someone, "Fear not or do not be afraid," there is *a reason to trust in Him*! "And the Lord said to Paul one night in a vision, 'Do not be afraid, but go on speaking and do not be silent, for I am with you'" (Acts 18:9).

Corrie and Betsie Ten Boom were watchmakers in the family business when the Nazis took over Holland. When they were arrested for helping Jews, they were taken to a labor camp at Ravensbruck, Germany. While other "prisoners" tried to hold onto their jewels or family heirlooms as they were brought into the prison camp, the Ten Boom sisters smuggled in a tiny precious Bible. They knew they had God's Words of life amidst the "hell" of survival in a labor camp, and stench from the ovens that constantly burned human flesh.[7]

As you grow to Love and bond with the Bible Map, it comes alive with the colors of history and feelings, truths, and steadfastness of its Writer. In its pages the Creator whispers, "You are so very Loved, let me show you." Mature humans will tell you that "falling in love" is the easiest part of a relationship. Bonding with and learning the Bible requires time and intensity, just as it does to learn anything. *A Christian's devotion to Bible study is the greatest of all adaptive behaviors for Fear.* The

Faithful *build* a Loving and obedient relationship with the Map. The Fearful *never* do. "So faith comes from hearing, and hearing through the word of Christ" (Rom. 10:17).

FEARBREAKER-JOYMAKER JOURNEY

"Finally brothers, whatever is true, whatever is honorable, whatever is just, whatever is pure, whatever is lovely, whatever is commendable, if there is any excellence, if there is anything worthy of praise, think about these things" (Philippians 4:8).

When you learn to handle "negative" thoughts and turn your mind to focus on the true, honorable, just, pure, lovely, and excellent that the Lord has provided for *you* in His Word—you will rejoice and *praise Him*. As you learn of Him, give thanks for the way He works in your life and the people He blesses you with. YOUR ONE-WAY JOURNEY HAS A MAP! Give *thanks* every day for the Bible! Meet the day with a Gratitude attitude and *that* will be the theme of your life movie. "I thank my God in all my remembrance of you, always in every prayer of mine for you all making my prayer with joy" (Philippians 1:3).

"Even if I am to be poured out as a drink offering upon the sacrificial offering of your faith, I am glad and rejoice with you all. Likewise you also should be glad and rejoice with me" (Philippians 2:17-18).

Are you wearing your cloak of responsibility with Joy as a visual aid of a life purchased by Jesus Christ? The Reality is: future generations will *thrive* or *suffer* in rebellion because of the gospel working through *you*. FEEL THAT RESPONSIBILITY. "[S]o that at the name of Jesus every knee should bow, in heaven and on earth and under the earth" (Philippians 2:10).

Transcending your Fears means accepting a Journey that is *led* by the Word of God. Focusing on serving the Cause keeps your tender-hearted compass pointed in the right direction. You can burst into Joy with these Reality questions:

- Am I growing to be more useful to the Lord?
- Can I honestly face the Lord and say I studied His teachings?
- Am I constantly remembering that I walk in His presence?
- Do I talk to Him and pray to Him constantly throughout my day?
- When adversity reveals my Fears, do I face and *grow* through them?

Your Divine purpose is the same as Paul's, the same as Lydia's and the same as the jailer's. Your Divine purpose is to be a Joy-filled Christian and glorify God in your life! In the deepest hardships, when you have no idea what is ahead and you are filled with Fear, you can choose to focus on Joy, regardless of your life circumstance. *Fear makes you feel small and insignificant—Divine purpose makes you feel strong, important, and Joyful!* "Rejoice in the Lord always; again I will say, Rejoice" (Philippians 4:4).

Paul wrote from prison to his beloved brothers and sisters, "I have learned in whatever situation I am to be content" (Phil. 4:11). Whether it is Paul's inner strength from prison or Lydia's courageous life change, you can celebrate being alive to serve the same Lord. You can only look forward to hearing the "rest of the story" in Heaven. "But our citizenship is in heaven, and from it we await a Savior, the Lord Jesus Christ" (Philippians 3:20).

GROWING THROUGH FEAR

1. What do you think was the Philippians' favorite day of the week? What is your favorite day of the week? Why?

2. As you pray and petition God for help with your Fears, a part of His answer is found in His Word that *you must study to learn.* How are you organizing your life to spend time training in the Word every day?

3. How do we overcome Fear of rejection when we want to reach out to others?

4. Since *you* are not your social status, bank balance, skin color, or background, what part of you does the Lord see? How did liberty and freedom come to a 1st century slave without a job change?

5. What advice would you give to a young married couple who visit a congregation where there are no other young married couples?

6. Challenge: Read through the book of Acts like a novel and track the main characters and plots. Follow a map of the missionary journeys and locate the congregations mentioned in the Letters.

~ 5 ~
The Magic Yearning
Satan and the power of suggestion
The prodigal son (Luke 15:11-32)

*I*n *the distance, the Heroine hears the sounds of party music and laughter. She follows that pathway toward a glittering carnival. The festival sight is breathtaking with beautifully colored tents, exotic smells, and cheerful people dressed in their finery. Great trumpets sound forth as a brightly-arrayed herald calls out to her, "Greetings to the lovely lady! Welcome to a world of splendor, where every wish can be fulfilled and dreams enchanted!" The glistening pageantry of the sight is overwhelming.*

She is drawn to the tent of a Magician who amazes the crowd with vanishing tricks and illusions. "What an exquisite young lady! Is it possible that one so beautiful, would also be so bold as to seize the magic thrill of ecstasy?" As she steps forward, the elated crowd purrs with anticipation. In the most charismatic undertone the Heroine has ever heard, the Magician says secretively, "Few are daring enough to ascend the magic pathway to bliss and have all their troubles disappear . . . is it possible you are the one?" As he gallantly takes her by the hand and helps her up the stairway, she closes her eyes with delight, anticipating the bliss of his promise. But in a sudden moment of terror, she is drawn through the tent onto a fierce gauntlet walkway. The party music is immediately drowned out by the screeching, grinding noise of the gauntlet. The floorboards move and

79

circle above boiling pots below. Steam obscures the end of the gauntlet, so she cannot see the obstacles ahead. Great steel balls rotate to knock her off into the flames as jagged circular blades come up from underneath. Large winches swing razor-sharp axe heads back and forth in front of her body. She cringes as she tries to pass them, holding her breath to step between the obstacles in motion. Shaking and trembling, the Heroine bursts into tears as she hears the laugh of the Magician ahead.

And he said, "There was a man who had two sons. And the younger of them said to his father, 'Father, give me the share of property that is coming to me.' And he divided his property between them. Not many days later, the younger son gathered all he had and took a journey into a far country, and there he squandered his property in reckless living. And when he had spent everything, a severe famine arose in that country, and he began to be in need. So he went and hired himself out to one of the citizens of that country, who sent him into his fields to feed pigs. And he was longing to be fed with the pods that the pigs ate, and no one gave him anything.

But when he came to himself, he said, 'How many of my father's hired servants have more than enough bread, but I perish here with hunger! I will arise and go to my father, and I will say to him, Father, I have sinned against heaven and before you. I am no longer worthy to be called your son. Treat me as one of your hired servants.' And he arose and came to his father. But while he was still a long way off, his father saw him and felt compassion, and ran and embraced him and kissed him. And the son said to him, 'Father, I have sinned against heaven and before you. I am no longer worthy to be called your son.' but the father said to his servants, 'Bring quickly the best robe, and put it on him, and put a ring on his hand, and shoes on his feet. And bring the fattened calf and kill it, and let us eat and celebrate. For this my son was dead, and is alive again; he was lost and is found.' And they began to celebrate.

Now his older son was in the field, and as he came and drew near to the house, he heard music and dancing. And he called one of the servants and asked what these things meant. And he said to him, 'Your brother has come, and your father has killed the fattened calf because he has received him back safe and sound.' But he was angry and refused to go in. His father came out and entreated him, but he answered his father, 'Look these many years I have served you, and I never disobeyed your command, yet you never gave me a goat, that I might celebrate with my friends. But when this son of yours came, who has devoured your property with prostitutes, you killed the fattened calf for him!' And he said to him, 'Son you are always with me, and all that is mine is yours. It was fitting to celebrate and be glad, for this your brother was dead, and is alive; he was lost and is found'" (Luke 15:11-32).

While family drama began with the family of Adam and Eve, it has continued through every era and culture. If your family has no Fear shown in *rebellion*, Fear manifested in *jealousy,* or Fear that is visible in *selfishness* among you, you are to be commended, or perhaps you are—deluded. Volumes have been written about this family, for they reveal the Fears within all of us (Psalm 56:3).

God's plan for human and church families is to radiate Love, and work together on this one-way life Journey. But too often, the powerful emotions of family relationships are what tear us apart. The Lord gives us different personalities and weaknesses, knowing that we will irritate each other, set boundaries, and challenge each other to rise to the occasion and *grow*. God did not plan for humans to be programmable robots. He intricately designed us with free will and feelings, and we must be grateful for His engineering (1 Cor. 12:25).

The story of the prodigal son does not have a fairy tale ending. The point is not: "They lived happily ever after," but rather, "They *grew* through their Fears." Within you and me, in our Joyous light and Fearful darkness dwell a mature father, immature prodigal, and jealous older son.

PRODIGAL SON

The prodigal in us wants to live as Peter Pan, soaring over Magic Never Grow-Up Island with no responsibilities. He lives for constant amusement and eats candy for every meal. He lands on the highest peak and crows, "I will never, ever, grow up and you can't make me!" What his heart is really saying is, "I am *afraid* to be a grown-up."

The Peter Pan prodigal rules within us when we:
- conceal our Fears deep inside
- say "I deserve this. . ."
- feel chronic restlessness with our lives
- envy the lives of the rich and famous
- pretend our Invented god is happy with our morals

- think "I want to do what I want to do, when I want to do it!"
- ignore wisdom
- yearn for the magic "out there"
- embrace immaturity and resist Reality
- believe that our choices are not hurting others

Part of every one of us would love to spend our lives as a child, with every need met and comforted; perfectly cared for and never disappointed.

When our Fears are not brought out into the open, that immature child down inside—controls us. We dig our heels in and refuse to grow up because we feel *entitled* to live in the magic bliss of a party. The prodigal in us spends a lot of time watching other people's movies and analyzing how he is missing out on the fun. The lure of the magic wins our hearts slowly, as we little by little become discontented with our Reality. No one wakes up one morning and says, "I am going to start sinful, selfish living today." It started with:

- watching someone get away with something
- learning to admire the famous and worldly
- seeing hypocrisy in a role model
- feeling that you are missing out on pleasure

The Magician's voice whispers *yearning* into your Thought storms by the *power of suggestion*. "Make your troubles vanish . . . come feel the thrill of the party." "The discerning sets his face toward wisdom, but the eyes of a fool are on the ends of the earth" (Proverbs 17:24).

When movies and television were invented in the 20th century, no one imagined they would change the course of society as they beamed the *values of others* into our lives. While the beguiling allure of life on the tightrope has bewitched humans since the beginning, prodigal encouragement now *casts a spell into our homes* through: television, movies, telephones, and internet. Disconnected and discontented, we *yearn* for an illusion world "out there" and not the Reality of the actual daily movie occurring in *our* lives.

Rebellion stems from Fear that:

- I am missing something that I am entitled to.
- being "good" is boring
- submission to the Lord is weakness

- standards are being imposed—to control me
- I am not good enough

OLDER SON

The older son carries the responsible, yet bitter part of our spirits, like they are heavy boulders. His self-imposed view of life's "obligations" may flow from a feeling of Fear-filled perfection that, "I am only worthy, if I am perfect" (Luke 15:29-30). When he Fears his "good work" is disrespected, he is angry that his efforts to gain the father's love have been ignored.

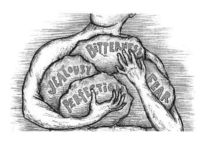

Quickly blaming his feelings on the father (v. 29), he tries to disconnect his perfect self, from the *soiled DNA* he shares with his brother—"this son of *yours*." (v. 30) Blame is a masterful tool of Fear-driven jealousy to point a magic "fix-it" wand on someone else's life and away from exposing the jealous person's heart. The Jealousy Club has a pledge song, "There Must be Something Wrong with You." The chorus goes, "Keep on a-blaming, keep on a-shaming, point the magic wand at them." The older brother's Fear-driven jealousy really means:

- You are rewarding his criminal behavior.
- I wish he had never come home.
- I want the limelight for being so "good."

The older son's plan for his "Perfect Son of the Year" award backfires into a life as a cheerless giver, unable to walk in Joy (2 Cor. 9:7). It is just too frightening for him to actually feel his Fears of, "I am scared that I am not good enough." *Self-righteous perfectionism is an elaborate costume of Fear.* When you carry boulders of Fear-driven jealousy and perfection with you on life's Journey, your spirit becomes hunched, sore, and twisted.

> But if you have bitter jealousy and selfish ambition in your hearts, do not boast and be false to the truth. This is not the wisdom that comes down from above, but is earthly, unspiritual, demonic. For where jealousy and selfish ambition exist, there will be disorder and every vile practice. But the wisdom from above is first pure, then peaceable, gentle, open to reason, full of mercy and good fruits, impartial and sincere. And a harvest of righteousness is sown in peace by those who make peace (James 3:14-18).

FATHER

Wisdom and maturity embody this father as he watches his precious son choose to walk into the gauntlet. What agony it is to watch someone be seduced by the world! The father part of us reasons with the prodigal, prays and waits—never giving up *hope,* that the beloved child will return (1 Cor. 13:7).

The wise father knew his power and limits. He had the:

- power to give the inheritance or not
- power to run after the boy or not
- power to pour out compassionate forgiveness at the boy's return
- wisdom to pray and never give up
- wisdom to counsel the older son to set himself aside and rejoice for his brother
- wisdom to know he could not reach inside and change the boy's heart. *The young man had to change himself.*

My grandmother had a very wise saying, "A man convinced against his will is of the same opinion still." *Except by inspiration and healthy boundaries, you cannot change another person.* "Whoever trusts in his own mind is a fool, but he who walks in wisdom will be delivered" (Proverbs 28:26).

Free will is a fearsome thing, but God *allows* it in every man and woman for *His* purpose (Isaiah 1:20). This earthly father showed his mental/emotional/spiritual health after his son was gone. He grieved and hoped—perhaps looking down the road each day, but there is no evidence that he "took to the bed" and gave up living because his son was being torn apart in the "gauntlet." *He accepted Reality.* This is an important step in conquering our own Fears when Loved ones are in rebellion (Proverbs 10:8).

MISSION CONTROL

While concern over someone destroying their life is a Reality, trying to control others with: criticism, pouting, anger, and guilt shows *your Fear* and will backfire on you. Fear-driven control tries to soothe anxiety within by seeking perfection in this imperfect world. *It is an illusion that perfection is possible.*

- If I were perfect, then I—he—she will always be happy.
- If I bend his will and change him, all will be well.
- If I can control _____, then I will be happy.

How difficult it is to give up trying to control someone, and let go! The prodigal's father knew what healthy boundaries were, and did not burn relationship bridges with his son. This wise father realized that the young man's heart would have to *return to godly living of his own free will* (Hebrews 12:11).

"Did you think that you could spend your days sitting on a velvet cushion, dressed in resplendent finery and not pay a price?" the Magician hollers at her sarcastically. "You promised me riches and pleasure and excitement . . ." she cries, as the axe blades swish back and forth before her. "I just wanted to feel happy all the time, without all of this Map work!" she screams as she falls to her knees and sobs.

SOMEWHERE OUT THERE

Satan, the great Illusionist and Magician, wants the thoughts of *your* mind to fall under *his spell* (2 Cor. 2:11). He preys upon your deepest Fears by whispering, "How very unfair life is." His sleight of hand and flattery are specifically designed to turn the tender compass hearts of the *immature parts of us*, away from Jesus—the North Star of all creation, and toward him. The prodigal and older brother's "negative" brains swirled with *unfulfilled yearning from the Magician's power of suggestion*. As they *allowed* their negative Thought storms to become captives of the Magician, they *chose* to let their hearts and feet—wander. "There is a way that seems right to a man, but its end is the way to death" (Proverbs 14:12).

Notice how *you* behave when you spend time with your friends of the "Live for the Magic Club," versus your friends of the "Reality Club." The "Missing Out on Pleasure Club" is filled with members who are just sure that life "out there" is constant holiday magic, wonderland, and dream fulfillment. Club members are not interested in the Reality of "right here" or any

Gratitude for the life they have been given. The worst thing they can imagine would be opening up and seeing what is "in here" within their spirit that keeps them so discontented and afraid.

> Alexis was a nice teenage girl. She helped her mother with her three younger sisters and had never been in trouble. She was an average student, with only a few friends at her high school. Suddenly one day, a new friend (girl) kissed her, and explained that she was a bisexual. Alexis was confused and told her parents, who mistakenly commented that some people are just born "different." As this new girl and her group befriended her, Alexis rehearsed a frightening memory from the year before when an older male neighbor made advances to her. Even though the incident had been dealt with at the time, constantly rehearsing the offense with these girls became the power for Alexis' new "girls only" beliefs. After she turned 18, she announced to her parents that she was a lesbian. Her lesbian friends "accepted and understood her," and the older ones bought her expensive gifts and took her on trips. They gave her "acceptance," for "who she was"—a prodigal daughter (Romans 1:26-27).

The lesbian girls said, "We love you! Why not savor the magic?" *The Magician wants your children and will travel the thought pathways of their Fearful loneliness and rebellion to magnetize the compass of their heart and every belief that is true and godly.*

Alexis' parents lack of intervention and clear teaching created distortion in the compass of this once tender heart. Without clear direction, her Fearful lonely heart bonded with these girls, and she was lured away. The voice of Fear in the "Missing Out on Pleasure Club" whispers sweetly, but *grows to be a life lived within the gauntlet.* "Resist the devil, and he will flee from you. Draw near to God, and he will draw near to you. Cleanse your hands, you sinners, and purify your hearts, you double-minded. Be wretched and mourn and weep. Let your laughter be turned to mourning and your joy to gloom. Humble yourselves before the Lord, and he will exalt you" (James 4:7-10).

FREE ESTIMATES

> Let no one say when he is tempted, 'I am being tempted by God,' for God cannot be tempted with evil, and he himself tempts no one. But each person is tempted when he is lured and enticed by his own desire. Then desire when it has conceived gives birth to sin, and sin when it is fully grown brings forth death (James 1:13-15).

Pulling my airplane carry-on behind me, I walked down the street toward my car. Not paying much attention to my surroundings, I glanced up at a large sign on the side of a building: "FREE ESTIMATES—SHOWROOM AVAILABLE." I thought, "I wish that young Christians would honestly ask an older Christian for a "Free Estimate" in the big decisions of life!" There is a showroom available of healthy friendships and marriage relationships in the Bible, and in your congregation. Who would be courageous enough to ask before choosing the "gauntlet?"

> Susan sent her daughter Elena to a Christian college for an education and perhaps—to find a mate. She chose Derek who had been raised in a troubled home and never embraced the truth about the gospel of Christ. As they were becoming more serious, Susan was learning that Derek had credit card debt, and had dropped in and out of college many times. When they came home for a weekend, she saw that Derek was taking some serious anti-depressant medication. Susan tried to reason with her daughter that money troubles, school failures, and emotional issues, added up to a lot of challenges in a young man. Elena rebelled and defended Derek. A few weeks before their wedding, Derek told Susan to stop e-mailing directly with her daughter, but rather use their new "joint" email address. Derek was "easing into job-hunting," and left the payments of his massive debts up to Elena. Susan was virtually cut off from communication with her daughter.

While anyone can make the *personal choice* to grow and change, Author Steve Farrar writes quite poignantly, "What you are before you are married is what you will be after you are married. . . . Right now is as good as it gets."[1] "Without counsel plans fail, but with many advisers they succeed" (Proverbs 15:22).

Had Elena listened to a "Free Estimate" instead of her Fear-driven rebellion, she might have heard: "HE IS NOT YOUR MISSION—HE NEEDS TO BE YOUR PARTNER." Before you lock your life into another's *will* ask 1) Does this person elevate my personal holiness level? 2) Will this person, more than any other on the planet, help me to reach Heaven? A "Free Estimate" includes the knowledge that some light or dark personality characteristics cluster together.

Light/maturing individuals:

- display honesty.
- accept personal responsibility for their actions
- manage their time and money.
- show interest in the needs of others.

Dark/immature individuals:

- act impulsively.
- have short tempers and are easily angered.
- are dishonest in personal/financial matters.
- look at life with self-centeredness.

Collecting information from past behavior yields insightful clues. For if Fear-motivators are not dealt with inside a person, they will drive their future behavior. The Reality is—emotional and spiritual growth are deeply connected. Read that over again: *The Reality is—emotional maturity and spiritual maturity are deeply connected*. It is not possible to be maturing spiritually, if you are emotionally immature. "[W]e proclaim, warning everyone and teaching everyone with all wisdom, that we may present everyone mature in Christ" (Col. 1:28).

NO SURRENDER MEANS NO SURRENDER – Time to grieve

Peter Pan never did grow up. He lives in delusion on Magic Never Grow-up Island today. As most real-life prodigal stories do not end with reconciliation, those who Love prodigals know the overwhelming grief of gazing out of their front door, and *never seeing the beloved return*. We grieve them:

- living the Fear-filled illusion that happiness is "out there"
- making terrible decisions that pull them away from the Lord
- wasting their days seeking pleasure
- believing a "Holiday of Sin" will not have everlasting consequences.
- never knowing *true* Joy—because they want to live in "magic"

Some prodigals look into the Magician's book of secrets and see how he plans for their destruction, but return to living under his spells of discontent and yearning. "The dog returns to its own vomit, and the sow, after washing herself, returns to wallow in the mire" (2 Pet. 2:22b). A prodigal's *Fears are so deep*, that he cannot see the destruction he causes in his *family*, or to his *own soul*. He fails to see the Lord's outpouring, steadfast Love (Luke 9:61-62).

As prodigals numb their Fearful—insecure—selfish feelings with maladaptive behaviors, the Lord *grieves* over their lost souls (Luke 18:24) and hardness of heart (Mark 3:1-6). Paul was concerned for the prodigals in the church and wrote, "I fear that when I come again my God may humble me before you, and I may have to mourn over many of those who sinned earlier and have not repented of the impurity, sexual immorality, and sensuality that they have practiced" (2 Cor. 12:21).

Living with the sadness of a beloved one destroying themselves involves a grieving process that takes time and *work*. Beware of your "negative" brain's desire to grip tightly to the anguish of the prodigal's choices and *focus your lifetime—mourning over them*. This is a walk of Fear and is a Joy-less pathway for you. But if your daughter is out in the world living in sin, and you have tried everything possible to bring her back, you must *grieve* that loss. Through studying God's devoted Love for you, and prayer, you will gain peace and resolve to never give up hope for her return—until her last breath. When you are able to attend the wedding of your best friend's pure, Christian daughter and feel only *true Joy for them*, you will know that you are growing and processing *your* grief (Ecc. 3:4).

As she lays crying on the moving planks, she brings from her memory a story in the Map about a knight who sought to use his bow for the Cause of the King, but often missed his target. At the point of his deepest torment, he realized the Magician's skillful work was in the power of suggestion. Once the knight put the King's words in his mind, he could draw his bow and send arrows with great skill. "Why do I have to keep walking this gauntlet?" the Heroine wonders. She gathers herself against the Magician, and turns back through the blades toward her Journey once more. The last edge slices the back of her shoulder, leaving a deep gash that scars her forever.

CAME TO HIMSELF

In your prayers today, did you pray for someone to "come to himself?" (Luke 15:17). Did you pray for the prodigal/older son part of *you* to "come to *yourself*?" When the noise of party life, money, and its contingent "friends" were gone, the prodigal son found himself at the bottom. In watching the providing hand of the Lord opening and closing life's doors, it is not accidental that the prodigal's Fear-driven choices brought him to a moment of solitude in a pig pen. God's hand was with the prodigal, even in the *Reality* of the pig pen. *There is no depth of mire that He is not deeper still* (Job 11:8; Matt. 28:20). Hungry, dirty, lonely, and at his lowest point:

- All "magic" illusions were gone.
- He saw himself in the Reality he had chosen.
- He knew he had been selfish and immature.
- He knew his father's nature was loving forgiveness.
- He wanted to return home—even as a servant.

"I called on your name, O Lord, from the depths of the pit; you heard my plea, 'Do not close your ear to my cry for help!' You came near when I called on you; you said, 'Do not fear!'" (Lamentations 3:55-57).

No matter where you are, *you* do not escape God's Loving attention. You may feel that you are a worthless piece of garbage in the mire with the swine, but Jesus came and died for *you*. As you humbly accept His Love, making *no excuses for yourself,* know that—all great personal change begins with repentance. "The Fear of the LORD is instruction in wisdom, and humility comes before honor" (Proverbs 15:33).

The greatest opportunity for a life direction shift is when our Journey is going badly. It is the realization that our life of yearning illusion is empty. Just as human Love is very, very real, but cannot be *seen* except in our actions. God's Loving hand of mercy extends down to us, right where we are (Psalm 136:12). Our responding actions *show* our Love. "Just as I am," is the voice of the repentant, coming in humility before the LORD.[2] It is not feeling, "I will just stay where I am—because my friends 'accept' me." We "accept" Reality, we do not "accept—meaning it's ok"—sin. God embraces and Loves the immature within us, but repentance means we leave our *sinful way of life* behind. The Sovereign King of the universe holds His children to a high standard of honor (Ex. 20:2-3). In a moment of complete humility, the prodigal and older son within us bows and says:

- I must overcome my Fear and look inside.
- *I take complete responsibility for everything I say and do.*

- I will face the *voice of discontent* that brought me here.
- I feel the pain I have caused my family and my Lord.
- I will reverse my course *daily* to bring glory to my King.

"But this is the one to whom I will look: he who is humble and contrite in spirit and trembles at my word" (Isaiah 66:2b).

LIVING THE SURRENDER

While an "Aha!" moment may turn the direction of a life Journey, it is maintaining that daily course by steering the small steps that makes heroic life change. "The law of his God is in his heart; his *steps* do not slip" (Psalm 37:31).

"He drew me up from the pit of destruction, out of the miry bog, and set my feet upon a rock, making my *steps* secure." (Psalm 40:2). *[Emphases added]*

Stepping out of the gauntlet and choosing a pathway of righteous living entails:

- managing the Magician's Fearful *power of suggestion* over us.
- nurturing our own inner *singing voice of contentment*.
- training our *powers of discernment*.

"But solid food is for the mature, for those who have their powers of discernment trained by constant practice to distinguish good from evil" (Hebrews 5:14).

A prodigal who is seeking to mature learns to:

1. *STOP AND DIAGNOSE THE FEAR BEFORE DECISION MAKING* – Rehearse what happened, the last time "I chose the gauntlet." *Feel the inner Fear that lured you by the power of suggestion.* Beware your amygdala reactions to feeling Fear, by stopping, detecting Fear, and choosing a response. Wisdom grows within you by finding your Fears, and *drawing back the curtain of mystery*. "Behold, you delight in truth in the inward being, and you teach me wisdom in the secret heart" (Psalm 51:6).

2. *REALITY* – The most powerful question to ask at a pig pen moment in your life is, "What is my responsibility in this?" Your *power of discernment* will grow exponentially when you listen to the answer and deal with the *yearning* that brought you there. The heartfelt statement, "*I take*

complete responsibility for my thoughts and actions," will change your life. The Magician has no "Abracadabra!" power over your thoughts, only the subtle *power of suggestion*. "A wicked man puts on a bold face, but the upright gives thought to his ways" (Proverbs 21:29).

3. *CONTENTMENT* – If happiness is "out there," it is out of your control to obtain it. When the Joyful *singing voice of contentment* is nurtured within you, you have *all power over your feelings*. Godly contentment comes from Gratitude and is anti-Fear. A strong and beautiful inner *singing voice of contentment* is louder than distant party music! "An evil man is ensnared in his transgression, but a righteous man sings and rejoices" (Proverbs 29:6).

"Not that I am speaking of being in need, for I have learned in whatever situation I am to be content" (Philippians 4:11).

4. *ACCEPTANCE* – We are all flawed and scared on this life Journey together. When you are angered by a prodigal, reminisce about a time that *you* felt afraid, unloved, and rebellious. Your powerful Loving acceptance heals, whereas self-righteous judgment damages. "For we do not have a high priest who is unable to sympathize with our weaknesses, but one who in every respect has been tempted as we are, yet without sin" (Hebrews 4:15).

5. *CONNECTION* – The prodigal son knew he could return to his father. Rarely do people turn their lives around, without a Loving, healing human relationship that is honest and open. If you cut yourself off from those bonds, you will not share God's Love flowing through human Love. Seek out relationships with other Christians who are serving the Cause faithfully. "[C]onfess your sins to one another and pray for one another, that you may be healed" (James 5:16a).

6. *LIMITS AND STRUCTURES* – Recovering alcoholics do not go to bars anymore. Reducing temptation is fundamental to moving away from a Fear-driven lifestyle. Delete the "Live for the Magic club" off your social network "friends" list. When you do not deal with your yearning, you

enable it. "Whoever walks with the wise becomes wise, but the companion of fools will suffer harm" (Proverbs 13:20).

7. *DIVINE PURPOSE* – When you grow to understand *how precious your life is to the Lord*, your Fears are transformed. As you feel your heavenly value, you will ask wide open, "How can I be useful?" "You are witnesses, and God also, how holy and righteous and blameless was our conduct toward you believers. For you know how, like a father with his children, we exhorted each one of you and encouraged you and charged you to walk in a manner worthy of God, who calls you into his own kingdom and glory" (1 Thessalonians 2:10-12).

8. *PERSONAL and SPIRITUAL GROWTH* – The cluster qualities of immaturity in "Free Estimates" show how growth is intertwined within you. You are not a mature Christian if you are lying to your husband about your credit card debt. As you begin to see all qualities within you linked together, you will see your spiritual maturing process as the *way to true Joy*! "Therefore, if anyone is in Christ, he is a new creation. The old has passed away; behold, the new has come" (2 Corinthians 5:17).

9. *GOD IS IN CHARGE* – Do you want to be less Fearful? Understand this clearly, God created you out of Love and He wants you to live a life of Joy! You can nurture your inner *singing voice of contentment* as you seek to please Him with your life. *He* is ultimately in charge of the world and everything in it. "But let all who take refuge in you rejoice; let them ever sing for joy, and spread your protection over them, that those who love your name may exult in you" (Psalm 5:11).

"Let those who delight in my righteousness shout for joy and be glad and say evermore, 'Great is the Lord, who delights in the welfare of his servant!'" (Psalm 35:27).

PRAY WITHOUT CEASING

Likewise the Spirit helps us in our weakness. For we do not know what to pray for as we ought, but the Spirit himself intercedes for us with groanings too deep for words. And he who searches hearts knows what is the mind of the Spirit, because the Spirit intercedes for the saints according to the will of God. And we know that for those who love God all things work together for good, for those who are called according to his purpose (Romans 8:26-28).

"The prayer of a righteous person has great power as it is working" (James 5:16b).

"Pray without ceasing" (Matt. 5:44; Luke 6:28, 18:1-7; 1 Thess. 5:17).

As we know that God's Loving hands, Jesus' intercession, and the Spirit's providing work receive our petitions, we continue to pray.

– *In prayer for yourself*, seek out every inconsistency or mixed priority. Examine yourself carefully, to be sure that the Fear-driven weaknesses that you see in a prodigal—you have walked away from yourself! You pray in accord with the Divine power of the universe, when you pray open ended: "I have no will but yours, Lord. I live to serve you. Your will be done." Study His will knowing *there are no magic tricks to gaining the wisdom in His Word* (Luke 6:12; James 5:16).

– *In prayer for others*, know that you are perfectly in synch with God's will, when you pray for someone to be faithful. He wants none to perish (Matthew 18:14). Appeal to Him *to allow the lessons that are needed* to turn a prodigal's heart. Ask Him to help you stay connected to the prodigal in the healthiest way possible, striving not to let anger hurt your influence. Keep in your heart that change must come from within *them* and that, a prodigal, *answers to God alone for his/her life choices* (2 Peter 3:9).

– *Give thanks* continually for what you are learning on your Journey. Snap your magic "fix it" wand in two pieces and *focus your life in Gratitude*. As you are growing closer to Him, depending on Him, and embracing the preciousness of the gift of salvation—praise Him! Enumerate your blessings daily and *celebrate* the little steps you took in the *right direction*. "Thank you, Lord! My inner *singing voice of contentment* was stronger than the lure of the party music!" Renew in your mind that your "negative" brain needs many repetitions of Gratitude, to counterbalance the tendency to focus on discontent (1 Cor. 9:23; James 5:13).

– *Pray for help*, to see the Fear in your-self and in others. Only *learning* brings change. The passage of time does nothing to mature you. *Recognize that Fear is the Magician's greatest power of suggestion, and practice being aware that he is using this sleight of hand trick on you—daily* (Matt. 16:23; Acts 5:3; James 4:7).

Remember, God allows us to make bad choices in our free will because sometimes that is the only way to get our attention. We must *freely* turn our wills to Him knowing that experiences are God-permitted lessons to help us do so! Jesus coerced no one to follow His Way. Pray to him in total subjection.

"Please help me share wisdom, Love, and set healthy boundaries, but know that you are in charge of f a m i l y and I am not. Help me be your servant and submit to being useful in whatever lies ahead. I know that you will care for me." Cherish that you breathe each day in *His* presence. "[C]asting all your anxieties on him, because he cares for you" (1 Peter 5:7).

FAMILY OF FORGIVERS – *God comes running*
"Brothers, if anyone is caught in any transgression, you who are spiritual should restore him in a spirit of gentleness. Keep watch on yourself, lest you too be tempted. Bear one another's burdens, and so fulfill the law of Christ" (Galatians 6:1-2).

Forgiveness is the fullness of Love. Forgiveness is:
- the fusion of free choice and surrender
- not saying that all is "ok," but letting go of the need to punish
- *not letting the memories control you*
- choosing to let go of your anger
- for *you*

Truly forgiving means letting Love for this struggling fellow sojourner of life be stronger than your anger. A very insightful unknown writer penned, "Not forgiving is like drinking poison and expecting the other person to die" (Col. 3:13).

Your Fear may whisper: "If I open my heart again, I am afraid they will hurt me." Unforgiveness and revenge are strengthening spells of Satan, the magician. *Forgiveness exemplifies spiritual maturity that you know the Lord will care for you, whatever is ahead.* In forgiving, God says, "You don't have to hold onto this, I will take care of it" (2 Cor. 2:7).

Toward everyone of us who is filled with Fear: God comes running with forgiveness! (v. 20) The earthly father in this story represents our gracious heavenly Father with arms outstretched; running down the road to meet us as we bring our foolish selves back to Him. Unlike the lost sheep and lost coin, the lost prodigal had to *freely choose* to come back to God. God's Loving embrace melts the Fear of separation, and the intensity of Joy speaks the truth of that painful distance—that we could have been lost *forever* (Matt. 6:15).

It is only by your choices that you are separated from Him. Grab on to Him as your labyrinth guide, and you will never fall into the fire. He comes running with open arms.

"My brothers, if anyone among you wanders from the truth and someone brings him back, let him know that whoever brings back a sinner from his wandering will save his soul from death and will cover a multitude of sins" (James 5:19-20).

FEARBREAKER-JOYMAKER JOURNEY
"Keep steady my steps according to your promise, and let no iniquity get dominion over me" (Psalm 119:133).

"For to this you have been called, because Christ also suffered for you, leaving you an example, so that you might follow in his steps" (1 Peter 2:21).

Like a head turn to the lure of magical party music in the distance, we will all have moments of immaturity. I call it "grow up and grow down." Step through your Fear and ask, "*Will this choice help me grow up and be more mature, or grow down and away from the Lord?* Growing up means taking complete responsibility for every choice, decision, and attitude within your power. As you learn the Treasure Map, you will see the high value in *your* Divine purpose and keep asking the question, "For what pathway was I created?" (Gal. 2:20).

A Christian life is *not a boring life* for those who *train their taste buds to true Joy.* Get excited about Christian living! Spend time enjoying your Christian friends and serving others. I shudder to think that some of my comedy skits from Bible camp may appear on "YouTube" one day. The Christian life is great in every way!

When God gives you an *opportunity* to grow through your Fear, don't tell Him "No!" Get rid of your delusion that there is a "vanishing troubles potion" or a "perpetual party" somewhere. Stand up off your soft cushion and say, "Thank you for this lesson, Lord!" Acknowledge how life's challenges are making you *stronger* and more *focused.* Your cloak of responsibility is light, when you stand straight and tall and walk in the pathway toward the Treasure. Only you choose a life in the gauntlet (John 6:53-58).

Ask these powerful questions?

- Is Fear driving this feeling?
- Am I listening to a hurtful Thought storm?
- What is my responsibility in this?
- What can I learn?

Becoming a Fearbreaker means:

- learning the Bible stories of how God cares for His children
- gaining wisdom from reflecting on my own life lessons
- knowing my life has Divine purpose and enjoying the quest
- desiring to please Him with every breath
- watching how God is working for those who hold His ever-loving hand

Take a moment right now and Stop. Bring your focus right here—right now—breathe in—breathe out—close your eyes and meditate on a Bible truth that brings you to contentment. Here is mine: "Isn't it great that the Lord is in charge?"

GROWING THROUGH FEAR

1. What part of you is a resistant prodigal? What part of you is a self-righteous older son? wise father?

2. How does the Magician lure you to live in a constant state of Fear-filled yearning? How does your "negative brain" encourage your prodigal and older son thoughts?

3. Discuss: "Emotional maturity and spiritual maturity are deeply connected."

4. How do healthy boundaries help people grow?

5. How can anger at a prodigal's behavior help or block your influence? Where does the DO NOT SIN line fall in dealing with a prodigal?

6. Share with someone a time when you found it hard to forgive? How have you grown through that?

~ 6 ~

The Plague from Within
Fearful insecurity that sickens
The Pharisee and the tax collector (Luke 18:9-14)

*T*he *walls of the Heroine's labyrinth passageway become higher and taller as she walks. At the base of this great wall, many sick people and invalids lie in distress. As she gasps at the scene, an old woman cries out to her, "Come protect yourself with this enchanted scarf." And as the old woman wraps the beautifully spun shawl around the Heroine's shoulders, she asks, "What is that exotic spicy scent?" The woman speaks softly, "Breathe deeply the aroma of protection, you are special . . . you are not like the others." She unties her cloak of responsibility and lets it drops to the ground as she draws in the perfume of the fine silver fabric. Moving through the crowd, she inhales the deep fragrance and whispers, "I am not like these wanderers, I am not diseased." But as she leans her back against the great wall of bricks to rest for a moment, a bell rings in the distance. Fighting hard to get a deep breath, there is no relief from the pounding headache and weakness. The cold wet bricks adhere to her sweaty back as she slumps down onto the ground, realizing the aching throughout her body is fever. . . .*

He also told this parable to some who trusted in themselves that they were righteous, and treated others with contempt. "Two men went up into the temple to pray, one a Pharisee and the other a tax collector. The Pharisee, standing by himself, prayed thus: 'God I thank you that I am not like other men, extortioners, unjust, adulterers, or even like this tax collector. I fast twice a week; I give tithes of all that I get.' But the tax collector, standing far off, would not even lift up his eyes to heaven, but beat his breast, saying, 'God, be merciful to me, a sinner!' I tell you, this man went down to his house justified, rather than the other. For everyone who exalts himself will be humbled, but the one who humbles himself will be exalted" (Luke 18:9-14).

PLAGUE

In 1346, The Mongols were battling European forces at the Black Sea port of Caffa. Bubonic plague was spreading quickly through the Mongol force and in the first known use of germ warfare, they began catapulting the plague-infected cadavers over the great siege-wall and into the city. As the European survivors fled by ship, they unknowingly carried the Black Death throughout the Mediterranean and into western Europe.

The close quarters and filthy conditions of medieval cities were the ideal host for the rats and their fleas that now transmitted the Plague. Within the next five years, 75 million people, more than half of the European population, would be destroyed by the bacteria introduced into the blood stream by a single flea bite. The Mongols passed the Black Death to the Europeans, but the *problem remained that they still had it themselves.* Even in our modern world, we suffer great plagues and pass on the epidemic, thinking that we will rid ourselves of the infirmity.

Fear as narcissism is a plague that has been around since the beginning of time, and is overtaking our modern world with its contagion—Fear shown in arrogance. Do you think of yourself as better than others? Would you put your needs above all else? Do you think that you are special and that "the rules" apply to others, but not you? Greet the insecurity that is Fear-driven narcissism: the Pharisee within.

PHARISEE

With the accuracy of a CAT scan, the Pharisee shows us his Fearful and arrogant heart. The scan test results say, "I am too frightened to look at who I really am, so I am pointing out how I am better than you." The bacteria of his Fear-filled heart explode wide open before us. He *is* the man who tries to extract the speck from the eye of another, while there is a huge log in his own.

> Judge not, that you be not judged. For with the judgment you pronounce you will be judged, and with the measure you use it will be measured to you. Why do you see the speck that is in your brother's eye, but do not notice the log that is in your own eye? Or how can you say to your brother, "Let me take the speck out of your eye," when there is the log in your own eye? You hypocrite, first take the log out of your own eye, and then you will see clearly to take the speck out of your brother's eye (Matt. 7:3-5).

The Pharisee, like part of each of us, was filled with a terror that prevented humble self-examination. He showed his Fearful arrogant heart as he bragged how "holy" he was by:

- standing in prayer, so all could view his "holiness"
- giving thanks that he was not like the "sinners"
- reporting his good deeds to God—for others to hear
- trying to manipulate the Lord with, "I thank you that I am not . . ."
- offering no repentance or sincere gratitude to the Lord

Narcissus of mythology, adored only himself. He saw no flaws or weaknesses within. As he gazed into a reflecting pool, he became so mesmerized with himself that he fell in and drowned.

The Pharisee felt he had no flaws and turned the lab microscope on the tax collector, to keep from having a check-up himself. "Examining" yourself for the disease of self-absorption is very painful. Diagnosing *others* seems like the best strategy. But like hurling the plague over the wall, you may have hurt your opponent, but *still have the bacteria yourself.* The Pharisee exists inside of you and me in our dark spiritual illness.

- Self-centered narcissism
- Arrogance
- Prideful disposition
- Personal ambition focus
- Passion-lust orientation
- Emptiness with a diminished capacity for Joy

TAX COLLECTOR

Great artists of the world have imagined this truly humble tax collector bowing in total submission before the Lord as he whispers, "Be merciful, I am a sinner" (Luke 18:13). This sincere man's spiritual temperature was feverish, but accurate. Diagnosis is the first step to wellness and *truth brings growth*. The tax collector:

- bowed his head in humility
- hit himself in the chest
- humbly begged the Lord for mercy
- called himself a sinner—as if he were the worst to live

THE BRICK WALL – *Built by Fear*

Like the siege wall between two armies, we build walls to protect our Fear-driven insecurities. The Enemy will tell us that building and main-taining our wall is the only way to be safe and secure. We may have watched our parents build walls around themselves and so our internal cruise control says, "Be a wall builder and you will be fine—never be exposed." As our Fear-driven insecurity builds our walls, it also *isolates* us from the Love of others. The harder we try to  impress, the thicker wall we build. We end up accomplishing the oppo-site of what we wanted, for now we are isolated—instead of connected (Proverbs 18:1).

The tightly walled European cities that withstood siege by humans for decades suffered the most devastation from the Plague. A fortified city had more humans in close quarters = more garbage = more rats = more fleas = more germs spread throughout the population. When you wall yourself in and keep from the sunshine, clean air, and fresh breezes, you give the bacteria of Fear as narcissism the perfect setting for rapid spread throughout your body.

IMMMUNE SYSTEM OF YOUR SPIRIT

Sickness and health dwell inside our spirits the same as light and dark-ness. The part of your spirit that is sick might feel self-centered, but the healthy part of your spirit is God-centered.

Healthy		*Sick*
God-centered		self-centered
safe		threatened
friendly		hostility
big		small
meek		opinionated
valued		unimportant
mature		immature

The bacteria of the internal Plague infection courses through the blood stream and damages organs. It is when the germs begin to power a high fever, cough, and swollen lymph nodes (buboes), that the Plague spreads to others. The bacteria of our Fear within becomes **visible** in our words and actions. "A fool's mouth is his ruin, and his lips are a snare to his soul" (Proverbs 18:7).

TEMPERATURE READING – *Know your Fear fever*

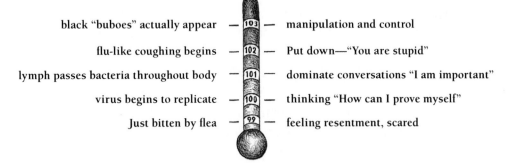

black "buboes" actually appear	— [103] —	manipulation and control
flu-like coughing begins	— [102] —	Put down—"You are stupid"
lymph passes bacteria throughout body	— [101] —	dominate conversations "I am important"
virus begins to replicate	— [100] —	thinking "How can I prove myself"
Just bitten by flea	— [99] —	feeling resentment, scared

A high Fear temperature will cause you to:

- be reactive & touchy
- resent others
- maintain bitterness
- be defensive in interactions

- show facial expression of disgust
- put others down with sarcasm
- insist you are *right and tell all your opinions*
- feel arrogance
- underestimate risks and damage
- be manipulative
- rage and be wrathful

Your childhood immune system learned to respond to disease with either an appropriate rally of protective white cells or surrender. Your spiritual immune system chooses to build thick walls, or clean and disinfect, to battle the Plague within. The first step in disease survival is learning to watch your Fear temperature rising and say, "What Fear am I feeling and what can I learn about myself?" "You have set our iniquities before you, our secret sins in the light of your presence" (Psalm 90:8).

Technology has provided a new thermometer the size of a bandaid to be used on the forehead of a patient. What if we had a thermometer display on our foreheads at all times, and everyone could read our Fear temperature? Actually, others read *far more* than we think they do. Our body's defenses are amazing. Fever is God's design to help us rally an immune defense against invading disease—even the internal disease of Fear.

Fear as narcissism it is not a new disease. It is a 24-hour Thought storm about myself, *my* feelings, *my* needs, *my* wants and *my* pleasures. It breeds Fearful anxiety bacteria within us because it totally consumes every cell. Do you know people who have a trauma-a-day? "I was slighted by a co-worker. I have a headache. My life/job/family is a disaster." Everyone is against them. They are the presidents of the "Trauma drama club" and the "Me First, Biggest, Best, Sorority." Their Fear as selfishness fever rules their every interaction and their Fear temperature is always raging. Fear ravages every cell of their bodies and steals all their Joy (Proverbs 26:12).

BLOOD TEST – *Results from under the Microscope*

The focus of a germ's life is reproduction. The moment a bacteria enters a new host its goal is "Let me find food, so that I can replicate." Infecting, destroying, and killing this host may be part of the process, but the bacteria's goal will be accomplished. Like an invading force from the East, germs can overtake a living host and produce millions of destructive self-copies in a short time. Satan/the Enemy, wants to devastate us with the illness of

Fear-driven insecurity and spread it throughout our thoughts and actions. Left untreated, a Fear illness will kill you (John 13:27).

What if that forehead thermometer displayed not only your fever, but "beeped" with alarm every time you had a Fearful/selfish/arrogant thought? How quickly would you control your feelings if you knew they were on display for others to read? What if a fever alarm kept ringing until you asked forgiveness of the Lord *and* the one you were thinking about? I think we would all get our acts together quickly, if we knew that 1) others were reading us 2) the Lord was reading us. The truth is—*they are.* "O Lord, you have searched me and known me! You know when I sit down and when I rise up; you discern my thoughts from afar (Psalm 139:1-2).

"For God will bring every deed into judgment, with every secret thing, whether good or evil" (Ecclesiastes 12:14).

Humans perceive micro-expressions and body language even when we think we hide them well. We communicate 93% non-verbally and only 7% is conveyed by actual verbal words.[1] Micro-expressions flash across our faces in a ½ second, displaying the emotions that we are trying to hide. Scientists who study body language can read the emotions on people's faces:

- If your smile causes crow's feet, you are displaying genuine joy.
- A one-sided raised lip or chin is the classic expression of contempt.
- Fear raises our upper eyelids/brows displaying its terror on our faces.[2]

Thoughts register within our entire bodies and are noted and felt by every cell. *Your feelings are circulating in your bloodstream.*

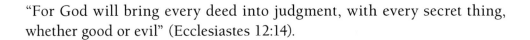

> And since they did not see fit to acknowledge God, God gave them up to a debased mind to do what ought not to be done. They were filled with all manner of unrighteousness, evil, covetousness, malice. They are full of envy, murder, strife, deceit, maliciousness. They are gossips, slanderers, haters of God, insolent, haughty, boastful, inventors of evil, disobedient to parents, foolish, faithless, heartless, ruthless (Romans 1:28-31).

Your *feelings* of Fear-driven insecurity/narcissism give you *powerful cellular information about you and what powers you.* "They show that the work of the law is written on their hearts, while their conscience also bears witness, and their conflicting thoughts accuse or even excuse them on that day when, according to my gospel, God judges the secrets of men by Christ Jesus" (Romans 2:15).

"But I can't be like these sick people," she whispers, as she slumps down near the wall. She wraps the shawl tightly to keep from smelling the stench. The more deeply she inhales its perfume, the more rapidly the infection spreads within her, "I am not dirty like them," she mumbles under her breath.

GERM WARFARE – *The contagion spreads outside by coughing*

I was looking forward to a few hours with my Viktor Frankl book and highlighter, so I snuggled into my window seat on the plane. As my mind slid back into history for a moment, a woman took the aisle seat next to me and I smiled politely and then returned to my book. Within a few seconds, the woman began talking. I asked some polite response questions, and then tried to return to my studies. She continued to tell me that her "son was a baseball player and was trying to choose between two different scholarships, and her daughter's softball bat was examined at the junior world cup of softball for forgery because she hit so many home runs. . . ." I smiled and tried again, to return to my book. For two hours, the woman told me every detail of her life and her children's lives. If there was any detail that she left out in the talking blitz, I am sure that she will track me down, and tell me the rest.

Irritated at the loss of precious study time, I thought, "Ok, if Fear is at the root of our negative behavior, what is she afraid of?" I realized, that perhaps *she is afraid that she is not important.* She wants to keep telling me her family's triumphs, so that she feels valuable. My compassion level grew for this woman as I reflected on times that I have talked too much, and been annoying also (Proverbs 29:11).

Call to mind that recognizing Fear gives us vital information. Learning to *take your Fear temperature* and the temperature of other "patients" on this life Journey, is one of the *most useful skills you can master.* As we learn to *see those who are irritating and angry as—suffering people,* we will better understand our own suffering. If we allow Fear-driven narcissism/insecurity to ravage our "negative" brain's tendencies, *we will view every interaction with our feverish eyes and the need to self-protect* (Proverbs 18:14).

Fear makes us act on the defensive:

1. *WALL BUILDING* – I have been hurt, so I must protect myself from pain. Every offense adds a brick to my wall and keeps me safe from more heartache.

2. *IMPATIENCE* – Inside I have no respect for you and think you are an "idiot." See how capable I am, why don't you just "get it?"

3. *TOUCHY* – Every action and word bothers me. I am so Fearfully insecure that I feel threatened and need to question the motive of every word.

4. *"I" DISEASE* – It really is "all about me." I don't listen in conversations that aren't about me. I share the thoughts and drama of my day with you and the worldwide web. "I" disease is the inner ailment of narcissism. Reality asks, "Are you really that self-absorbed?" Narcissism answers, "Yes I am." Count how many times you say, "I" in conversations.

5. *POUTING* – Sets an emotional and communication wall with the hope of manipulating others. I have the Fear-filled control and "upper hand" over you when I stone-wall. If I don't receive constant attention, I will pout.

6. *SELF-RIGHTEOUS* – I am just so good, but I don't know why everyone does not listen to me. I cannot listen to your wisdom or take your advice, because that would mean I have been wrong—not perfect.

7. *MISUNDERSTOOD* – Nobody understands me. I do not know what I did to cause this. The Thought storm of "My wife does not understand me" powers the Fear-driven narcissism of adultery. The "misunderstood" have no idea how their actions hurt others.

8. *VICTIM* – Everyone is so unsupportive and everything bad happens to me. No one cares about me or thinks about my needs. To a victim, everyone looks like a potential executioner, poised to inflict pain.

9. *PROJECTOR* – Puts the blame on others. My Fearful arrogance is so large, that I cannot possibly be weak/sick. It must be you. In prayer, the Pharisee tried to *convince God* how bad the tax collector was by contrasting how *good* he was. Reality check: *God does not need to do blood tests. He knows your DNA and the truth of what is going on inside you.*

The bacteria of Fear as insecurity lodges in our lungs and becomes a deadly cough of hurtful actions toward others. *When your Thought storms are still inside, you have the opportunity to deal with them in privacy.* But those Fearful thoughts drive you to *action* as you cross the DO NOT SIN line and insult others. When you throw disease-filled comments/actions over the wall at others, you show that you are so terrified of what is inside yourself, that you go on the offensive. "If anyone says, 'I love God,' and hates his brother, he is a liar; for he who does not love his brother whom he has seen cannot love God whom he has not seen" (1 Jn. 4:20).

Fear makes us go on the offensive:

1. *ANNOYING/OPINIONATED* – My opinion, my idea, my suffering is worse than yours. Whether for pity or attention, we are saying, "I think that I am nothing, so I must convince *you* that I am something." How much time do you spend inside your head trying to find support for ideas that you want to be true? (Proverbs 18:2).

2. *ARROGANCE* – Rules are for others not me. I am above the law. I can lie, live on credit, cheat on my wife, because I am special. Arrogant narcissists underestimate risk and truly think they will "get away with it." I get to insult people, because I am being "honest" with them. Of course, the last person the arrogant would be honest with is him/herself. That is the terror he/she is avoiding (Proverbs 21:24).

3. *CRITICISM* – Critics pass out poison cupcakes. You can frost them up beautifully, but they will still make you sick. The "cooks" believe that criticizing *you* implies praise of me. You may want to test them and then throw the poison cupcakes away. Fault-finders/critics put everyone under the microscope, to examine the bacteria inside them (Romans 2:3).

"If you look for the bad in people expecting to find it, you surely will."
—Abraham Lincoln

4. *HARSH JUDGMENT* – While Christians seek to grow by the Lord's standards, harsh judges feel it is their job to sentence others. Everything is a competition—win/lose. Judges determine guilt/innocence and keep the focus on the "criminal." If you want a career as a judge, remember, they sit on high benches in isolation (James 2:4).

5. *SARCASM* – The Greek root of this word means, "to tear the flesh" and reflects the underlying *mean* message that the speaker wants to convey. "My that dress is reallllly bright!" is not actually a compliment. Sarcasm is a scab over deep infection that even allows its speakers to "smile," when injecting plague in their victim. This is not the same as joking or loving teasing of hilarious things, that friends/families enjoy. Sarcasm comes from a deep Fear-driven insecurity and is fatal to trust in relationships (Matt. 15:19).

6. *BRAGGING* – Fear within arrogance insists that, "I am first, biggest, best!" It is the outward contagion of the inward disease of pride, whether over your own "accomplishments," or those of your family. Pride or "credit grabbing" can be spoken in person, or shared on the web. Do you think that Mary would have used social networking to brag about her Son? Consider the "humble brag" of your status read—*seriously* (Proverbs 25:27).

7. *PUT-DOWNS* – Fear-driven evaluation can power you to dislike those who are prettier/smarter/happier than you. If you are afraid they are better, you might talk "bad" about their parenting/cooking in hopes of showing how "good" you are. You seek to heal *your illness* by putting others down and making them "sick" too. "Put-down clubs" gather to examine all the "stupid things she said" and the "hideous" outfit she wore. Families sometimes teach this skill as they bond through making fun of others (Proverbs 25:23).

8. *BULLYING* – Fear is the root of bullying. You are weaker/lower/less powerful than I, and I have the ability to pick on you. Since I am superior and you are inferior, then I am better than you are. Bullying injects cancerous microbes into put-downs to create words and actions that sicken and kill (Romans 12:3).

9. *RAGING* – A little dog postures and growls with his teeth bared to make himself seem bigger than he is. His rage is saying, "Look at me, I am not

small; I am going to act big so I will feel important." "Acting up" in children is easy to see, but the most out-of-control adult is likely the most Fear-filled insecure person (Psalm 112:10).

Trying to take the *Fear temperature* of someone raging at you, or in the delusion of "I" disease is difficult. Lashing back at them is an amygdala fight reaction. When we step back and *read vital signs*, we may begin to understand the Fear bacteria breeding thoughts in *our* spirits, and the spirits of others. *If we do not deal with the bacteria, we will never get well* (Psalm 69:5).

Patient #1

Susanna's husband rages. When he is irritated or frustrated, he stands tall and hollers—at her. He tells her to "shut up" when she asks questions and calls her "stupid." As his career and health have worsened, so has the raging. Susanna confides in Jackie the tearful truth about how her husband treats her. Jackie says wisely, "I think he does not love himself and is *very frightened of you*." "Are you serious?" replies Susanna between sobs. "I am half his weight and only two-thirds of his height. Why would he be afraid of me?" Jackie replies, "He is afraid of you because you represent truths he does not want to see. He would rather lash out at *you* in anger, than to *feel* his inner Fears."

While Susanna's husband had some serious issues and needed spiritual/emotional maturing, she had to set clear DO NOT SIN boundaries (Psalm 4:4; Eph. 4:26) with him by:

- having godly Integrity herself
- remembering that he is frightened
- speaking the truth in Love
- focusing on the behavior that crosses the DO NOT SIN line
- seeking Christian counseling for herself and encouraging him to do the same

Seeing him as *afraid* helped her deal with the upset of his bullying/raging behavior. When you can stay calm and *keep gathering information*, dealing with Fearful people can be like a vast medical library, filled with knowledge about them and about you.

Patient #2

Ashley had competed in beauty pageants since she was young. She played piano for the talent competition and wore beautiful glittering gowns. Her hair and make-up took hours. John was a devoted Christian man who fell deeply in Love with her. As the years of marriage ticked by, Ashley became discontented with their ordinary life of bills and children. Even though she was still attractive, her inner Fear as narcissism could not make peace with the fact that she was no longer the beauty queen and this feverish Thought storm powered her to sin. She found a man who "adored" her and in the moments of adultery's passionate romp, felt "worshipped."

As the evil queen of Snow White attempted murder when she was no longer "the fairest of them all," Ashley infected her marriage and the lives of her children by her Fear-driven narcissism/insecurity. Without constant attention for her beauty, she felt "unloved."

Reading blood tests and taking temperatures for *bacteria levels of Fear* is the first step into the Joy of Reality (Psalm 139:1-2). If you constantly compare yourself to others, "She is better/worse/prettier/more spiritual/ less sinful/happier than I am"—you are filled with the bacteria of *Fear.* Ask yourself, "What is my motive? *Am I seeking to walk my life Journey in Joy and Love, or do I want to be right?*"

"Not that we dare to classify or compare ourselves with some of those who are commending themselves. But when they measure themselves by one another and compare themselves with one another, they are without understanding" (2 Cor. 10:12).

"But if you bite and devour one another, watch out that you are not consumed by one another" (Galatians 5:15).

God designed human lives to intersect so that we would learn from each other! Remember, the ability to *take Fear temperatures* and vital signs of yourself and others, allows you to see life as a great laboratory filled with exciting wisdom about how to increase *your* health and true Joy in living. "Search me, O God, and know my heart! Try me and know my thoughts! And see if there be any grievous way in me, and lead me in the way everlasting!" (Psalm 139:23-24).

DIAGNOSIS AND TREATMENT – *Empathy all around*

What if for a moment the Pharisee and the tax collector got to switch places into each other's skin and read each other's spiritual/medical history? What if they could take notes on the Fears that the other was experiencing inside?

"I became a Pharisee because my parents expected it. My prideful arrogance comes from Fear that I have to be the best, or God will not Love me. I need to put you down to prove that I am better."

"I became a tax collector so I could make a lot of money. I thought that was the way to power and respect. I know that I am a sinner and I humble myself before the Lord, and beg Him to be merciful to me."

Having empathy and compassion means that we feel for each other, but humbly realize everyone is a recovering "patient" of Fear illness. When you accidentally cough your germs on someone, do you simply apologize, but if your husband does the same, do you get angry? You had empathy for yourself, but harsh put-down toward him. When you become upset with Fear-driven narcissism in another, recall a time that *you behaved similarly*. If you sound forth *your goodness* and *his badness*, you may be afraid to look inside. Be the person you want *him* to be (Rom. 2:1-5).

While the Pharisee could see what disgusted him in the tax collector, he needed intensive *treatment* for himself. *You can put the diseases/faults of others under the most powerful microscope and see every one of them, but you are still sick.* Memorize the history that—you can catapult bodies over the wall, but you still have the Plague.

As you learn to Love others *as* fellow sojourners, you learn to Love yourself. How could you Love your neighbor as yourself, if you did not first *Love* yourself? (Romans 13:9). Intimate Love of self is not narcissism, but acceptance of *how perfectly Loved and cherished you are by God.* He knows your diseases and gives you complete empathy and compassion, asking you to do the *same* for others. *True empathy is true Love.* True Fear beneath respect is submitting that the Lord is in charge of others. You are not.

"One's pride will bring him low, but he who is lowly in spirit will obtain honor" (Proverbs 29:23).

As you learn empathy and watch for the *fever of Fear* within, you realize there are *no lifetime vaccinations* for the Fear-driven superiority that feels—you have "arrived" spiritually and others are sick. When you judge the spiritual disease symptoms within others, you may find *their most irritating qualities are what scare you most about yourself!* Beware of "Mouth disease" that allows anger and frustrations to cross the DO NOT SIN line.

- A loose tongue that wags when you are overtired/hungry/hormonal.
- Unfiltered comments made without considering the listener's feelings.
- Germy opinions that roll off the tongue.
- Apologies cannot rewind time to the moment before words were spoken.
- Joy is never lessened by thinking through your words before speaking.

"For out of the abundance of the heart the mouth speaks" (Matthew 12:34).

You can live your life with the chronic illness of Fear-driven narcissism, infecting others with every breath, or in an isolation room with hand-built walls. And you may receive some get well cards in your self-quarantined ICU, but you will never receive a card that says, "YOU BRING ME SO MUCH JOY!" (Philippians 4:1; Proverbs 27:5).

YOU ARE WHAT YOU REPEATEDLY DO

Aristotle, 384–322 B.C. wrote: "We are what we repeatedly do. Excellence, then, is not an act, but a habit." Apply this to your behavior and your character.

- If you repeatedly act mean, you are a bully.
- If you repeatedly point out faults, you are a critic.
- If you repeatedly act self-centered, you are a narcissist.

"For if anyone thinks he is something, when he is nothing, he deceives himself" (Gal. 6:3).

While we know that spiritual health and sickness dwell in *all* of us, we are *identified* by our actions that come over the DO NOT SIN line. People say, "But that is not who I really am." Well of course it is, because *your character is what comes from your mouth, hands, and feet* (Psalm 119:57-60).

When you increase your Integrity, your Fear level drops, because it is clear what is *your* responsibility and what is another's responsibility. *The Lord knows the truth of what is said and done.* When your heart is filled with spiritual wellness, your inside person Joyfully shines through, and your *Love* temperature is easily visible to all (1 Peter 1:8).

Drifting in and out of consciousness, she awakens to the voices of others who are sick around her. She hears them talking of themselves, their glories and importance. One woman speaks of her family, listing every member's weakness and failure. A man tells of his prominent social status and says, "I am a man of great influence, I don't deserve this." The Heroine realizes that she thinks of herself in the same way and removes the silver scarf of superiority to humble herself and serve once again.

HUMILITY – *The Great Physician's prescription*

Jesus prescribed the cure for the Pharisee's Fear-filled arrogance as he read his "heart-function" test. *Humility* is the prescription to heal Fear-driven narcissism illness and thrive. The Great Physician is never unsure of what treatment you need. He never has to wait for an MRI. He gives you the prescription, and it is absolutely FREE. That does not mean that His cures taste good or have no adverse reactions, it just means that they work. "I tell you, this man went down to his house justified, rather than the other. For everyone who exalts himself will be humbled, but the one who humbles himself will be exalted" (Luke 18:14; James 4:10; 1 Peter 5:6).

Even secular "success" writers focus on the dual values of courage and humility. In Jim Collins' book, *Good to Great*, he writes, "Level 5 leaders embody a paradoxical mix of personal humility and professional will." He goes on to cite studies of top level business leaders who did not grab the credit for their business success, and: "When things go poorly, however, they look in the mirror and blame themselves, taking full responsibility. Unsuccessful CEO's, did just the opposite—they looked in the mirror to take credit for success, but out the window to assign blame to others around them."[3] "[H]ave unity of mind, sympathy, brotherly love, a tender heart, and a humble mind" (1 Peter 3:8).

Bear in mind that the two most powerful motivators are *Love* and *Fear*. God Loves you so much that He does not want you living behind a wall of Fear-driven selfishness and anger. But, *He is not neutral on the state of you inner spiritual health!* True humility is seeking to see yourself as God sees you. "Whoever has a haughty look and an arrogant heart I will not endure" (Psalm 101:5b).

"Do nothing from selfish ambition or conceit, but in humility count others more significant than yourselves" (Philippians 2:3).

Jesus:

- never acted, faked, or pouted to get attention
- knew game-playing was for children—not mature relationships
- did not "play" detached
- was the ultimate "grown-up"
- opened his heart with sacrificial Love and kindness

Jesus was *real*. He was not afraid to launch out and Love tax collectors, prostitutes, dirty lepers, rich and poor, with an intense passion we can only glimpse. Jesus wants you to throw off that bacteria-laden perfume scarf of narcissism, and tie on your cloak of responsibility. "Put on then, as God's chosen ones, holy and beloved, compassionate hearts, kindness, humility, meekness, and patience" (Colossians 3:12).

With greater skill than a microsurgeon who reattaches nerves thinner than a human hair, our *delicate feelings were designed by the one who understands the softest touch and the slightest temptation. God knows you better than a microscope*! He knows you carry the virus of Fear and He has the only remedy—His Love. "In this is love, not that we have loved God, but that he loved us and sent his Son to be the propitiation for our sins" (1 John 4:10).

The Enemy's greatest weapon is Fear and he knows that your high bacteria count will keep you from a life of Joy! *Your Divine purpose is powered by the Loving acceptance of God's cure*. As you allow God's Love inside you, His great Love *changes* you—and how you *look at* being alive. *There is no antidote for human Fear but—Love*.

"Let all bitterness and wrath and anger and clamor and slander be put away from you, along with all malice. Be kind to one another, tenderhearted, forgiving one another, as God in Christ forgave you" (Eph. 4:31-32).

THE BATTERING RAM

Medieval battering rams required many men and hours/days of repetitive force to besiege a great wall. Once a crack was established, the wall masonry would begin to crumble. Determined persistence demolished the siege walls men built to protect themselves. As the Love and humility cure takes hold within you and overpowers each Fear-filled germ, your strength will grow to be able to wield a battering ram from within *your* brick isolation walls. *Bricks that once kept you quarantined can now be used to build bridges to Love others.* Keep asking yourself these courageous questions:

- Do I believe Jesus died just for me? (John 3:16)
- Can I honestly list my inadequacies? (James 5:16)
- Have I asked for help with the beam in my own eye? (Luke 6:41-42)
- How much energy do I spend looking at the imperfections of others? (James 3:5-12)
- Will I do what it takes to live a high standard of personal holiness? (1 Peter 1:15-16)

> For we ourselves were once foolish, disobedient, led astray, slaves to various passions and pleasures, passing our days in malice and envy, hated by others and hating one another. But when the goodness and loving kindness of God our Savior appeared, he saved us, not because of works done by us in righteousness, but according to his own mercy, by the washing of regeneration and the renewal of the Holy Spirit, whom he poured out on us richly through Jesus Christ our Savior, so that being justified by his grace we might become heirs according to the hope of eternal life (Titus 3:3-7).

FEARBREAKER-JOYMAKER JOURNEY

"Love is patient and kind; love does not envy or boast; it is not arrogant or rude. It does not insist on its own way; it is not irritable or resentful; it does not rejoice at wrongdoing, but rejoices with the truth. Love bears all things, believes all things, hopes all things, endures all things" (1 Cor. 13:4-7).

The sickness of a *Fearmaker* lifestyle is: empty—helpless—victimized—reactive—blames others—quarantined—a Fearful life.

The wellness of a *Joymaker* lifestyle is: peace of mind—contentment—self-confidence—thoughtful response—building a Joyful life of Divine purpose.

Humbly studying God's Word, praying, and continually thanking Him for His providing hand are *the* vitamin habits for good health. A high Fear fever is not developed overnight and there are *no magic pills* for healing Fear-driven insecurity. When you desire to push yourself forward to feel important, think of Jesus saying, "You are worth my life sacrifice." *Wrapping yourself in that Love brings wellness to your spirit and increases your desire to honor Him with a healthy heart.*

Pray before you interact with others asking, "How will my words make other people feel?" When you pray for spiritual vigor, sincerely reflect and:

- Tell Him your deepest, darkest Fears (Matt. 5:10).
- Admit that you trust Him completely (Psalm 13:5).
- Ask forgiveness for your specific weaknesses (2 Cor. 12:9).
- Give thanks to the Lord in everything (Eph. 5:20; Col. 3:17).
- In humility say—"Your will be done" (Matt. 26:42).
- Break down the walls around your heart and say, "I will be who the Lord wants me to be" (1 Samuel 12:24).

PRAY

- Constantly—as you walk in His presence
- Concentrated—focused or "on your knees"
- Courageously—open to serve Him as He wills

Ask Him, "Please show me how to glorify you." Vibrant Christian living does not seek to spread disease, but thrives in the cause and effect of a spiritual health quest. Daily devotion to a clean bill of spiritual health strengthens a constitution of JOY! "And walk in love, as Christ loved us and gave himself up for us, a fragrant offering and sacrifice to God" (Eph. 5:2).

GROWING THROUGH FEAR

1. Is a Fear-filled Christian more/less useful to the Lord? Why?

2. Do you think "I"-disease (thinking of myself only) is a problem? How does your "negative" brain promote "I"-disease? As alcoholics and credit abusers have no idea how their behaviors hurt others, what other damage do people do who only think of themselves?

3. Do you follow through with commitments? How does dependability relate to Fear-driven narcissism?

4. Sing the song: "Humble yourself in the sight of the Lord" every day this week.

5. What is the fine line between a happy, celebratory comment on your social network: "I just got engaged!" and cyber-bragging (or cyber-whining)? Does cyber-bragging hurt your "friends?" How do you think posting daily thoughts and feelings is changing the hearts of women?

6. How would nurturing the inner *singing voice of contentment* (Ch. 5) strengthen the immune system against the plague of narcissism?

7. Read the story of Hannah and Penninah. Is bullying anything new? What was the root Fear that drove Penninah's bullying? (1 Samuel 1:1-8) Share a time when you tried to fill up your hurt by putting someone else down.

~ 7 ~

Predators on the Savanna

Fears from the sensual world

Simon and the woman in repentance (Luke 7:36-50)

WARNING: THIS CHAPTER CONTAINS MATERIAL FOR MATURE ADULT STUDY

The Heroine rests in a cave of a great crater that opens out onto the grass-lands. She awakens at sunrise to feel scorpions crawling on her legs. Snakes slither in through cracks in the rock while spiders and lizards descend the wall where she is resting. As she gets up to run, hundreds of bats swoop in through the cave entrance fleeing the rising sun, and she shields her head with her hands. A lizard drops on her neck and wriggles under her collar as spiders bite into her legs. Screaming as she tries to run, her toe catches in the rock and she falls flat out onto the floor—filled with poisonous snakes.

One of the Pharisees asked him to eat with him, and he went into the Pharisee's house and took his place at the table. And behold, a woman of the city, who was a sinner, when she learned that he was reclining at table in the Pharisee's house, brought an alabaster flask of ointment, and standing behind him at his feet, weeping, she began to wet his feet with her tears and wiped them with the hair of her head and kissed his feet and anointed them with the ointment. Now when the Pharisee who had invited him saw this, he said to himself, "If this man were a prophet, he would have known who and what sort of woman this is who is touching him for she is a sinner." And Jesus answering said to him, "Simon, I have something to say to you." And he answered, "Say it, Teacher." "A certain money lender had two debtors. One owed five hundred denarii, and the other fifty. When they could not pay, he cancelled the debt of both. Now which of them will love him more?" Simon answered, "The one, I suppose, for whom he cancelled the larger debt." And he said to him "You have judged rightly." Then turning toward the woman he said to Simon, "Do you see this woman? I entered your house; you gave me not water for my feet, but she has wet my feet with her tears and wiped them with her hair. You gave me no kiss, but from the time I came in she has not ceased to kiss my feet. You did not anoint my head with oil, but she has anointed my feet with ointment. Therefore I tell you, her sins, which are many are forgiven, for she loved much. But he who is forgiven little, loves little." And he said to her, "Your sins are forgiven." Then those who were at table with him began to say among themselves, "Who is this, who even forgives sins?" And he said to the woman, "Your faith has saved you; go in peace" (Luke 7:36-50).

Starving for affection and belonging, some humans search out sexual contact to fill their emptiness. Sex outside of the bonds of a godly marriage becomes a poisonous toxin exchange that seeks to fill the loneliness. Whether we are 8 or 80, loneliness is a powerful Fear. God planted a need for Love deep within us that drives us to connect with other humans. Fear-filled emptiness can *pretend* we are feeling Love, when in Reality we are transacting pain, suffering, and sin.

God's Word does not specify that this precious woman in repentance was a prostitute, but she came to the Lord on her knees with a heart filled with sorrow for a life of sin. Had she heard Jesus speak, and began to hope there was more to life than Fear and loneliness? Would she be slapped down again and find out that Jesus would want something more from her? Perhaps this genuine repentance is the first decision that she ever made that brought her peace. No one knows how this precious woman began a wayward life. But her honesty and humility came together at the feet of Jesus, who did not want anything from her, except her choice to follow Him. *He was the one doing the giving, not taking.* It may have been the first time in her Fearful lonely life, that she *encountered true Love.* A Love that only asked her to turn from her old life, and *receive* the blessings of a new walk of Joy (Psalm 16:11).

Pressing through her Fear of being rejected, Jesus forgave her Fear-filled wounded heart in essence saying, "You now belong to me, you never have to go back to that life of sin again." What an amazing example this precious woman is to us as we watch her repent, grieve, and stay close to Jesus. Her feelings of sincere Love poured out for the one who rescued her from the jaws of death. Her overwhelming Gratitude came from *living life in the depths of a predator's cave.* Who would be more thankful for rescue from spiders and snakes; the one who has seen them from a distance or the one who had endured their poisonous bites?

SIMON

This grieving woman made Simon uncomfortable. For such a woman to make a scene, cry, and unfurl her hair to wipe Jesus' feet was offensive. Can you see Simon crossing his arms in rejection and curling up his lip as he evaluated her? Were his Thoughts storming with Fear-driven judgment?

- I am nothing like her. I am superior.
- This raw emotion is embarrassing.
- If I empathize with her, I might look like a sinner.
- I would never do anything that needed forgiveness.

Simon told his heart that he needed no forgiveness, and he received none. It is likely that within all of us there is a judgmental Simon and a repentant precious woman. He saw no need to change his self-righteous, Fear-driven, arrogant ways, and therein lay the monster. *Simon's delusion was that he himself was not covered with spiders.*

WILD KINGDOM – Lure

The safari grassland is beautiful and teeming with adventure. Wildlife abounds on the savanna in graceful giraffes and antelope, and life is simultaneously beautiful and dangerous. Herds of elephants, zebras, wildebeest, and ostrich co-exist in balance, but they are always watchful for the predator lions, leopards, and poisonous snakes that kill.

Animals do not play with predators that can kill them. Man has not yet learned this lesson. The longer we play with the monsters/predators of our world, the greater likelihood that they will bite us. Satan is the master Poacher. His goal is to slaughter all the peaceful wildlife of our world and reign with the predators. The Poacher is friendly and gets our cooperation for his wildlife management by teaching us "risky play" with predators and convincing us that is cool. He knows us so well that He even knows which type of predator we would enjoy playing with most.

"Be sober-minded; be watchful. Your adversary the devil prowls around like a roaring lion, seeking someone to devour. Resist him, firm in your faith, knowing that the same kinds of suffering are being experienced by your brotherhood throughout the world" (1 Peter 5:8-9).

Predators:

- have an allure of charm and power
- know their prey and how to subdue them
- try to isolate their victims from the help of their family
- hate exposure and work best from the shadows
- inject deadly poisons that destroy nerves and organs
- overpower their prey and bite pieces out of them

Modern-day Predatory monsters use two basic strategies for taking the lives of their prey:

1. *Pleasures: Sex and Vulgarity* – The body contains millions of nerve endings and microscopic capillaries. The intimacy of sex was designed to connect two people on a physical, emotional, and spiritual level. Whenever a man and woman engage in sexual intercourse, the woman's body stretches to accommodate the man. It is in that stretching, that tiny fissures or cuts are formed in the woman, and the blood products of the man's semen actually cross into her blood stream. That is how intimately bonded two people are when they share their bodies, and that is why God made this special ceremony for a husband and wife only. As *your body is the vessel of your mind and your spirit*, having sex with someone you are not life-promised to in marriage can leave you laden with guilt. The body and spirit hold onto that guilt and try to cover over it with maladaptive behaviors to keep the wound from bleeding. The intimacy ceremony that God intended for

bonding is now cheapened by sharing with an uncommitted. "Therefore a man shall leave his father and his mother and hold fast to his wife, and the two shall become one flesh" (Matt. 19:5).

In order to ease the sadness, people joke, brag, and invent polluted words for a ceremony God designed for Love, intimacy, and Joy. All vulgarity is based in disrespecting that which should be cherished, special, or just personal and private. Whether sexual innuendo, sensual attire, or dirty language, the result is the same: the vulgar monster wants you to look at a God-created body/activity and *degrade it*. "Put away . . . obscene talk out of your mouth" (Col. 3:8). "Let no corrupting talk come out of your mouths" (Eph. 4:29).

2. *Venom/Poisons: Alcohol and Drugs – the statistics speak*

- "Substance abuse is the nation's #1 health problem."[1]
- "Alcohol is the #1 substance problem for America's youth with 80,000 deaths per year . . . 18 million alcoholics."[2]
- A 2010 Lancet article stated that alcohol was the #1 most dangerous drug because it harms not only the individual physically and emotionally, but hurts families and society as well.[3]
- Why would anyone play with the monster of alcohol or drugs that damage the body, depress the spirit and destroy the family? Would you drink a little poison?[4] "And do not get drunk with wine, for that is debauchery, but be filled with the Spirit" (Eph. 5:18).

"For the time that is past suffices for doing what the Gentiles want to do, living in sensuality, passions, drunkenness, orgies, drinking parties, and lawless idolatry" (1 Peter 4:3; Proverbs 23:29-35).

After 30 years of Las Vegas magic and tiger shows, on October 4, 2003, a 380-pound tiger mauled Roy Horn, leaving him disfigured and partially paralyzed. You can be thrilled by predators and call them "kitty," but their instinct is to harm you. If a predatory monster can convince you that *playing with him will bring you an express slide to happiness, you will succumb to the temptation.* You can make-believe that they are your pets, but that is not Reality (Proverbs 6:27).

PREDATORS WORK IN THE DARK

There was complete darkness below as we landed in the abandoned jungle air base. Carved out of an acacia tree forest in northeast India, the base would serve as our waiting place for the journey home at the end of WWII. Only the full moon illumined our way, as 50 exhausted pilots and navigators packed into the unlit bamboo basha hut for a longed-for night of sleep. I unrolled my bedroll and arranged my mosquito netting on the woven bamboo rack closest to the front opening of the thatched bunk house. All GI's had been required to turn in their weapons the previous week when the war ended, but I had held onto my .45, concerned about our journey home, and hoping to keep it for a souvenir. Having secured a bunk at the front and the .45 under my pillow, I went back outside to drink in the mesmerizing full moon that had risen while the other guys filtered in.

A high-pitched shriek pierced the darkness. A sound that a man only releases in his last moment's of living. Flashlights pointed to the back corner of the basha revealed a skinny young corporal almost completely enveloped in a python's coils. The snake had clamped its fangs into the man's thigh and within seconds was working hard to coil its way around his torso. This latecomer had taken one of the last beds, and the snakes habitat had been disturbed. The young victim desperately fought to breathe, as every GI tried to pull at the 19-foot Burmese python's coils in effort to free their buddy. Bamboo beds and netting poles splintered everywhere as men stumbled and knocked each other over. Men fought mosquito netting on their hands, their heads and feet, and many were injured in the panic.

With flashlights beaming in every direction, they finally dragged the furious snake and half-dead young man outside to see how they could help. GI's screamed instructions from everywhere and swarmed the scene all pulling at the lower coils of the hungry reptile and trying to extricate the victim. The scrambling men looked like a mass of maggots multiplying in the wound of a horse. Someone got a jeep from the motor pool and used the headlights to shine light on the melee. Having retrieved my contraband .45 from under my pillow, I kept digging at the other guys trying to get to the snake's body, but without success. Knowing that in my hand I held the only solution and only hope for this man's survival, I fought my way around the pile of men to where the snakes teeth pierced the man's body and with one hand on his leg, put a bullet in the snake's brain.

As I was writing Dad's story I asked him, "What rank was this guy?" Dad said, "He was probably a corporal." Then Dad chuckled, as only an 88-year-old man can do, and said, "He obviously wasn't too bright! We had been in India for two years and everybody knew what could inhabit abandoned bamboo huts in the dark."

You can pretend that there are no python's in the darkness and you can try to ignore them, but you will pay the price for lack of Reality vigilance. The young corporal thought that he could hang out and talk with his buddies and then grab whatever bunk was left. Perhaps some who witnessed this scene learned a lesson in vigilance.

The Poacher would like you to believe that predators ruling the world is the norm. If you walk through the zoo of "The Invented god of What Feels Good," you will see that "everybody" plays with predators for fun. As you pass their cages, their lies keep you listening and playing with them by saying: "Numb the hurt and you will feel fine."

Predator Clubs tantalize you to feel great and powerful *as they edge you away from your family group.* They have a strategy to turn you to *them* for comfort by whispering, "We know your Fears and your emptiness, let us help you feel better." They capitalize on your sadness and speak softly within your Thought storms: "You will never know happiness because your mother was horrible—your life will always be disappointing." Their movie is *Play with us and Forget,* and club mixer activities include the *Tame Blame Game.* Members of the Predator Club get certificates in rationalizing behavior:

- Girl/boy sexual touching is not as bad as homosexuality (Rom. 1:26-27).
- Dirty words/music are just my way of expressing myself (Col. 3:8).
- Television's influence is just part of life, you can't stop it (Phil. 4:8).
- Divorce is fine because when I'm happy—you will be happy (Matt. 19:8).
- Watching movies of people having sex is not like doing it (Matt. 5:28).
- Abortion is not actually killing a baby (Proverbs 6:17).

A predator's goal is to convince you to *open their cage* and let them come near you. They must get close to accomplish their objective: you and your family becoming their *prey.* With proximity they can latch on and pump venom into your blood stream, killing your nerves and shutting down your organs. Poisoning and *killing your spirit and flesh* is how predatory monsters grow stronger. They will lie, cheat, and steal to obtain your body and soul (Proverbs 27:12).

There is debate among top medical professionals over the meteoric rise in mental illness and parallel pharmaceutical company profits. Ask yourself this question, "Why do we have more crime, divorce, adultery, teen pregnancy, child molestation, alcoholism, and drug use than we did 100 years ago?" Can it really be a plague of "brain disease" requiring medication throughout the developed nations? The answer cannot be in a prescription, the answer is in dealing with the Fear-driven sins that are so close to us, and yet distance us from our Loving God.

Realistic Christians who desire the walk of Joy are completely aware of the Poacher's traits. Sex, alcohol, and dirty words *bother* righteous souls (2 Peter 2:7-8). You don't get to be naive (Proverbs 24:11-12). Naivete is a gift for the young. Naivete in grown-ups is illusion. Illusions entertain us in a dream world of stuffed animals, instead of teaching us to pay attention to the real life-safari we are actually walking. The Poacher wants you to believe the Fear-driven illusion that you can play with predators, turn them into pets, and not be bitten.

PREDATORY MONSTERS EAT THE YOUNG

Most human parents would declare that they care deeply for their children. My experience with the 500 students I teach each week is that they use the language and actions that they have seen in their homes. With electronic access to sin, children experience life in Reality, but also virtually as other people's lives are displayed before them on screens. And for most, the "bad words" that they hear on the playground are no surprise to them because, "Dad says it all the time."

Realistically, parents don't want to give up their own cursing, television programs, jokes, and movies and change *their* behavior. *Admitting that a lifetime of Fear-filled anxiety is exploded within a child because of failure to shield them from predators—is more truth than most people want to hear.* Crazy-making occurs in the mental stability of children when adults *say* one thing, but *act* another.

As I teach the same children year after year, I see:

- The use of foul language become more and more prevalent.
- Children withdraw or act out when their parents' divorce.
- The violence level of the "gamer" kids intensify.
- Jokes about sex get more and more common.

- The girls who wore the shorts with "cute" on the rear end—become boy-crazy.
- Teachers working harder and harder to help children understand honest values, when their home "habitats" do not have them.

I Love being a teacher! Making music with kids is truly Joyful work. But in the few decades that I have taught school, I have watched a stampede of the prey by the predators, and the school is not to blame. The internet is not to blame. Satan, the Poacher, and his luring *you* to open his cages and let his predators into your life, is to blame. *The habitat of the Poacher is pervasive, growing stronger, and his predators are eating our young.*

*Danielle (not her real name) is a beautiful and talented 13 year-old who has come to me for private lessons since she was very young. She has a rare blend of sweet nature, maturity, giftedness, and interest in working hard that is delightful. She shared with me one day that the #1 conversation subject in middle school is "Are you bisexual?"

*A disturbed third-grade boy preyed upon a sweet little girl in his class throughout the year. The teacher did everything possible and the boy was frequently suspended, but when the teacher was not looking, he often pinched that one girl's chest and rear end and whispered vulgar comments to her.

*As I walked with the second-graders to my classroom portable, the wild rabbits were out in the field nearby. One boy exclaimed, "Look, there is a "##%%**'n bunny!" Even though I disciplined the boy, the words had been spoken for all the children to hear.

Perhaps *you* are working hard to protect your children (and yourself) from the predators. You use a TV Guardian foul language filter, and monitor the content of programs.[5] Maybe you are reading Bible stories everyday and limiting video games. You take seriously the task of creating a home "habitat" that turns everyone's hearts to the Lord. *Are you sending them to spend all day at school with other children who exhibit predator values and telling them, "Don't act like them?"*

When children receive mixed messages about the world, it sets up a wound of Fear-filled doubt in their hearts—not Loving dependability. The inner terror that there is no truly protective God-Love breeds Fearful insecurity. Adversity will be a part of every child's life, but no survival-oriented creature on the savanna locks its defenseless young in a cage with a predator. Every parent must choose their child's schooling knowing that they will stand before God and give account for their children's moral and Fear development—which happens during every waking moment! (Psalm 119:63).

Make this statement, "I am not afraid of information." Now go spend the day with a family who is successfully homeschooling their children, visit a private school, and then visit the public school classes where your children would attend. Do that every year of their lives remembering that the steps of this one-way Journey cannot be re-traced. Pray about and make the decision knowing that you will be accountable to God for your choice. Ignoring predators helps them grow stronger. Ignoring cause and effect shows Fear.

> Six hundred elementary students gathered for the assembly as dozens of our local high school students came to perform. The belly dancers shook their breasts and arms to the new-style eastern music. The lyrics rang out, "back and forth, roll your hips round, now slow down, don't make a sound. . . ." as the high school girls now rotated and squatted before the young audience. I stood in the back where I could keep an eye on my second grade music class and—prayed. The cheerful student government announcer explained, "We have come to perform for you today to encourage you to do well on the upcoming standardized tests!" The predators were well advertised today. The prey watched closely.

Perchance you do not relate the lifelong Fears that become generated in a child's spirit with the loss of *innocence* that is taken forever.

> I was in the third grade when I first heard the Madrigal singers of the high school perform. The six young men in tuxedos and six young ladies in formal gowns sang acapella harmonics that thrilled my senses. Laying awake that night, I vowed that I would be a Madrigal singer one day and it became the greatest Joy of my high school years. Imagine if I had made that determined vow after watching the belly dancing club! Where would I be today—in a life lived very differently.

The habitat of the life-safari is different than when I traveled as a well-protected fawn. Today, truly loving fathers and mothers *put their lives on the line to safeguard* the beautiful innocence in their child. Wise parents use caution and gradually educate their young in the wisdom of living on the savanna, so they are not overtaken by it. Your job is to "keep yourself pure and virtuous, unstained by the world" (James 1:27)—not be naïve about it. This is what pleases the Lord (Col. 1:10).

UNCAGED – *Predator groups running wild*

> John had played sports throughout his younger years and enjoyed the physical activity and camaraderie. At a weekend tournament, one of the older boys on his team offered him marijuana. As the only freshman in the group, he had wanted to fit in with the older boys and feel accepted. Soon he began buying drugs from another teammate and was "hooked."

Alcohol, drugs, sex, homosexuality, sensuality, and filthy talk *are introduced by a person.* Perhaps you saw your mother joyfully comforted by a drink in the evening or a guy admired *you* when you wore a string tank top. Somehow, you had a desire to *connect* and please that *person* or duplicate the feeling you saw them enjoy. Fear of rejection said, *"If I do not participate in this, I will not be loved by them."* Predators say, "I can fill your Fearful loneliness by connecting you with 'love' from these people." The toxic/maladaptive behavior is just the bridge. *When a predator or venom is your connect with the "love" of other humans, it makes releasing them very difficult.*

Over time, the desire to avoid rejection and cover the Fear-filled shame must be increasingly tantalized to receive the same thrill. The Poacher keeps using camouflage to set his snares and provide the *exact temptation bait*— tailor-made for our weaknesses. *There are many predators, but the emptiness, the root of it all, is the same.* Fear-filled emptiness creates:

* false connections through drinking parties and sharing drugs
* false "love" in sexual compromises
* false lifestyles and affections based on mutual dependency
* false belief that you are worthless and do not belong to anyone
* a need to avoid *rejection* at all costs

Powerful Fear of rejection may press you for desperate measures to cover your loneliness. You may feel, "If I admit that I am scared and lonely, I will be perceived as a weak loser." In Reality, *feeling and admitting that Fear is the only way to open up and let the Lord's Love fill your lonely heart* (Luke 7:36-50). The Poacher tells you that you are *nothing* without the approval of the predator pack, and you can only accept "love" on their terms.

Jessica felt like her family was falling apart. Her father raged, and she and her volatile teenage sister fought constantly. A family counselor recommended that Jessica stay at college on the weekends to provide some distance between her and her volatile sister. Jessica, feeling frightened and all alone, turned to an intimate relationship with a young man. She had been solid in her Christian values all through high school, but in her Fearful loneliness turned to a sexual relationship for comfort.

When we feel rejected, we look around in Fear for something to hold on to. It takes great courage to stand up to the predatory monsters when you are at your **weakest** and even more *fortitude to stand up to the "friends" who introduce you to them* (1 Cor. 15:33). Remember, the human heart *yearns* for acceptance and connected Love. Fearful loneliness allows the predators to cut you in pieces and bind you, never to walk in the sunshine of Joyous abundant living.

SURVIVAL OF THE FITTEST EFFECTS – *Wounds and scars*
Ok, but life is about survival of the fittest, right? The "fittest" learn to fight off predators by using:

- Monster identification—there are many wildlife books available to educate you in naming and confronting worldly predators.
- Strength and skill training—learning the Map and keeping your tender compass heart pointing correctly, not toward momentary pleasure.
- Exposure prevention—protecting a habitat conducive to survival. Predators will whisper, "You cannot live without me."
- Strategy development—staying under the wings of The Protector. Predators lure away those who feel lonely.
- Defense—against the bites that permanently scar. Predators lurk ready to sink their teeth in at the moment of weakness.
- Clean breaks—the only way out of their dominance. Proximity lets predators claw you into pieces taking parts of you with them.

After you have lived the bite of a monster, that piece of you is missing forever. Instead of the freedom the monster promised, your *scar fastens you forever to the fangs that injected their venom and altered your nervous system.* Yet, there are great lessons in that scar.

Ignoring the Fear scar allows the Poacher to wrap his tentacles into all the seasons of your life as you keep struggling to *avoid rejection* and *feel Love.* A Thought storm might whisper, "If I get pregnant, then he will want to marry me. I will have him *and* a baby to love me—and never be alone again." The poison love in sexual attention is the Poacher's lure. But, in *the moment of crossing* the Sin line, you leave a portion of yourself behind—forever.

Remember, *Love and Fear are the greatest motivators*! If you believe this action will: 1) bring you Love and 2) reduce your Fear and loneliness, you will give your precious body and soul to it. Look at every one of these maladaptive behaviors and *reason* how they are a result of inner Fear:

"Now the works of the flesh are evident: sexual immorality, impurity, sensuality, idolatry, sorcery, enmity, strife, jealousy, fits of anger, rivalries, dissensions, divisions, envy, drunkennness, orgies, and things like these" (Gal. 5:19-20).

Do you see how in the same self-punishing acts there is a desperate outcry *from* Fear and *for* Love? Because your body houses your spirit, when you allow sin inside you, the hurt *creates a wound of separation. Your hurt festers and spreads infection as you now live to protect and cover up that loss of yourself.*

These spiritual/physical choices make the wound grow septic, and eventually bring death (Rev. 21:8). Whether our life movies are titled: *Predators Tore Me To Shreds,* or *My Courageous Life On The Savanna* is really up to us. Reaching down into our spirits to look at the Fear of rejection, and the great loneliness, may be one of the most courageous things we will ever do. The Great Protector offers you the only antidote for the poison of Fearful loneliness—BELONGING.

THE PROTECTOR AND THE GREAT BELONGING

You did not have a perfect earthly father or family. They do not exist. The voices of the predators entice you to believe that a momentary pleasure in the midnight of your wilderness Journey will fill your Fearful emptiness wound. In Reality, the Love and affirmation and delighted blessing of the Father that you long for—is as the sun above the savanna; always available, abundantly radiant, and warming for every cell of your spirit.

You are not alone on your life Journey. You belong to the real perfect Father and He is the Protector of all His children. The Protector says: "You belong to me. You are my child. I gave you life at conception for this one-way Journey. You have my devoted Love and attention. I always want us to be close. I always care about what you are feeling, and my arms are open to you. Only you can choose to separate us." You are the Lord's most precious possession. You *belong* to Him and He will never leave you behind.

- "Including you who are called to *belong* to Jesus Christ" (Rom. 1:6).
- "For this very night there stood before me an angel of the God to whom I *belong*" (Acts 27:23).
- "And those who *belong* to Christ Jesus have crucified the flesh with its passions and desires" (Gal. 5:24).
- "See what kind of love the Father has given to use, that we should be called *children of God;* and so we are" (1 John 3:1).
- "Fear not, for I have redeemed you; I have called you by name, *you are mine*" (Isaiah 43:1). *[Emphases added]*

Belonging to the perfect Father means He will never disappoint or let you down (Heb. 6:18, 12:6; 1 John 4:8). *God put the need for Love/connection/belonging inside you* and *He* is able to fill it! As you accept God's Love for you, you will long *to please Him with every breath* (Heb. 13:20-21).

Jesus was NEVER cool. Popular friends, parties, clothes, and money meant nothing to Him. He never networked with the "right" people. Do you remember the question I asked you from Chapter 1? What if you gave up being afraid of everything *except disappointing God*? What if *belonging to Him* was the only thing of importance to you?

Jesus LOVED *people.* That radiant, affectionate, overflowing Love for *you—was the motive for His sacrifice!* (John 8:29). The precious woman in repentance (Luke 7) dealt with her Fear of rejection because she *wanted His Love for herself!* She was ready to give up everything for the Joy and belonging to Him. She had the courage to get on her knees and show how much she appreciated receiving His Love, do you? (1 John 4:8-10).

HEALING – Empathy and compassion

I once visited with a woman who endured her childhood starving in a Nazi concentration camp. The allotment of a watery bowl of broth and crust of bread was never given to children, so she had to beg from the starving adult prisoners for crumbs to sustain her life. She admitted to me that sixty years later, she still kept crackers in her purse at all times. You see, she knew how precious food could be.

A valuable GIFT is opened when we learn to connect our past Fears with our present choices by asking the question, "What can this scar teach me?" Simon, the Pharisee, never saw the spiders crawling on him, for he thought he had no Fears. Since he felt he needed no compassion himself, he may never have developed compassion for others. *Simon may never have opened his gift, but always wondered why he was covered with spider bites.*

As you watch the repentant woman of Luke 7 step from her past life, think back to a moment in *your* past. Perhaps you had sex without the commitment of marriage, or another regret. A moment of compromise—when *part of you was left behind.* Play that movie on the screen of your memories for just a moment and *feel the Fear* that powered your decision. Did you feel, "If I do not do this, I will never be loved—accepted." Now rewind the scene again. When you get to the moment of compromise, grieve for the lost piece of yourself from that monster's claw. Grieve the part of yourself that you left behind trying to *please* someone else or *be* someone else. Feel the Fear and have compassion for your loneliness. Know that the Lord's arms are around you at this very moment, and He Loves you.

Imagine the look of compassion on the Lord's face as the woman in repentance humbled herself and cried. Notice how He did not push her emotions away, but let her grieve, and even extolled her compassionate gestures to Simon. Envision how she might have felt after His death and resurrection. "Jesus Loved me so much that He died for *me*. I am that valuable."

As you begin to fill the lost places of yourself with the character traits of courage, wisdom, and peace, your inner spirit now lines up with your outside actions. This great gift can power you the next time you feel Fearful loneliness and are tempted to play with a predator.

The steadfast Love of the Lord pours forgiveness over us like rain on the grasslands, running down over our mistakes. Heartfelt repentance is one of the most liberating, freedom-filled moments of wholeness you will ever experience. Some want to revisit their predator's cage often, and surely this is a life choice. However, *many have wasted their lives staring through the bars of a cage at one who hurt them, rather than living life on the beautiful savanna of God's creation.*

APPETITE DEVELOPMENT

"I hold back my feet from every evil way, in order to keep your word" (Psalm 119:101).

My friend Dan Jensen gave a wonderful explanation of God's design for marriage intimacy. "God meant for a man to undress only one woman in his *mind* and in his *eyes*—the one he is married to." "Let marriage be held in honor among all, and let the marriage bed be undefiled, for God will judge the sexually immoral and adulterous" (Hebrews 13:4).

Dissatisfaction with Reality explodes in the hearts of those who view pornography and sensual acting. It causes men to fantasize that women should be choreographed and paid actresses in performance—trained to meet a man's every desire. Once you have viewed powerful sexual images, they will *never, ever, be erased from your mind*. Right now, can you recall an unfortunate scene that is scarred into your mind from a movie long ago? Satan uses porn/sensuality to desensitize your taste to what is private and intended for commitment.

A tour of any Roman museum evidences the sensuality that ruled the ancient world, as it rules our sex-saturated culture. Even within recent history, when photography was invented around the time of the Civil War, one of its first uses was for pornographic snapshots sold to the fighting men.[6] "[T]here is nothing new under the sun" (Eccles. 1:9).

Christians work throughout their lives to develop godly hearts and appetites for purity. The early Christians did not want to be like those around them. They shunned the indulgent and sensual culture of the Roman world, and history records them as choosing to be "different." Keeping themselves and their children pure for the Lord's service *was* their new life (2 Cor. 11:3). Their focus was on pleasing the Lord (Eph. 5:10). We inaccurately mislabel wishing, thinking, and intending, as CHANGE. Only the works of:

- studying the Bible as a road Map for living
- choosing Christian companions
- refusing to watch sensuality in any form
- understanding why we dress modestly
- reflecting on what is true personal holiness
- walking each day in your Divine purpose
- praying to God constantly for strength—are what make real change.

"Since we have these promises, beloved, let us cleanse ourselves from every defilement of body and spirit, bringing holiness to completion in the fear of God" (2 Corinthians 7:1).

What if you carried around a sign that said, "Would you like to look at my cleavage?" Would you and your words be responsible for promoting sensual thoughts in a man's mind and body? Do you think it is ok to wear a shirt that *shows* your cleavage? If you are responsible for your words (Ch. 6), then are you responsible for your actions? What if you wore your underwear—bra and panties—around town one day? Would you be responsible for contributing to sensual thoughts in the minds/bodies of the men who saw you? Then is it ok to wear them because you are near a pool and the fabric is a different color? What if the next time you wore shorts and a string tank top you carried a sign that said, "If you have sensual thoughts when you look at me—that is your problem." Is it really? (Matt. 5:28; 12:37).

> We were just newlyweds when we invited the young people from our new congregation over for a barbecue. I had no understanding about modesty, nor that I was encouraging "thought processes" within others. I wore some cute, tiny, little, red shorts and did not think twice about it. Even though it was summer, I noticed that the young people who came wore t-shirts, jeans, and capris. It was only through a very gentle and thought-provoking lesson by our preacher, Darrell Perry, and some casual conversations with older women, that my mind started percolating about *my* responsibility to be modest. No one was harsh with me, but the Words in the Bible and my desire to please the Lord—were changing me. As I learned to wear my cloak of responsibility daily, I began understanding about covering my God-given body. "For this is the will of God, your sanctification: that you abstain from sexual immorality" (1 Thess. 4:3).

The excavated paintings and mosaics of the Roman World reveal a widespread and pervasive appetite for sexual promiscuity. Human life was cheap and deviant behavior reigned. We know from the evidence that early Christians covered their torsos and thighs, knowing that these lead to the more private parts of our bodies. "[T]hat women should adorn themselves in respectable apparel, with modesty and self-control . . ." (1 Tim. 2:9; 1 Pet. 3:3-4).

1. *Early Christian writings* consistently emphasize the principles of covering the body *for helping the purity of heart and mind of all*. Clement of

Alexandria wrote about "clothing, clinging close to the body . . . outlines the woman's figure, so that the whole shape of her body is visible to spectators . . . such clothing is meant for looking, not for covering." Clement died in the year 215.[7]

2. ***Early Christian art*** shows men and women who are dressed modestly, which was completely different from the clothing of the day.[8] The art of an ancient culture does not lie. It is the "picture that tells a thousand words." As their minds were being renewed to Love the Lord, the early Christians covered their intimate bodies and kept them private. They dressed differently out of devotion and Love of God.

> I appeal to you therefore, brothers, by the mercies of God, to present your bodies as a living sacrifice, holy and acceptable to God, which is our spiritual worship. Do not be conformed to this world, but be transformed by the renewal of your mind, that by testing you may discern what is the will of God, what is good and acceptable and perfect (Romans 12:1-2).

The Poacher wants our bodies to be open for public, cheap, and unrestricted viewing. He wants us to rub together dancing and call it "innocent fun." Many young women do not understand (as I did not when I was young) that they are hurting a man's ability to have pure thoughts when they reveal or move sensually in front of him (Gal. 5:19-21). If you do not believe this is true, ask a deeply spiritual Christian man. Now ask yourself, would you wear those clothes or act that way with Paul and Timothy? "And whatever you do, in word or deed, do *everything* in the name of the Lord Jesus, giving thanks to God the Father through him" (Col. 3:17). *[Emphasis added]*

Early Christians avoided the public baths that were the center of Roman culture, and did not view the violent games of the arena. Christians did not attend the theatre when the drama and comedy themes focused on immorality. Lactantius wrote, "I am inclined to think that the corrupting influence of the stage is even worse (than that of the arena). The subjects of comedies are the deflowering of virgins or the loves of prostitutes . . . *They teach adultery by acting it out.* How do we expect our young people to respond when they see that these things are *practiced without shame* and that everyone eagerly *watches*."[9] Lactantius became a Christian in his adult years and died in the year 320 A.D. Would he write the same commentary on our movies today that "teach adultery by acting it out?" How is it we think we can *watch* and not be affected? (1 Timothy 2:2-3).

Would you watch *that* movie or use *those* words with the apostle Paul or the repentant woman of Luke 7? Would you look back into the cage and wistfully brood over the predators of your old ways that left you with scars? "Oh, I loved wearing low necklines before I was a Christian." or "I miss drinking wine and dancing." You work on behalf of the Poacher when you make light about *poisons or scars*.

> Put to death therefore what is earthly in you: sexual immorality, impurity, passion, evil desire, and covetousness, which is idolatry. On account of these the wrath of God is coming. In these you too once walked, when you were living in them. But now you must put them all away: anger, wrath, malice, slander, and obscene talk from your mouth. Do not lie to one another, seeing that you have put off the old self with its practices and have put on the new self, which is being renewed in knowledge after the image of its creator (Col. 3:5-10).

The rich oil deposits that are mined from beneath the savanna come from *decayed* animals and vegetation from thousands of years ago. When our Fear-filled earthly ways are put to *death*, we reap an infinite bounty in true Joy by learning the ways of the Creator.

> But the fruit of the Spirit is love, joy, peace, patience, kindness, goodness, faithfulness, gentleness, self-control; against such things there is not law. And those who belong to Christ Jesus have crucified the flesh with its passions and desires. If we live by the Spirit, let us also keep in step with the Spirit (Gal. 5:22-25).

True Joy is:
- listening to college girls encourage younger girls to live godly lives
- having good clean fun with your Christian friends
- asking yourself, "Is this pleasing to the Lord?" then changing the channel
- a "That is amazing!" moment when you are reading the Bible
- wearing the same "coverage" amount of clothes to church as elsewhere
- using the *same* vocabulary 24 hours a day and 7 days of the week
- *remembering that Jesus inside spirit and outside behavior were the same*

LIVING IN A PROTECTED WILDLIFE HABITAT – *Safari*
The parents of the animal kingdom *teach* their young how to stay close, use awareness and defense, in order to stay alive. God has laid out blue-print formulas for the family in His Word. For millennia men and women who have built lives on the foundation of respect and self-control, honored the Lord and reaped the benefit, in a stable, godly home and children. Christians who

"survive as the fittest" on this part of the one-way Journey hone their skills to combat predators, and constantly train to live morally on the savanna He created (2 Peter 1:4).

While the protective habitat enclosure of the Love of God ensures your spiritual security, realize that the choice of eternal separation, eternal neediness, emptiness, loneliness, and hurt will not occur without your consent. Only you climb outside the shield and into the snare—to compromise your safety. It is terrifying to most of us to admit that we bear the responsibility for our behavior—whether under pressure or not. *When we make decisions in Fear, we will likely have regrets.*

As long as you draw breath, there will be things on this earth to Fear. *Your character is formed as you respond to your Fears.* Read Galatians 5:19-25 again and ask the Lord to help you with the predators you are playing with. Do you want to reduce your Fear and walk in Joy? *Walk by the Spirit purifying what enters your eyes, ears, and heart each day.* Keep your spirit and body serving Him in the purest union by refusing to be torn apart by a predator.

FEARBREAKER-JOYMAKER JOURNEY

"Am I willing to give up eternity with God for _____ (predator)?" Ask the Lord, "Is this pleasing to you?" throughout *every* day. I keep pink heart-shaped post-it notes on my television and mirror with that question "Is this pleasing to the Lord?" (Eph. 5:10). As you grow in your *power of discernment* (Hebrews 5:14), train your heart with *positive statements* to lovingly focus on the *Joy of being pleasing.* "And it is my prayer that your love may abound more and more, with knowledge and all discernment" (Phil. 1:9).

Believe deep inside you that the strongest motivation is Love! Christian living is not just about *avoiding* predators, but rather about *embracing* God's steadfast Father Love. The mutual Love that you give and receive from God cannot be forced—it is poured out with thanksgiving!

Make a Fear growth plan:
- Acknowledge you are *feeling* Fear when tempted by a predator.
- Honestly list the bites this predator will take from you.
- Understand you cannot change/fix/heal the predator.

- Seek strength from His Word which is the Map for this one-way Journey.
- Get ongoing help from mature Christians with your battles.
- Focus on how vital your strength is to your Divine purpose.

Praise Him and keep saying, "Thank you," to the Lord that lost pieces of your spirit can be filled with Love and wisdom. Know that wearing your cloak of responsibility in abiding Joy, allows you to glorify Him. "May the Lord direct your hearts to the love of God and to the steadfastness of Christ" (2 Thess. 3:5).

GROWING THROUGH FEAR

1. Which predators do you play with the most? Name and tell someone about them. Pray together and ask the Lord's help.

2. How do you try to make distinctions between "big" and "small" sins? Is watching a movie with adultery in it ok with the Lord?

3. If true repentance means dealing with your Fear, is there something in the past or present that you need to grieve for and repent of?

4. "Why did you do that?" is an often-asked question. How can you teach yourself to ask, "What Fear were you feeling when you did/said that?"

5. How you can you grow in your *power of discernment* to be more pleasing to the Lord? (Ephesians 5:10; Colossians 1:10; Psalm 104:34).

~ 8 ~
Frightened Little Women
Fear-driven decision making
Lot's daughters (Genesis 18:22-19:29)

*T*he *door opens onto a ledge about half-way up the cliff side. Their ropes sway with the breeze as the Heroine and her climbing partner begin their ascent up the face of the rock to the summit destination. As each girl pulls herself up, shale and stones fall from above. Choking from the dust and with burning hands, they persevere as the wind becomes stronger and dark clouds roll in. Clinging to her rope, the Heroine notices other doorways in the ledges around them. As her rope sways, she hollers to her partner below, "I am not going up to the summit, there are other doors along the way, I am just going to take one of them." Her less-experienced climbing partner follows her lead, but when reaching for a ledge, loses her grip on the rope and plunges down toward the crevasse.*

Please read the prequel to this story in Genesis 18:22-19:29.

> Then the LORD rained on Sodom and Gomorrah sulfur and fire from the LORD out of heaven. And he overthrew those cities, and all the valley, and all the inhabitants of the cities, and what grew on the ground. But Lot's wife, behind him, looked back, and she became a pillar of salt (Genesis 19:23-26). Now Lot went

141

up out of Zoar and lived in the hills with his two daughters, for he was afraid to live in Zoar. So he lived in a cave with his two daughters. And the firstborn said to the younger, "Our father is old, and there is not a man on earth to come in to us after the manner of all the earth. Come let us make our father drink wine, and we will lie with him, that we may preserve offspring from our father." So they made their father drink wine that night. And the firstborn went in and lay with her father. He did not know when she lay down or when she arose. The next day, the firstborn said to the younger, "Behold, I lay last night with my father, Let us make him drink wine tonight also then you go in and lie with him, that we may preserve offspring from our father." So they made their father drink wine that night also. And the younger arose and lay with him, and he did not know when she lay down or when she arose. Thus both the daughters of Lot became pregnant by their father. The firstborn bore a son and called his name Moab. He is the father of the Moabites to this day. The younger also bore a son and called his name Ben-ammi. He is the father of the Ammonites to this day (Genesis 19:30-38).

God sent angels from the heavenly realm to rescue this little family. Lot's faithfulness was always in the Lord's view and divine rescue was dispatched to bring him, his wife, and daughters away from harm and on a Journey to safety. But even after the angel asked the survivors not to look back at the destruction and keep their eyes on the path of deliverance, Lot's wife could not resist her Thought storms, and in one turn of her head exchanged her life of freedom—for a pillar of salt. Lot and his family had tried to build their life in the tornado alley of vice, the city for which the sin of sodomy was named (Rom. 1:24-27; Rev. 21:8). While their bodies had been rescued, the wickedness living in those cities traveled deep within those daughters, as dangerous Fear disease (1 Corinthians 15:33).

Who could not have compassion for these two girls who watched two cities, their fiances, their home, and their mother be destroyed? Their lives had been decimated and their world forever changed. But, instead of rising up to meet adversity with faith, Lot's daughters' allowed a Thought storm of Fear to rush in their minds:

- We were raised to be wives and mothers.
- We will have no sons to carry on the name.
- If we have no children—we have no value.
- We are going to die out here with dad.
- We must get dad drunk and have sex with him.

Their Fears for the future pushed them off a cliff to extreme actions as they sought to alleviate their pain. Believing that the end (giving birth to sons), would justify any means, they conspired to alter their father's mental/moral status, so they could become pregnant by him.

Perhaps they did not prepare the standard wine dilution or progressively strengthened it as the evening wore on. As water sources were often polluted, small amounts of alcoholic wine were added in order to sanitize the water. Ancient writings cite dilutions of 20:1 to 3:1 (water to wine), and this diluted wine was the standard "wine" beverage of the day. Only "barbarians" drank undiluted or "unmixed" wine.[1]

It is not likely that "righteous Lot" (2 Peter 2:7), would have ever partaken of undiluted wine and suffered its mind-altering effects—if he had known about it.[2] "So they made their father drink wine that night also. And the firstborn arose and lay with him, and he did not know when she lay down or when she arose"(Genesis 19:33). But if you wanted to get a grown man drunk without his knowledge, gradually "strengthening" the wine mix would do it. These girls' Fear of the future was so great that they plotted incest to control their destiny, with *their father as the pawn*. "For out of the heart come evil thoughts, murder, adultery, sexual immorality, theft, false witness, slander" (Matthew 15:19).

CRISIS – Dreams shattered

The tornado sirens had been sounding intermittently all day, but everything was planned and paid for, so our families and friends gathered in the white church building that morning to watch me marry my best friend. We had known each other since high school, and he was the steady, thoughtful, loving, Christian man I had always dreamed of. The turn-of-the-century church building where generations of my family had worshipped and married was decorated with yards of white tulle, hundreds of deep blue hydrangea and glowing candles.

As Mom was pinning on my veil, all my bridesmaids were busy admiring the thousands of pearls and crystals that my "Nana" had sewn on my satin bridal gown—with a loving prayer in every stitch. Everyone was a bit teary-eyed in the basement beneath the church building when the twister hit. The noise was horrendous, but all the bridesmaids and mothers huddled together and cried in the corner of a children's classroom where we had dressed. The basement windows blew in and glass shattered everywhere. We heard a crashing overhead as if the world had ended. Hours later, we were rescued from the basement to find that my grandfather, many of our guests, and my beloved fiance were gone. The entire building above us, and our lives, were a pile of rubble.

What is the worst thing that could happen to you? _____ You know that moment you wake up from a bad dream and your Reality is blurred. Then the haunting Fear grips you, "Oh, it wasn't a dream, my daughter is pregnant, my house did burn down, and I still have cancer. My life really *is* that bad."

Life-changing events feel like ground zero of a bomb explosion. You are completely destabilized and consumed by grief. The pit of your sadness cannot go any deeper and you feel as though you might crack from the strain. Your very existence is threatened and there is no future predictable. When your world has exploded—the trauma changes everything. The trauma changes *you*. Even though the Lord's compassionate arms wrap around your grieving heart, the agonizing Fear of change remains. "But, I had it all planned . . . my life has changed forever . . . what do I do now?" (Psalm 6:4).

The daughters of Lot, like many people, found their traumas too horrible to stop and face, so they kept on trying to "quick fix" their lives. When they found themselves at ground zero, they titled their new life movie, *I am Taking Control of Life From Now On.* By listening to their Fear of the unknown and manipulating an "outcome," they tried to soothe their hurt. A Thought storm of Fear became disastrous actions of evil. They let the destabilizers of life push them to cut their ropes and *they* fell into the abyss. When you are de-stabilized by a life crisis you can:

- be angry for the rest of your life, now that you are a victim
- give in to Fearful Thought storms like Lot's wife
- pretend that the destabilizer does not affect you and put on a happy face
- feel your feelings and choose to be a *stabilizer* in a daunting situation

"Commit your way to the Lord; trust in him, and he will act" (Psalm 37:5).

In Louisa May Alcott's, **Little Women,** Jo says repeatedly, "Why do things have to change?" She constantly clings to the past and struggles when life twists and turns around her. Throughout their lives, Jo, Beth, Meg, and Amy felt stronger with each other nearby, and faced living and dying courageously wrapped in each other's arms. Unlike them, Lot's wife and daughters met with crisis opportunity and changed—*from treasured women under the Lord's protection—to a pillar of salt and the mothers of pagan nations!* (Psalm 85:8).

In Chinese, the word for *crisis* is two words joined together. One character is danger the other is opportunity.[3] If in the midst of life turmoil you stop and *feel your Fear of change,* you may meet face-to-face the growth *opportunity* in that crisis. You may open a door that you never knew existed. As you lean in and *accept* what has happened

to you, you have your *first hand grasp on the rope toward growth.* If you ask, "Why doesn't God care about me?", you may be feeling that His Love can be disconnected from you—by a twister. Is the Creator of the universe that small? Do you think you are off His radar?

> Who shall separate us from the love of Christ? Shall tribulation, or distress, or persecution, or famine, or nakedness, or danger, or sword? . . . No, in all these things we are more than conquerors through him who loved us. For I am sure that neither death nor life, nor angels nor rulers, nor things present, nor things to come, nor powers, nor height nor depth, nor anything else in all creation, will be able to separate us from the love of God in Christ Jesus our Lord (Romans 8:35, 37-39).

IDENTITY – I dropped my tiara!

The Bible recounts many stories of women who struggled to have children: Sara – Genesis 18; Hannah – 1 Samuel 1; Elizabeth – Luke 1. It was a devastating thing for a woman of ancient times to be unable to bear children and never achieve the identity of "mother." Even today some feel pressure to have children to create the improved version of—"who I could have been" or the "perfect child to fulfill my hopes and dreams." It is the same Fear-driven expectation as these sisters (Lot's daughters) felt 4,000 years ago. Technology offers other temptations to be cautious about as "extra" in vitro babies are DNA "harvested" or washed down the drain. Christians believe that every life is precious and must be centered that *the reason* for having children is to raise them to serve the Lord (Genesis 2:7).

Inside each of us is the princess *plan* that we mapped out as little girls: the perfect wedding to the perfect man with the perfect children, house, and cars. That dream plan becomes part of our identity. Our Fears can tell us that any obstacle to that dream must be eliminated (Isaiah 65:2).

With your hand-written *Wish List for my Life,* everything goes well on your life Journey for awhile. Then one day, a tempest hits you and leaves you *hanging by a rope on a cliff.* You hold down your tiara with your free hand and holler down into the canyon, "YOU MEAN I AM NOT GOING TO BE CINDERELLA?" and the echo returns . . . "Cinderella, Cinderella, Cinderella . . ." As you cling to your rope in despair, you daydream a narrator's voice responding from the canyon, "Cinderella is a fantasy-fiction story meant to stimulate discussion on stepfamilies and bullying. *It is not a true story*—this will not happen to you." Your life-identity has just detonated along with the tempest (Job 13:15).

STRESS IS – *You expect a princess life and you get your life!*

Why do we think that we get to have perfect lives? Too many princess movies? If Jesus learned obedience by the things which he *suffered* (Hebrews 5:8), how is it that we think we get a perfect life? Suffering offers us a chance to lay down our tiaras and grow up (Job 38:4).

Every Heroine is driven by a truth. A truth that she holds in her deepest core and ties around her waist like a rope when life is a cliffhanger. If when left dangling at the end of her rope, she determinedly pulls *herself* inch by inch to safety, her character will burst with the strength of a woman determined to surrender—only to the Lord. But if she loosens her grip on the rope in order to reach back for her childhood princess wish list—she will end up twisted, hanging upside down, and swinging.

Courage comes in recognizing that tempests and their aftermath have the *meaning* that *you give them*. If your "life is over" because you lost your job or house, it is because you have written that into *your definition* of what it means to have a "life of value." Did God tell you that *you* get to set the "This is a worthy life" standard? Wisdom within you might ask that powerful question instead, "What lesson do I get to learn from this experience?" (Proverbs 8:14).

God knows and Loves your insides, but does not care about your glow-in-the-dark magic wand or plastic tiara. These are things of *childhood* and will block your emergence of womanhood here in Reality. When all external identities are broken, the real *you* remains. *Remember your life here has a Divine purpose to serve and glorify the Lord, not a Cinderella purpose*! (Luke 9:23).

In this you rejoice, though now for a little while, if necessary, you have been grieved by various trials, so that the tested genuineness of your faith—more precious than gold that perishes though it is tested by fire—may be found to result in praise and glory and honor at the revelation of Jesus Christ. Though you have not seen him, you love him. Though you do not now see him, you believe in him and rejoice with joy that is inexpressible and filled with glory, obtaining the outcome of your faith, the salvation of your souls (1 Peter 1:6-9).

ATTITUDE LENSES – Do you watch your movies – IMAX or 3D?

Have you ever put on someone else's prescription glasses? It gives you quite a shock to see the world with the correction that they require. Several times a day, you *actually* change lenses to view different events and people. Lenses are chosen by your Thought storms and your heart, and they show your light/dark, valuable/not valuable pieces of yourself. If you have hurt my feelings in the past, I look at you through attitude glasses that see you as an *enemy*. If you are my *friend*, I put on my attitude glasses to see you with kindness. My heart attitude tells me which glasses to choose and there are thousands of attitude lenses available.

- Dark lenses maintain your hidden identity and keep probing eyes out.
- Movie lenses help you experience the lives of others.
- Panic-stricken lenses keep you reacting and lashing out at everything.
- Problem-solving lenses help you analyze and respond to information.
- Fear lenses always give you blurry vision.

As you dangle from your rope after a cliffhanger event, a telescope attitude lens lets you dream of the future far away where everything is "perfect." Your close-up lenses only allow you to look at the fibers on your rope as it tears blisters into your hands and think about how miserable you are at this moment. Your lenses affect how you see events and *others*, but because you wear *some* lens at all times, when you look in the mirror, they affect how you see *yourself* also. You can increase or decrease your suffering in life, depending upon the attitude lenses you put on. "Whoever trusts in his own mind is a fool, but he who walks in wisdom will be delivered" (Proverbs 28:26).

You write the narration script of your life story through the lenses you wear as you are living it. How you *retell* your stories determines how you *use* them in your spiritual growth. Siblings often have completely different recollections of cliffhanger events because they wear different attitude lenses. One sibling *focuses* his attitude on the happy memories, and the other focuses and rehearses her "negative" brain on every angry or unfair moment that occurred.

Maximizer lenses (Pessimists) have built in flashing strobe-lights. Their daily movie is a panic-stricken emergency and the Rescue Trauma Club is always playing a horror flick. Even running errands and grocery shopping are distressing episodes for them. Every human interaction produces an I MAX 3D movie event titled, *The Trauma that Defined Misery*.

Minimizer lenses (Naive Optimists) are always pretty and dismiss feelings and pain as nothing. The La-la land Club watches the same IMAX 3D movie event and titles it, *It's all a Princess Dream!*

Reality lenses watch daily action and know that the same event can be given many different meanings. Keep in view that *you decide what an experience means in your life.*

Within every one of us are maximizer, minimizer, and Reality lenses. If we receive lots of attention by wearing our pessimism maximizer lenses, we will never be motivated to put them away. The Adversary will continue to steal every moment of our life's Joy—with negativity. If our Fears make denial more comfortable, minimizer lenses will help make everything look "just fine." "In the pride of his face the wicked does not seek him; all his thoughts are, 'There is no God'" (Psalm 10:4).

Changing my lenses transforms the way I view trauma, life change, and those around me. Reality and positive thinking patterns, like rock wall climbing, must be practiced, and this is *work*. I have taught myself to say, "Ok, Fear glasses off, let's stop and take a deep breath." When I calm my thoughts and open my eyes to Reality, I can see around the canyon all the wondrous choices and blessings I have and say, "It *is* a wonderful life!" Which glasses are your favorite choices? "Love what is good and hate what is evil" (Romans 12:9).

"The good person out of the good treasure of his heart produces good, and the evil person out of his evil treasure produces evil, for out of the abundance of the heart his mouth speaks" (Luke 6:45).

FEAR/CONTROL – I did it myyyyy wayyyyyyy !!!
"Be angry, and do not sin; ponder in your own hearts on your beds, and be silent" (Psalm 4:4).

The attitude lens of Fear-driven control detects constant threat and may push you to think, "If I can control the lives of others, I will have more control in my life." Smart women work very hard to *help* everything! Imagine if you could just input requests to God and *He* would comply. What a mess you would have if you controlled every door of your destiny! Ask yourself, "If I had everything that I *wanted*, would I be perfectly happy?"

Fear-driven control is NOT: (these are good things!)
- being proactive and planning
- teaching biblical and godly living
- learning from experiences
- setting healthy boundaries

Fear-driven control is:
- an illusion based in a fantasy of perfection
- bending the will of another person to our own
- manipulating circumstances
- "If you would see it my way, everything will be fine"
- a reaction to not getting your own way
- believing that *you* know best
- any activity that crosses the DO NOT SIN line (Eph. 5:10)

The "sisters'" powerful Thoughts stormed that *God needed their help in managing the future.* Was it true that they only had two choices—incest or die alone? Fear pressures us to believe that there are *only two doors* to choose from—*black and white*—when really there are a rainbow of door choices! In their frustration and anger the sisters forgot that no matter what Fear-driven control tells you, the godly choice is *never* to cross the DO NOT SIN line (Eph. 4:26; Ps. 4:4). NEVER. "In your struggle against sin you have not yet resisted to the point of shedding your blood" (Hebrews 12:4).

Sometimes we tell the Lord, "I know what I want. I want *this* solution to *that* adversity." "With problem A—I want Answer C; I DO NOT WANT ANSWER D!" News flash: *You do not get to choose your adversity.* Do you think you can say, "I don't want X or Y, but I will accept adversity Z? I CAN ONLY BE HAPPY IF I GET MY WAY!" It is in this anxious and Joy-less state that we make Fear-driven decisions and suffer greatly as Satan continues to win. While you control *much* of your destiny with your choices, you may need a Reality check of who is really in charge of the *world*. God's Loving, providing hands are at work caring for *His children*—that means *you*! Ask yourself, "If I trust in the Lord, what spiritual harm can actually come upon me?" "The fear of the Lord leads to life, and whoever has it rests satisfied; he will not be visited by harm" (Proverbs 19:23; 1 Peter 3:13-17, 4:16).

Beneath Fear-driven control there is a hidden "needy" agenda. The sisters' inner Fears whispered, "I will be *nobody* if I am childless. I will be *somebody* if I have a son." They saw no value in *their* own lives. They had no trust in God's Love for them, nor *Love* of themselves (Mark 12:30-31).

Loving yourself means:

- honoring your unique preciousness to the Lord
- seeing your Divine purpose on this one-way life Journey
- honestly questioning *your* life choices
- accepting your *power* of choice and human *limits*
- humbly facing each day as a trusting *servant* of God
- keeping a daily awareness of the DO NOT SIN line
- giving up the quest for the perfect princess life
- *looking from the end of your life backward when making decisions*

If you believe you need to help God "fix things," you might think, "But Lord, you had *this* plan and purpose for me, right?" As if He had written your life story with a Cinderella plot and purpose! Or is that *your* idea of your purpose? *Fear-driven control is a deep impatience.* It is the instant gratification that says, "I AM SMARTER THAN GOD . . . I KNOW BETTER THAN HE DOES." Do you really?

The World is still haunted by the Fear-filled, controlling choices of Lot's daughters as they drugged their father with wine—had incestuous relations—and created the evil and idolatrous nations of Moab and Ammon (Genesis 19:38). The offspring of the sisters, the Moabites and Ammonites, have plagued the world for thousands of years.

Moabites: 156 times cited in the Scriptures

- Worshipped pagan gods of Chemosh and Baal
- Sacrificed infants and used virgin prostitutes

Ammonites: 105 references

- Worshipped pagan god Molech and offered child sacrifice
- "cruelty of the Ammonites" (1 Samuel 11:2; Amos 1:13).

To this day, the disobedient descendants of these sisters torment the Christian world. *Two young women changed the course of civilization with sinful acts.*

As you learn why *not* to be afraid (Fearful anxiety), you must rehearse why *to* be afraid (Fear within respect). Don't misunderstand God's patience. His standards are clear and violation brings enduring consequences. Do you want to be haunted by Fear? Make a bad decision that changes the course of history. Your choices are *bigger* than you are. "In the fear of the Lord one has strong confidence and his children will find refuge" (Proverbs 14:26).

THE GREAT FEAR LEAP

Do you ever think, "I lost my keys this morning, I must have Alzheimer's?" Can you count the times that you have mentally jumped to a wrong conclusion? When you look at a great chasm of disappointment in your life and see no way to cross it, you sometimes *make a Fear leap into a future that does not exist.* Thinking, "I am on *this* cliff and I want to be on *that* cliff and the only way between the two is—to jump," can send you plunging down into a crevasse. In trying to manipulate "the mark that you will leave on the world," you may tragically leave a legacy of Fear in lieu of faith. Fear leaps begin with *faulty assessments* of the door choices in your

life labyrinth. Instead of praying and assessing which door choice might be according to God's will, a *Fear leap takes you over the chasm in panic*, to the Invented god of "The Ends Justifies the Means."

An employee who needs more money to "feed his family," takes the Fear leap of "I must do this to keep from starving" to justify stealing from the company. Lot's daughters' (the sisters) Thought storms clamored and swirled within them until they believed *what they plotted to do was ok*! Imagine what they must have seen/heard of alcohol and sexuality growing up in wicked Sodom in order to be *able* to concoct such a plan! Fear of the future drives people to do crazy things! As they pondered whether the "ends justify the means," they might have asked the question, "Will there be any *honor* in the end?" (1 Peter 2:12). When a Fear leap goes into action, it cannot be withdrawn. Fear leaps are:

- jumps away from God and His will
- always downhill
- disguised as shortcuts to happiness
- *Thought storms that become evil plots and actions*
- begun out of Fear-driven control and *impatience*
- actions in your life story that cannot be re-wound or recorded over
- ways of trying to manipulate your destiny

A huge goal of Satan, the Adversary, is to *rip the hope from your heart* by preying upon your Fear of the future. He wants to convince your "negative" brain that it is hopeless to trust in the Sovereign Lord. The Adversary designed Fear leaps to get you to give in and *jump the chasm when making decisions*. As your fingers are clinging to the ledge, Satan will grind his boot in and kick at your grasp to try to get you to fall to your death by choosing one of his "shorter routes to dream fulfillment." He does not care that your choice right now *will haunt your future and keep you from eternal glory!* (1 Cor. 10:13). *With every grasp on the ledge, you are determining what kind of woman you are going to be in this life and where you will spend the next.* Look Satan in the eye and say, "You may smash my bleeding fingers on this cliff, but my grip holds fast to the arms of the Lord." "Say to those who have an anxious heart, 'Be strong; fear not! Behold, your God will come with vengeance, with the recompense of God. He will come and save you'"(Isaiah 35:4).

THE SPACE

Wartime prison camp survivors know how it feels to live in a powerless state of Fear and under constant threat of death. Their daily goal to preserve their own life meant persistent vigilance. Viktor Frankl, MD, PhD wrote about starvation and daily beatings as he struggled to survive mentally and physically in Auschwitz. "We who lived in the concentration camps can remember the men who walked through the huts comforting others, giving away their last piece of bread. They may have been few in number, but they offer sufficient proof that everything can be taken from a man, but one thing: the last of the human freedoms—*to choose one's attitude* in any given set of circumstances, to choose one's own way."[4] *[Emphases added]*

"Between stimulus and response there is a space. In that space is our power to choose our response. In our response lies our growth and our freedom." —Viktor E. Frankl

Think of that moment of *space* between what has happened/been spoken to you—and—how you respond to it—as a *pause button* in time. A moment of the purest freedom to choose from the *billions of possible responses* that you  can give. When you STOP—feel—think and pray, "Help me Lord, I don't want to make a Fear-driven choice," you get to *consciously choose* what your body/spirit are now doing with your *life*.

If "You are what you repeatedly do," then be aware that sometimes there is *one moment of time that will define you forever*. One Fear leap in your life can haunt you and change the course of history. It is in the choices constructed in the freedom of your *SPACE* that you discover *who you really are*. What moment will define you? *Your character and your life are formed as your respond to the moment of Fear.*

We can choose to "take every thought captive to obey Christ." (2 Corinthians 10:5). Or we can let our thoughts/actions push us over the edge. When we Fear that God *really isn't who He says He is* and will not do what He promises, we will justify our actions out of our *own inner terror*. "Behold, God is my helper; the Lord is the upholder of my life" (Psalm 54:4). "The Lord is my helper; I will not fear; what can man do to me?" (Hebrews 13:6).

Overwhelmed by the weight and pain of her partner's tandem rope below, the Heroine clings tightly as her rope sways in the breeze. On the opposite rock wall, she notices some words painted on the stone and blinks her tear-filled eyes to read them.

"You Don't Know Everything That Is Ahead In Life . . . Keep Climbing."

REALITY AND TENACITY CHECK

"The pessimist complains about the wind; the optimist expects it to change; the realist adjusts the sails." —William A Ward

Realists ask, "What is the Lord giving me the opportunity to learn?" —Kathleen Ferrell

Well, it is not as poetic or profound as Ward's lovely words, but it is the phrase that I ask myself many times a day. If spiritual growth is my goal, tough experiences can *benefit* me.

Imagine if the "sisters" sat down in the cave and said, "Ok, let's make a list of all the things we can learn from the events in our lives."

- Our fiances would not come with us to escape the city (Gen. 19:14).
- Thousands died because of their wickedness and sexual sin.
- Our home and everything we owned was destroyed.
- Mom was killed because she disobeyed.
- Let's write all this down, so we don't make those same mistakes.

What did these girls miss the opportunity to learn? Reality acceptance does not mean paralysis; it means *you* get to grow! Author Joan Borysenko wrote, "Accepting reality means buying a one-way ticket out of la-la land."[5] And "When you argue with reality—you lose!"[6] The first step on your Journey of Divine purpose *accepts* where you are standing and asks, "Lord, how can I be useful to *you*?"

Survivors of Nazi, Japanese, North Korean and Vietnamese prisoner-of-war camps had one thing in common: "[T]hose who knew that there was a task waiting for them to fulfill were most apt to survive."[7] Their life purpose kept them focused on a goal to live for. In Frankl's case, it was reconstructing the manuscript of his life's work as a researcher. He began rewriting manuscript sections on little scraps of paper and felt that his dedication to that effort and the hope of seeing his beloved wife again helped him survive through starvation, beatings, and the ravages of typhus. *Accepting Reality and having a purpose inspired him to wake up each morning and keep living.*

The highest peak of prisoner death rates in Auschwitz occurred in the week between Christmas and New Year 1944. No changes in work, weather, or food caused this spike. Most prisoners held to a purely "naive" super-optimistic belief that they would be liberated by Christmas and the *disenchantment* of their hope lowered their resistance so that they succumbed to death.[8]

Admiral Jim Stockdale was held captive and tortured by the Viet Cong for eight years. When interviewed and asked which type of man died in the prison camps he replied, "Oh, that's easy. It was the optimists. . . . You know, I think they all died of broken hearts." Similar to the Auschwitz prisoners, the super-optimistic men would get their hearts "set" on being liberated by Thanksgiving or Fourth of July and could not deal with the despair when those hopes were dashed.[9]

Studies of survivors who were able to move on in life without depression after these horrific experiences showed that these realistic and positive (not naive or super-optimistic) thinkers held character traits showing they were "altruistic, had a moral compass based on firmly held beliefs, used humor, had strong role models, and were guided by a sense of mission or purpose in life."[10] *These are all traits of Christians with a strong Divine purpose to glorify God even in the brutally honest Realities of life.* It is the not the NAIVE-OPTIMISTS (minimizers), or the PESSIMISTS (maximizers), but the REALISTS, who survive and thrive after trauma! Real people who we think of as Heroes know that:

- Heroism is very, very hard.
- Heroism is an attitude long before it is action.
- Heroism can mean balancing necessary toughness-tenacity-guts-courage, but also patience-meekness-submission.
- Heroism has a backward-looking lens from the end of life to a moment of choice that says, "I would like the Lord to be pleased with me."

Take a moment and mentally rewind the story of Lot and his daughters to the "moment" of those girls' decision to get their father drunk and . . . Now imagine that they stopped their evil plot at the Thought storm and did not go through with it. How many potential ending possibilities can you imagine? Can you think of a dozen? More? What if these "sisters" lived to be little old ladies and had the opportunity to tell their life story. Think about them recounting all the trauma of losing their mother and fiances and how upset everyone was. What if they admitted they had some really evil thoughts while waiting in that cave? Then imagine that they might share how they learned one of the greatest of all virtues: *godly endurance* as they patiently worked, waited, and tried to *honor* their father. Think of their Joy to be able to tell how the Lord "opened a door" for them?

Even if they died in that cave with their father, and there was no "rest of the story," they could have been received up to the Lord leaving behind a legacy of faithfulness! Every spirit begotten into flesh at conception lives beyond that body's earthly Journey to spend eternity—in either Heaven or hell. If their bones and flesh were never found, the sisters' imperishable spirits could be in eternal glory! (Rom. 6:22-23; Gal. 6:8; Titus 1:1-3).

Do you suppose that once God rescued this family from mass destruction by the hand of an angel—He then turned His back on them? (Jude 7). Do you think that the God who created and sustains *you* turns His back on you when you need Him the most?

The attitude lens of Heroism knows that there is a swinging rope bridge spanning *necessary toughness* and *patience* that you must learn to cross in order to survive and thrive on this sheer rock climb of life. When your footing slips and a hailstorm bombards you with frozen buckshot, will you let go of the rope or will you wrap it hard around your wrist again and hold on?

Why be courageous?—Eternal glory, that's why.

"And after you have suffered a little while, the God of all grace, who has called you to his eternal glory in Christ, will himself restore, confirm, strengthen, and establish you" (1 Peter 5:10).

SHE AIN'T HEAVY . . . SHE'S MY SISTER

"Sisters . . . sisters . . . would you look at such a pair of sisters . . ." As we read about this true family, can you think of a family that you have known where one person led a Fear-driven change within the group? Perhaps like

Lot's wife, it was a "pillar of salt" type of change within the group? "One who is righteous is a guide to his neighbor, but the wicked leads them astray" (Proverbs 12:26; Proverbs 10:17; 1 Peter 4:3-5).

> Kelly had been a stay-at-home mom, but decided that she wanted to go to work full-time. Very quickly, the Lord's day became her "catch up and relax" day, and there was no need for church. Jim and the kids came to Sunday services for awhile, but then gradually fell away. Within a few years, Jim committed adultery and wanted a divorce, and Kelly "needing some support," stopped in to visit when the church assembled. Her children grew up to be troubled, have multiple babies outside of marriage, and none became Christians. Kelly thought she could create a happy family *her way* and dropped the Bible Map down the abyss. Her family followed.

"Enter by the narrow gate. For the gate is wide and the way is easy that leads to destruction, and those who enter by it are many. For the gate is narrow and the way is hard that leads to life, and those who find it are few" (Matt. 7:13-14).

God's plan for physical and spiritual families is that we link up our ropes and tandem climb together in the same direction. Unfortunately, the climbers you depend on the most may cause *you* to slip and plummet. *It takes great courage to stand up to temptation offered to you by someone you Love* (1 Corinthians 8:9).

I want to encourage everyone in their life Journey toward the heavenly Treasure, but let there be no misunderstanding. *If you are tempting me to cut my rope and fall away from godly living, I will pray for you and crawl over your body in order to keep climbing—up to the Lord's side* (Matthew 5:43-45). Do you know why? Because I Love Him. I know His goodness and I want to be with *Him*. I actually let my mind meditate on what *Jesus' blood is saving me from!* (eternal separation and torment) (Hebrews 10:12; 2 Thess. 1:9). I believe that sinless Jesus Christ stepped in front and took the punishment I deserve—that is why I trust *Him* (Col. 2:14). *I serve Him in this life battle with Satan because I want to be on His side!* The *winning* side. I pray that no relationship keeps me from obtaining eternal Heaven. We make grave mistakes when we follow humans instead of reading the detailed Map that God has given to us. Godly adult relationships should:

• respect differences in tastes, ideas, and perceptions

- have the same focus in pleasing the Lord
- encourage each other in living that is consecrated before God
- provide comfort, support, and promote confidence
- be characterized by kind honesty and Reality checks
- rejoice and give thanks for the "buddy system" provided by the Lord

Christian friendships should encourage you to pick up the Map and examine yourself. Sincerity and affectionate candor mark my closest friendships, and it is a Joy to be able to share my hopes and failures freely and ask for advice, without criticism. Building relationships means growing in responsibility for other climbers who share the ascent of life's mountain with you. When you are scared, you need Love and reassurance from sisters you trust. Accept your differences, climb in tandem, and learn that meeting adversity can help you grow from a novice to an experienced climber—on the cliffs of life. God designed us to climb together (1 John 4:20-21).

A few years ago, I took some of my young singers to perform in England. After I had dealt with some challenges and frustrations on the trip, the chaperone mom, Tarianne, said something to me that shocked me. She said, "If I needed to survive and could choose my team, I would choose you." I will never forget the feeling that came over me. I never thought of myself as benefitting *any* survivor team. I was never even "picked first" for dodge ball!! My scrawny body is certainly not "survival team" material. While it is likely that she has encouraged many people with that same phrase, what rose up within *me* from her words was a tenacity to maintain an Integrity level—*worthy* of that confidence. This is one of the major tenets defining "adulthood"—to *take complete responsibility for every one of your actions*. I may be a half-dead woman pulling a corpse on the end of my rope, but my goal is—I will not let *you* down. I pray daily for help in keeping my grip on the rope and strength to keep inching in the right direction (John 16:33).

While the elder of Lot's daughters set fire to her own rope and passed the match to her sister, determine that *you will cheer on* other climbers that you meet on the cliffs of life. Holler over to them, "The Lord is in charge and He Loves you!" Resolve that the Lord will be the master of any climbing buddy team that you are part of. "The LORD is my strength and my shield; in him my heart trusts, and I am helped; my heart exults, and with my song I give thanks to him" (Psalm 28:7).

Develop a patient Love for your sisters knowing that their arms of encouragement are a pure golden gift from the Lord on this part of your one-way

Journey. The cloak of responsibility folds elegantly on the shoulders of those who understand how important *their attitude glasses and deeds* are to others. We are all knitted together as a great lace tablecloth of intersecting threads. We hold each other from unraveling, but also create beauty in our connections.

> [T]herefore be self-controlled and sober-minded for the sake of your prayers. Above all, keep loving one another earnestly, since love covers a multitude of sins. Show hospitality to one another without grumbling. As each has received a gift, use it to serve one another, as good stewards of God's varied grace: whoever speaks, as one who speaks oracles of God; whoever serves, as one who serves by the strength that God supplies—in order that in everything God may be glorified through Jesus Christ. To him belong glory and dominion forever and ever. Amen (1 Peter 4:7b-11).

The Heroine grasps the tandem rope tightly through both arms as it bears the weight of her partner. She hollers down below, "Are you ok?" and hears her soft cries. "Can you hold on?" she calls down to her, hearing only crying in return. Wrapping the rope over her shoulder, she begins the ascent with her partner in tow. "If our instructions were to go to the summit, then somehow He will give me the strength to do so," she whispers to herself. With blood from her hands soaking into every grasp of the rope, and every muscle in her body strained with agony, she pulls up and climbs slowly—inch by inch, hand over bleeding hand.

DECISIONS, DECISIONS – How to . . .

"Preserve my life, for I am godly; save your servant, who trusts in you—you are my God" (Psalm 86:2).

> While he was in Auschwitz, Viktor Frankl volunteered for transfer to a work crew in another camp. It would only be in hindsight that he knew if his choice took him to extermination, or better/worse conditions. His friends were afraid for him as he got onto the train to go to the unknown. As it turned out, his circumstances became improved with the move, but months later, he found out that thousands died in his original camp of starvation and cannibalism.[11]

So, how do you make life decisions that please God and are not driven by Fear? "And I tell you, ask, and it will be given to you; seek, and you will find; knock, and it will be opened to you. For everyone who asks receives, and the one who seeks finds, and to the one who knocks it will be opened" (Luke 11:9-10; James 4:15).

- Pray wide open with no hidden agenda.
- Admit what your desires are—He wants you to acknowledge them.
- Look at all the facts about each door and where it may lead you.
- Consult the Map history of others who made similar choices.
- Never cross the DO NOT SIN LINE.
- Get a Free Estimate from a mature Christian who has made good life choices.
- Keep reading Hebrews 5:14: "But solid food is for the mature, for those who have their powers of discernment trained by constant *practice* to distinguish good from evil." *[Emphasis added]*

God wants you to grow in spiritual discernment! "And it is my prayer that your love may abound more and more, with knowledge and all discernment" (Phil. 1:9). As God is in charge of everything, hold tightly in your heart that He understands about the door choices in your labyrinth! "I am the door. If anyone enters by me, he will be saved and will go in and out and find pasture" (John 10:9). "Strive to enter through the narrow door. For many, I tell you, will seek to enter and will not be able" (Luke 13:24).

As you grow to take responsibility for your choices, you may sense the *awe and terror that you leave a legacy behind in every interaction*. If you live life tormented by Fear and your poor decisions, you will never know how magnificent it feels to be—*brave*. There are no magic formulas for decision-making, but you will *not* choose well if you act in Fear. One thing is for sure:

- If you *cling* to the past—"Why didn't? How come? But I . . ."
- Fantasize/*leap* to a future that does not exist
- *Deny* the Reality of your present situation—You will be driven by Fear. Joy is in *Reality* (Psalm 63:7).

When you feel you are stuck in a cave with only two life choices and a long list of Fears, disappointments, and reasons-to-be-angry, can you DEPEND ON—RELY ON—*God?* That the one who created you is working to take care of you? Absolutely! (1 Peter 5:7). God's Love for you—*His daughter*—is deeper than the darkest cave or abyss of any canyon. *He is on your side* and wants you to make great decisions!! Make sure that you:

Stop: Never make a big decision while your ropes are still swaying after a storm—you may still be *grieving*. Lot and his daughters may have been suffering "post-traumatic stress" at a very deep level. Pretending to "fix" your life without *accepting* a tragic change is a plunge of death. GET YOUR ROPES SECURED, admit the Fear, pray about the Fear. Focus on the virtue of godly *endurance* and contemplate the lessons you are being offered. "But for you, O LORD, do I wait; it is you, O Lord my God who will answer" (Psalm 38:15).

Look: The Holy Spirit's *providing hand* is available in every door opening and closing. The best door choice always glorifies and *never* leads you into sin! Wisdom looks for God to unlock doors *without trying to kick them open*. Watching for providence and waiting on the Lord can be a great act of courage. Highly-skilled rock climbers constantly look ahead for a strong ledge to grasp and a sure foothold. "You open your hand; you satisfy the desire of every living thing" (Psalm 145:16).

Embrace: That in the midst of the wreckage of your life there is a way to *glorify Him*. Perhaps this moment is not just about avoiding a "bad" decision, but making a choice of HONOR. It may not be the most beautiful and surely not the easiest to open, but *one of the doors he offers you is a way of honor* (1 Cor. 10:13). As you rise up with a heart full of courage, you manifest the invincibility of the spirit that God placed *within you* when He breathed in your life. "Teach me your way, O LORD, that I may walk in your truth; unite my heart to fear your name. I give thanks to you, O Lord my God with my whole heart and I will glorify your name forever" (Psalm 86:11-12).

Submit: Prepare yourself to listen and obey Him. Had Lot's wife and daughters prepared their hearts to be obedient, their life movies would have had very different endings! Patience may mean setting aside what *you want* in order to remain open to God's timing. Begin by thinking, *"This is not what I had planned, but I trust you, Lord. I will walk in the Joy of living before you, no matter what occurs around me."* "For my thoughts are not your thoughts, neither are your ways my ways, declares the Lord" (Isaiah 55:8).

HUMOR LENSES – *Clean windows make the whole world look brighter*

A well-developed sense of humor is the pole that adds balance to your steps as you walk the tightrope of life. —William A. Ward

> Viktor Frankl wrote: "I practically trained a friend of mine who worked next to me on the building site to develop a sense of humor. I suggested to him that we would promise each other to invent at least one amusing story daily, about some incident that could happen one day after our liberation." The Auschwitz prisoners' daily food allotment was one bowl of watery broth "soup" and a crust of bread. As they stood in line each day, every man hoped that the ladle containing *his* serving of broth might have scraped the bottom of the great soup pot and caught a few precious peas, or a longed-for scrap of cabbage. One day as they labored, digging tunnels in the frozen earth, they began laughing as one of the starving men—forecasted that after the war, "during a future dinner engagement they might forget themselves when the soup was served and beg the hostess to ladle it 'from the bottom.'"[12]

These men learned to crack inside jokes regularly in order to bring relief from the continuous strain. What a skill for mental and physical survival training to liberate the mind! Imagine, if as the "sisters" sat there in that cave, the elder turned to the younger and said, "Well, I guess we can stop arguing about who has the cuter boyfriend, huh?" God gave us the ability to use humor in the aftermath of Fear to say, "Life has changed, but we are right here. It is going to be ok!" Well-timed humor allows us to elevate and find Joy amid the gravity of life. "Then our mouth was filled with laughter, and our tongue with shouts of Joy; then they said among the nations, 'The LORD has done great things for them.' The Lord has done great things for us; we are glad" (Psalm 126:2-3).

Every emotion has an *appropriate* outlet, and humor can be a bonding experience after a terror is over. Humor activates the dopamine pleasure centers in your brain and is a way of saying, "We are all on this Journey together." The starving Auschwitz prisoners *themselves* made the jokes, and in that musing over the quest for peas from the bottom of a soup pot were saying, "You can starve and torture me, but you cannot have my mind or attitude" (Eccl. 3:4).

When we are reduced to a quivering, Fearful existence, a sense of humor helps us focus on the tiniest of Joys! Humor is a great adaptive behavior to the helplessness of our circumstance. *In the release valve of humor, we accept that trying to control things is futile.* The Lord is completely in charge. "[I]n God I trust; I shall not be afraid. What can man do to me?" (Psalm 56:11).

FEARBREAKER-JOYMAKER – *Joyful resilience*

> Count it all joy, my brothers, when you meet trials of various kinds, for you know that the testing of your faith produces steadfastness. And let steadfastness have its full effect, that you may be perfect and complete, lacking in nothing. If any of you lacks wisdom, let him ask God, who gives generously to all without reproach, and it will be given him. But let him ask in faith, with no doubting, for the one who doubts is like a wave of the sea that is driven and tossed by the wind. For that person must not suppose that he will receive anything from the Lord; he is a double-minded man, unstable in all his ways (James 1: 2-8).

God was right there in the cliff-side cave with those sisters. He needed no search and rescue climbers to find them—they were never lost. Even if you die as a young woman in a cave with your father, only *your* choices will be what separate you from *eternal glory*! (Chapter 13) If you are serving Him, you are exactly where you should be. He knows your sorrows and your Fears and how much you want to please Him. There is never a moment that the Lord has forgotten you. *You are not lost.* "Fear not, for I am with you; be not dismayed, for I am your God; I will strengthen you, I will help you, I will uphold you with my righteous right hand" (Isaiah 41:10).

As the Heroine of *My Life Serving the Cause* movie, you can live each day as a walking meditation in the Lord's presence. In praying the Hebrew word "Amen" (so be it), you step out believing in Him. In His presence, you obey, act lovingly and then *release* control, knowing that *He is in charge of the outcomes.* That is Joyful resilience. By your trust-filled choices, you hand Him control of your soul's destiny and say, "so be it." Joyful resilience says, "Whatever happens, the Lord will help me handle it." "He will not let your foot be moved; he who keeps you will not slumber. Behold, he who keeps Israel will neither slumber nor sleep" (Psalm 121:3-4).

Frankl wrote that even in their deepest suffering, the tiniest little thing would bring them Joy. A moment alone to throw pebbles or a small wildflower seen through the electric fence was *precious. Joyfully resilient Christians learn to be thankful to the Lord, in their darkest moments.* They realize that true Gratitude is the climbing platform for Joy and Divine purpose. Joyful lives are lived in Reality. (Psalm 106:1; 1 Thess. 5:18). Joyfully resilient Christians:

- believe that they live in the presence of the Lord every moment
- accept Reality

- deal with their Thought storms
- know that He is ultimately in charge of the universe
- practice being Thankful—especially when times are hard
- realize there may be *great gifts* that come from this horrible trial
- feel the Joy that *comes from* living their Divine purpose
- pray with total surrender, "Lord, what will you have me do today?"
- understand God's Word represents Him
- *bounce back* after Fearful events by training their brains to focus on the lessons and the Love they have been shown

"Blessed is the man who remains steadfast under trial, for when he has stood the test he will receive the crown of life, which God has promised to those who love him" (James 1:12).

Real Heroines survive cliffhangers and persevere to tell about it. Your Joyful resilience shows that in the midst of sickness, job loss, family troubles, and intense Fear of the unknown, that your life, right now at *this* moment—can be *meaningful by serving the Lord.* If you are a Heroine-servant, your *reward* and your true, glorious crown await you in Heaven. The most important relationship that you maintain is with God! He wants you to reach the summit and He will *never* fail to hold His end of your rope! When Fear of the unknown makes you feel lost and insignificant—your Divine purpose makes you feel strong! "[R]ooted and built up in him and established in faith, just as you were taught, abounding in thanksgiving" (Col. 2:7). "Great is the Lord!" (Psalm 40:16).

Meditation: When my greatest Fear is of the unknown, my greatest Joy is that I am entirely known and Loved by my God.

GROWING THROUGH FEAR

1. In what ways are you Fearfully controlling your life? What would happen if you surrendered that control to the Lord?

2. It is under the most extremely stressful situations that our real character is exposed. How can suffering help you yearn for the next world? What does the quality of "necessary toughness" have to do with being a faithful Christian?

3. As we look from the end of our lives back to the present moment, we get the opportunity to live with the consequences of our choices before we act. How did the "sisters" explain to their young sons who their father was and how they were conceived?

4. How do we confuse our Cinderella purpose with our Divine purpose?

5. When have you felt like there were only two door choices, black and white? Share a time when you were at the end of your rope and tempted to make a Fear leap.

6. Do you think that you could make a decision that would change the course of history? What legacy will live beyond you? How do you leave a legacy in every interaction?

7. How do you know that Lot's wife listened to a Thought storm of Fear? If the same-sex parent is the most powerful role model in a child's life, what did these girls learn from their mother?

8. While Lot is noted for *his* righteousness, (2 Peter 2:7-10), how do we know that living in the wickedness of Sodom influenced these women's choices? How does deepening your understanding of what Jesus Christ has saved you *from* help you make better life decisions?

~ 9 ~

Like a Long-Abandoned Garden,
You have Forgotten Why You are Here

Fear of rejection that paralyzes

Parable of the talents (Matthew 25:14-30)

A great wrought iron key peeks out from beneath the leaves in the pathway of the maze. The stature of the massive boxwood walls blocks any view of the horizon and only the wispy clouds directly above are visible. With heightened curiosity, the Heroine picks up the key and continues along that pathway in the maze which ends at a large iron gate. The gate is so overgrown with vines that it is impossible to see through it, so she struggles to turn the key and forces it open. Within the walls is an overgrown garden, where flowers and shrubs that flourished long ago now lay in rot. The weeds are so tall that she must part her way through them to find a resting spot by the leaf-filled pond. As she lays back in the leaves, she thinks, "It would be impossible to bring this garden back to life," and closes her eyes to rest in the shade. As she sleeps, creeping vines grow silently around her engulfing her—into the layers of decay.

For it will be like a man going on a journey, who called his servants and entrusted to them his property. To one he gave five talents, to another two, to another one, to each according to his ability, Then he went away. He who had received the five talents went at once and traded with them, and he made five talents more. So also he who had the two talents made two talents more. But he who had received the one talent went and dug in the ground and hid his master's money. Now after a long time the master of those servants came and settled accounts with them. And he who had received the five talents came forward, bringing five talents more, saying, "Master, you delivered to me five talents; here I have made five talents more." His master said to him, "Well done, good and faithful servant. You have been faithful over a little; I will set you over much. Enter into the joy of your master." And he also who had the two talents came forward, saying, "Master, you delivered to me two talents; here I have made two talents more." His master said to him, "Well done, good and faithful servant. You have been faithful over a little; I will set you over much. Enter into the joy of your master." He also who had received the one talent came forward, saying, "Master, I knew you to be a hard man, reaping where you did not sow, and gathering where you scattered no seed, so I was afraid, and I went and hid your talent in the ground. Here you have what is yours." But his master answered him, "You wicked and slothful servant! You knew that I reap where I have not sown and gather where I scattered no seed? Then you ought to have invested my money with the bankers, and at my coming I should have received what was my own with interest. So take the talent from him and give it to him who has the ten talents. For to everyone who has will more be given and he will have an abundance. But from the one who has not, even what he has will be taken away. And cast the worthless servant into the outer darkness. In that place there will be weeping and gnashing teeth" (Matthew 25:14-30).

While we all hope to take personal responsibility like the two and five talent men of this poignant parable, we can certainly relate to the one talent man's Fear that made him sit on his ability. When the moment of accounting came, the Fear that he was caught made him lash back at the master and say, "I knew you to be a hard man, reaping where you did not sow and gathering where you scattered no seed." He speaks a classic Fear reaction projecting—YOU are mean. YOU are unethical. YOU caused me to do it. It can't possibly be me, this is YOUR fault. Like Adam blaming the Creator, "It was the woman that YOU gave me" (Genesis 3:12). *[Emphasis added]*

Fear-driven excuses

- keep us from taking personal responsibility for our actions (Romans 14:22)
- remind us of the possibility of failure (2 Corinthians 13:5)
- stop us from listening to the Lord's instructions (Proverbs 8:34)
- limit us receiving more blessings from God (Psalm 40:4)

As our life garden grows through its many seasons, the Master Gardener expects us to become *more skilled* at tending our talent/gift. Every season of our life garden is painted in detailed watercolor and those paintings are stored for exhibition in a great viewing by Him. Daily garden tours allow us to examine the evidence of *how our time is spent on this earth* and watch the growth from our labors. While the Master Gardener sees all, the exhibit of our paintings at life's end will be the final gallery showing (Matt.12:36).

There is a unique giftedness in each of us, distinctively individual and well-known by the Master Gardener who gave it. If you choose to rest, in lieu of using your gift and *working* in your garden of life, creeping vines will eventually grow out and tie you very tightly. The longer you rest, the more tightly you are bound until you are immobile and suffocating (Mark 11:20).

THE ROTTED GARDEN – *Fear/paralysis*

The longer you lie amidst the overgrown garden, the more overwhelming the task feels. When the rains come, the mud increases the decay of rotting leaves and weeds, and you find it difficult to even dream of what the garden could be. The Fear-filled and paralyzed do not enjoy problem-solving and feel they live in this earth garden to *tolerate life*. Their paralysis is an emotional standstill that stems from being deeply hurt. Fear pulls us to withdraw inside, with the hope of avoiding another painful experience (Psalm 34:15).

> Viktor Frankl watched apathy overtake the personalities of men after daily beatings in the prison camps. The protective defense mechanism of apathy was a stage of "mortification of feeling" observed by Frankl, where caring was just not possible. The prisoners grew a "very necessary protective shell."[1] In fact, *very few* used the hardships of life to "test their inner strength . . . or attain human greatness." The majority of prisoners chose to "vegetate," not considering that there was an opportunity for any triumph in their suffering.[2]

When faced with challenges, most of us take on the role of sufferers and only live to solidify the *reasons* for our Fear-driven apathy paintings of this life-season. We move the sticks and weeds of our disappointments around in different positions to repaint the scenes in more dramatic versions. Fear-filled paralysis Thought storms say that we are, "serving the time," here

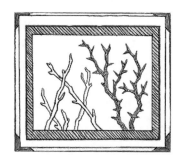

on earth and not "redeeming the time" (Eph. 5:16 KJV). As there is no help, nor purpose to life, a feeling of ambivalence would be our highest hope for a "good day."

Satan, the Weedmaster, wants you to believe that doing nothing will make you feel better and suffer less, but actually, over time, his lethal vines harden into wood. Even in a strangulated life of apathy, you *still get the suffering you have sought to avoid*, because your mind is controlled by worry and Fear. The quest for the *absence* of Fear opens a *chasm* that fills deeper and deeper with rot. In Reality, your influence within life's intersecting maze is felt, *even if it is the negative influence of a couch potato.* "Whoever is slack in his work is a brother to him who destroys" (Proverbs 18:9).

The Fearfully paralyzed live a *half-life*, walking downhill in the labyrinth-path-of-least-resistance because they are just too terrified to examine their Fears. Half-lifers just survive, rotating in a circle from the bed—to refrigerator—to sofa—around the TV god. Imagine the commercial for a "Half-lifers Reality show"—"Stagnant, she sleeps, eats, turns over on the couch and watches TV of others watching her, 24/7—premieres Wednesday, 9 pm." ZZZzzzzzzz. Like a scene from a futuristic movie where arms and legs atrophy from lack of use, the "interest in vibrant living" muscles atrophy from insufficient exercise. Fear-filled paralysis is very safe and like the one talent man, comforting to know that things cannot get any worse. The *status quo is familiar and allows neither growth nor challenge.* "A little sleep, a little slumber, a little folding of the hands to rest, and poverty will come upon you like a robber, and want like an armed man" (Proverbs 24:33-34).

No one needs to look far to find the man who walks through the door in the evening and heads for the TV remote. He nods at his children and restricts his wife to talking to him—only during commercials. Or the woman who plays the TV from the moment she awakens (likely during her sleep also), throughout every meal and activity. Life is just too difficult for them, and they do not want to *feel* or *hear* any Realities.

- 2011 statistics record that Americans *averaged* 158 hours a month in front of the TV—22 minutes more than last year.[3]
- There are only 166 *work* hours in a month!

If you have sought a relationship with someone who turns for comfort from or worships the TV god, you have known a falling-down-a-black-hole experience (Proverbs 19:15).

Our inner gifts and talents begin to rot, because the tending and effort required is just Fearsome. Old blossoms from years gone by dry up and are never replaced by new ones because their nourishing bushes are never pruned or watered.

> Go to the ant, O sluggard; consider her ways, and be wise. Without having any chief, officer, or ruler, she prepares her bread in summer and gathers her food in harvest. How long will you lie there, O sluggard? When will you arise from your sleep? A little sleep, a little slumber, a little folding of the hands to rest, and poverty will come upon you like a robber, and want like an armed man (Proverbs 6:6-11).

THE SLEEPING GARDENER – Fear-filled laziness

Fear-filled laziness is modeled in and receives acceptance in *families*. Six-year olds who have learned this helplessness do not want to exert the effort to walk across the room in order to play a game. The weeds of Fear-filled laziness are particularly insidious Fear manifestations because they are so *easy*. "I am just an easy-going and relaxed person," she says, as she rolls to her other side on the couch. "I don't want to be competitive or anxious about life, so I just take it easy," as if *those* were the only life choices. "As a door turns on its hinges, so does a sluggard on his bed" (Proverbs 26:14).

Fear-filled laziness thrives on:

- the support of others who also worship the TV god
- saying "I will try . . ." with no intention of follow through
- "What can I get you to do for me?"
- the *minimum* effort expended to "get by"

Laziness is like an old garden gazebo covered with weeds that desperately needs repair and repainting, but "*It is just not worth the effort—the reward is not that great.*" Satan, the Weedmaster, relishes Fear-filled laziness for he must only convince you *to remain as you are*—at ease and comfortable! If laziness is your "Invented god," then everything you do is planned around that pleasure. Your *problem-solving exists to please your laziness*. Laziness is a crippler. "Like vinegar to the teeth and smoke to the eyes, so is the sluggard to those who send him" (Proverbs 10:26).

Fear-filled laziness is also Fear-driven control. Perhaps the one talent man thought: "You are not going to control me. I will just do nothing and give you your money back. I mean, why work so hard?"

The passive-aggressive element of Fear-filled laziness feels, "I will be ready when I am ready. If I am late, then things will begin when I get there!" Sue said, "Sorry, I *had* to be late." The Reality was—she tried on three outfits and talked on the phone instead of watching the time. Reality does not confuse genuine challenges with inconsiderate *manipulation*. The Fear-driven lazy/controlling are chronically late for departures and appointments, and never seem to turn their "I will try to"—into *getting it done.* "I passed by the field of a sluggard, by the vineyard of a man lacking sense, and behold, it was all overgrown with thorns; the ground was covered with nettles, and its stone wall was broken down" (Proverbs 24:30-31).

As in all strengths and weaknesses, there is laziness and industry within every one of us. The self-centered Fear within laziness thinks, "What can I get you to do for me?" If I can get you to "do that for me," I am *special and valuable.* I have the "upper hand" and I am important. This is *playing games* in relationships and is dishonest. The Fearful/lazy game-playing cannot see how learning to *manage* their Fear is better than manipulation. This Fearful laziness is a denial that the Master Gardener views the seasons of your garden, and the paintings they inspire, throughout your one-way life Journey. *Every time your industry rises up and overpowers your laziness—you please the Lord.* "The sluggard is wiser in his own eyes than seven men who can answer sensibly" (Proverbs 26:16).

Fearful laziness uses the distractions of life to allow the years to blur by in a fog without asking, "What have I done for the Cause? What garden have I grown with my talents?" Laziness' daily question is, "Why would anyone want to grow?" Few scriptures are repeated almost verbatim twice in the Bible. This one is: "The sluggard buries his hand in the dish and it wears him out to bring it back to his mouth" (Proverbs 19:24 and Proverbs 26:15).

THE DEFEATED GARDENER – *Fear of failure*
The thorns of Fear of failure damage the flesh of every gardener who accidentally bumps against them. Fear of rejection/failure wants you to *become so cautious* that you see no *potential*—only *decay.* Fear wants you to repeat the memory, "I failed once and it was awful. I don't ever want to do that again" (Galatians 5:13).

Fear of rejection/failure keeps us living in "hope of no mistakes." If we Fear leap into what might *possibly* go wrong, we will never risk extending ourselves to do the necessary work and clean away the decay. Remember, it takes no effort at all for our brains to focus on negative experiences. "The sluggard says, 'There is a lion outside! I shall be killed in the streets!'" (Proverbs 22:13).

"Thorny brush of Failure" Thought storms incubate negativity about what lies ahead and justify the paralysis that follows. While the scout motto is, "Be Prepared," the "Future Failures of America Club" says, "Be Terrified." Club members rehearse their Fears and negativity—bonding together by complaining that, "If I had been given HER talent, then I would be successful." Their group uses Fear-driven excuses as a hallmark of belonging. "The way of a sluggard is like a hedge of thorns, but the path of the upright is a level highway" (Proverbs 15:19).

My dear friend, Cathy, reminds me that, "You are worrying about something that has not happened yet." Fear leap. Think about this exact week in your life last year. What Fears of the unknown were you worrying about? How many of your Fears of the future never happened? How did you deal with the ones that did? While ruminating over people we Love or situations that concern us is part of being inter-planted with others, successful gardeners focus on *their own power and limits* as a worker in God's garden. If you want to grow through Fear of failure/rejection ask yourself:

- What opportunities did the Lord provide in the last 525,600 minutes (year)?
- How did I grow from them?
- Where would I like to be one year from now?
- What life-change can I really make with my *own* hands?
- Does this decision freeze me in a decayed past or help me grow in Joy?

Knowing that weather and insects touch every garden, life gardeners always have in their minds a plan A and plan B. They have studied the Map, prayed for guidance, examined the doors/gates, sought Free Estimates, and then made a choice. If that choice fails, they say, "What can I learn from this?" and continue to seek the Lord's will.

Perfectionist gardeners who Fear failure say, "Just one false move and you might mess things up!" They cannot Love the parts of *themselves* that are not *perfect*, and therefore they *cannot Love you*, if you are not ideal. In actuality, the great gardeners of the earth learn by 1) researching and 2) making mistakes. The most basic and boring gardens are grown by those who *Fear taking the risks of being alive!* Perfection is an air-brushed, Hollywood-glossy painting of your garden, not a *real* garden. Reality life gardeners know that hard *work* and risk always precede *reward.* Your greatest danger is not the loss of life from the elements or disease, *but an unlived life for the LORD.* Fear of failure's only *power* is within you. "The soul of the sluggard craves and gets nothing, while the soul of the diligent is richly supplied" (Proverbs 13:4).

THE MULE WITHIN – *Vows of stubbornness*

"English daisies love cooler temperatures," the matronly gardener told her neighbor. "Well, I am sure they will be fine here," said the young woman, as she planted them in full sun. July temperatures in the area hit the 100 mark often, but the young gardener squared her shoulders and filled her front flower bed with the delicate blossoms. Of course, within a few weeks, no matter how much she watered them, they were dried and brittle.

Greet the stubborn mule within you. Mules, like any grazing animal, will break in and eat every beautiful plant in your garden, and then dig their heels into the earth—never to be moved. *The mule within you will keep your life stuck in stubborn immaturity* (Jeremiah 17:23). Think through these questions:

- Do you enjoy arguing?
- Do you ignore cause and effect?
- Do you have frequent personal problems, job, and financial problems?
- Do you feel threatened by the concept of problem-solving?
- Do you make a lot of negative comments?
- Do you think that you know best?
- Do you hold fast to your opinions whether they are biblical or not?

Mules live by their own stubborn oaths thinking, "This is who I am . . . and how much I am gonna grow . . . take it or leave it." Mules "invent" gods to justify their desires, ignoring the true God who sets the seasons and standards. Their stubborn oaths can sound like confidence or loyalty, but they usually have poisonous roots in refusal to accept the way of the Lord. A stubborn and Joy-less life complains away the meaning of Jesus' devoted sacrifice by thinking, "Why work to grow a beautiful garden? I want to live life my way!" NEVER CONFUSE STUBBORNNESS WITH STRENGTH.

"So I gave them over to their stubborn hearts, to follow their own counsels" (Psalm 81:12).

Out of the cold dampness of winter peek the softly strengthening sun's rays. Deep beneath the decayed leaves, the earth warms from its lazy sleep and the awakening blood of spring pumps through its veins. As a pulse bringing up blood pressure from a heart deep within, the first crocus of spring pushes open the earth and begins the explosion of color with the vivid rainbow of a painter's palette. As the Heroine-servant rises up and begins to rake away the dead leaves and vines, she realizes that the gifts in this garden were only sleeping—in the cold winter of neglect.

Her foot bumps into an old metal sign under some rotted leaves. As she wipes the surface, a glow of copper shines through. Rubbing at the patina with her sleeve, she can read the beautifully etched words from long ago:

"With All of Your Gifts, How Did You Glorify Me?"

An old shepherd's hook thickly covered in vines shows that the sign once hung at the center of the garden. This is the question that will be asked at the great Garden viewing at her life's end.

THEN COMES THE SPRING – A great awakening

The winter days of our lives are lived as the one talent man, sealed up inside with blame and excuses. Everyone in the "Suffering Gardeners Club," sits in the cold of their homes and reads, **The Art of Excusitis**. This epic work masterfully lists all the excuses available for "failure to thrive," in life gardening. Insects and plant diseases are easily blamed for disenchantment because they are the ever-present tools of the Weedmaster. *Those who are uncommitted to their Divine purpose are the best at Excusitis*. Concluding chapters confess: "Growing a beautiful life garden is quite impossible. Just lay back in the weeds and take it easy" (Proverbs 20:13).

It is likely that the one talent man lived out his life within that one season painting, "The Winter of Excusitis." "The Awakening Joy of Spring" painting is only created by those who *desire* such a beautiful season of life and know that getting down in the dirt is the only way to achieve it. *Growing a Joyful life is dirty and not for the fainthearted*. In giving up the "Winter of Excusitis" and learning to paint "The Awakening Joy of Spring," there is a great shift in *attitude* toward life. Gardeners of life know that *skill growth* and *character growth* are parallel. "For as the earth brings forth its sprouts, and as a garden causes what is sown in it to sprout up, so the Lord GOD will cause righteousness and praise to sprout up before all the nations" (Isaiah 61:11).

1. *SPEAK THE FEAR* – "I am afraid to change. I have been lazy/negative/stubborn—Fearful. I am afraid of making mistakes and don't know where to begin in this overgrown life-garden." *Feel the grief for your half-life that you have spent with your talent buried in the backyard.* Ask your-

   self, "Why have I been so Fearful?" Like the tiny Bermuda grass that roots six feet beneath the earth, your "negative" weeds are rooted deeply in your brain! If you do not deal with the *roots* of your Fears, they will continue to support your laziness and you will keep wondering why you are growing *weeds*. Looking at
   garden paintings of your past life seasons will help you say, "This is what happened, and I felt this, it could have been different, but it was not . . . this is Reality." You will struggle with the same Fears throughout your life, if you do not *admit*, *grieve,* and *deal* with them asking, "How did I feel when I failed? Did I feel rejected—unloved?"

   God's arms are poised to *fill* the hole that Fear's wound leaves in you with beautiful flow-ering Love and a new Divine purpose. Filling the "weeded out" spaces of your garden with the fullness of His Love for *you*, will bring you to the Joy of being full grown and in the delight of serving Him. *As you become completely con-vinced of the passionate Love Jesus has for you, your lazy motives will melt.* Your Fear will be overgrown with Love (1 John 4:18).

2. *A GARDEN CLOAK OF RESPONSIBILITY* – "Willingness to serve" is your new mission! Admit that you have dropped your cloak of
   responsibility in the dirt and are having a new attitude shift to grow a beautiful life garden. The one, two, and five talent men had *separate* life business with the Master. While everyone's Divine purpose is to glorify God, what another was given/expected was not the *other* individual's

business. Your Divine purpose now says: "I take complete responsibility for all of my feelings and actions because I am *useful* and *important* to the Lord's work." When you have repented and "changed your heart" with the Lord, He has no anger toward you. Are you mad at yourself for the past? It is an act of WILL to accept complete responsibility for your actions and say, "Lord help me, I want to seize the moment, extend myself and—grow!" You are never a failure with God as long as you are growing. Joyful gardeners wear a blossom-covered cloak of responsibility. "Create in me a clean heart, O God, and renew a right spirit within me" (Psalm 51:10).

3. *TAKE GARDENING CLASSES AND LEARN TO FERTILIZE* – When I learn the Gardener's Almanac evidence about the Master Gardener, I judge Him worthy of my obedience. Every true story in the Bible is *packed* with real information on how men and women dealt with Fear of failure. Reading of the young boy David stepping out with a heart of valor and a sling-shot talent to slay the giant Goliath, fills me with courage for my life's work. Although he was small and young, David had experience defending himself from lions and bears. He was *preparing to be useful*. When I feel small, I remember this boy's unabashed courage defending the Lord's Cause (1 Samuel 17:34-37, 45-47). "For the Lord sees not as man sees: man looks on the outward appearance but the Lord looks on the heart." (1 Samuel 16:7).

As you read the Bible, find the Fears in every character and look for how they overcame Fear of failure or were paralyzed by it. Search for examples of those who *wanted* to do God's will in their current circumstance, *before they had any idea of how they were going to be used!* Keep a list of those who felt: "I am wide open to serve you Lord!" Prepare *yourself* to be useful and to be *added to that list*! (Psalm 52:8).

- Fall in Love with the Master Gardener's Almanac, the Bible, every day that you breathe. "I will not lie down to rest until I have studied His Word and deepened my understanding of my Divine purpose" (Hebrews 4:12).
- Learn memory verses about *work:* "Well done, good and faithful servant. You have been faithful over a little; I will set you over much. Enter into the joy of your master" (Matt. 25:23). (Remind yourself the verse does not say, "Well done, good and faithful slacker.")

- Listen to the *roots* not the Fear-filled Thought storms beating down your flowers: When you offer *no excuses* and take personal responsibility for everything you feel, say, and do, your "Victim's Garden" now can be replaced by a "Victory Garden" (Gal. 6:9-10).

4. *PASSION* – Where is your gift/talent? In my first season as a gardener, I killed a lot of plants! "Crispy Critters" died by the dozens in the heat of the afternoon sun and the slugs had an all-you-can-eat festival in the shady flower beds. It took me many seasons of reading books, chatting with gardening experts and a lot of trial and error to develop the garden that I enjoy today. "Talent" relies heavily on training and dirty fingernails.

God has taken the initiative in giving you talents and every resource you need to complete your life Journey. He knows exactly what you are *capable* of and asks you to work within those talents that *He entrusted* to you. Your capabilities are not synonymous with your *comfort zone*, as you may learn to *germinate and ripen* within you, something that you have never tried! When you keep looking for gates to new parts of your garden, and asking, "What do I get to learn from this, Lord?" you are growing in your *power of discernment*. Vibrance and devotion are the fertilizers that transform a Fearfully dull and useless life. Abundant living involves risk! Your gifts and talents do not show your character as much as your choices.

> [F]or as in one body we have many members, and the members do not all have the same function, so we, though many, are one body in Christ, and individually members one of another. Having gifts that differ according to the grace given to us, let us use them: . . . if service, in our serving; the one who teachers, in his teaching; the one who exhorts, in his exhortation; the one who contributes, in generosity; the one who leads, with zeal; the one who does acts of mercy, with cheerfulness. Let love be genuine. Abhor what is evil; hold fast to what is good. Love one another with brotherly affection. Outdo one another in showing honor. Do not be slothful in zeal, be fervent in spirit, serve the Lord. Rejoice in hope, be patient in tribulation, be constant in prayer. Contribute to the needs of the saints and seek to show hospitality (Rom. 12:4-13).

You have a niche in the Lord's garden. Perhaps you are the encourager that we all need, the generous giver, or the merciful. You have an abundant talent within you that is waiting to burst forth like that first crocus of spring. *Your gift is as unique as your combination of the DNA helix* (Psalm 85:10).

While some types of flowers quickly become compost in my garden, I get along very well with hydrangea and fuschia that flourish with abundant watering. Their phenomenal beauty is *worth* my work!!! *That is the secret to using your gift: you Love the product, GLORIFYING GOD so much, that the labor is worth the work.* Your openness to Joy and conviction of His amazing steadfast Love will push you to live a life pleasing Him. You can never know God's will for you if when a gate swings open, you are afraid to go through it and serve. The beauty of your garden blooms—as your desire to be pleasing to God grows (Colossians 1:10).

Anita Roddick wrote, "If you think you're too small to have an impact, try going to bed with a mosquito in the room."

5. *PRIORITIES – HOW IMPORTANT IS YOUR GARDEN IS TO YOU?* Fresh out of college, I worked at a company where the finance manager would roam daily between different offices and cubicles telling jokes and chatting with people. Intermittently, he would sit at his desk crunching the company's financial numbers, at which he was quite skilled. At 5 pm, when the office staff was departing, we would hear him on the phone with his wife saying, "I need to work late again tonight." You could almost hear her end of the conversation as they had children at home and his having "too much work to do" was habitual. He received a lot of Fear-powered ego massage spinning his stories and jokes throughout the office, but his underlying self-centeredness hurt his entire family. Clearly, he may have *said* that his family was important, but he did not spend his time in a way that demonstrated that (Psalm 127:3).

Try keeping a log of "How I spend the time of my life," for one month. Sink into your mind that your time management *shows* your priorities, just like your *actions show your character.* What does it say when you are passionate about your recreation and job, and ambivalent toward working for the Lord? What will awaken you? (Proverbs 16:3). Be honest about how you are *problem-solving your life* to your priorities. No one forgets to go pick up $1,000 that someone wants to give them! When you decide to spend your time on worldly causes or just revolving around the TV god with non-existent spiritual labor, you are clearly *showing the Lord* your priorities.

I have retrained myself to say, "I did not *make* time for that . . ." instead of, "I did not *have* time." Everyone has the same 86,400 seconds in a day and the moments of life are *precious.* As you use the words "quality time or quality of life," feel the Reality of how much is in the grasp of *your* hands. Five minutes of time can be spent Lovingly listening and caring for someone or—watching TV commercials. Does your time management answer the question, "Why am I here?" As I remember the finance manager's priorities from observing him 30 years ago, what painted scenes of *your life* will be on display in the minds of others?

6. *PICK UP A SHOVEL AND GET DIRTY* – In writing this book, I set a summer schedule of writing 8–10 hours a day. I got up at the same time every morning and put on grey sweat-capris and an old Bible camp t-shirt. My favorite shirt has a crown of thorns drawn on the front and says, "He's my Friend, He's my King, He's my Saviour." As I write for you now, this 10 year-old camp t-shirt reminds me why I am doing this project. I confess that my writing room is a "creative space" with laundry baskets mounded with notebooks, a reference book stash, my exercise bike, and even more piles of books on the tables. There are door-sized charts on two walls with notes scrawled all over them, a cereal bowl, some water glasses, and post-it notes *everywhere.* If you need to use my iron, you might take your life in your hands entering this room to get it. But don't panic, the rest of the house is cleaned up. I confess all this to you to make the point that: *work makes a mess sometimes.* Growing a garden means getting some grass stains. Extending yourself is not a neat and tidy process. "As for me and my house, we will serve the Lord" (Joshua 24:15b).

Lethargy is a win for the Weedmaster and words like "industrious" or "disciplined" have virtually been choked out of the vocabulary of most Americans. Thomas Edison holds a world record for 1,093 patents and wrote: "Opportunity is missed by most people because it is dressed in overalls and looks like work."

Discipline says, "there is something more important than this moment and what I *want* to do." Every breath, every word, every gesture needs to be fulfilling your Divine purpose or *you are just taking up space.* Boredom is unknown in a Heroine-servant's life. After all your excuses fail you, *try growing in self-discipline. Anything worth doing is hard* (2 Thess. 3:7).

Know this by heart, the *size of the blossoms in your spiritual garden reflects the root depths of your committed Love for the Master gardener.* When you feel the Fear of failure/rejection, it is helpful to ask, "What is the worst thing that will happen if I try this good work?" If you are doing a good work, and later hear someone is "making fun of you," what have you lost? (Heb. 12:4). The Lord says over and over in the book of Revelation, "I know your works" (Rev. 2, 3, 14:13). He views the paintings of your life! Roll up your sleeves, pick up a spade, and get dirty! Is there a servant's heart beating within your chest? "A healthy tree cannot bear bad fruit, nor can a diseased tree bear good fruit. Every tree that does not bear good fruit is cut down and thrown into the fire. Thus you will recognize them by their fruits" (Matthew 7:18-20).

7. *CULTIVATE* – Thomas Aquinas (1225–1274) wrote, "Repeticio est mater studiorum: Repetition is the mother of all learning." This is the truth! Daily commitments close the discrepancy gap between your goals and actions. Make lists and cross them off to increase your accountability to: Bible study, devoted prayer time, attending every service, and visiting others. Now make that list again tomorrow and cross it off *again*. Keep in mind that Aristotle pointed out that you are, "what you *repeatedly* do," and remember that one of the greatest virtues is *godly endurance*. When you ask, "Does this work precede a reward?" Be mindful that *your real reward is in Heaven!* "Whatever you do, work heartily, as for the Lord and not for men, knowing that from the Lord you will receive the inheritance as your reward. You are serving the Lord Christ" (Colossians 3:23-24).

The women chatted vivaciously about the Ladies' Day speaker and lovely flowers as they filed out of the restroom during the lunch break. In their exuberance and haste, they had left many paper towels on the floor. Becky entered the restroom a few minutes later only to find the elderly Keynote speaker, who suffered from a debilitating spine disease, bending over one by one to pick up each towel scattered around the room. Becky exclaimed, "Oh no, please let me do that!" But, as the elderly woman rose up slowly, her face beamed, "I am just so happy to be able to serve."

As you keep weeding and pulling up vines in your life, plant into your mind that—*The goal of your life is not to retire, but to serve God.* If you want to be less Fearful, trust God with open arms. There is one personality that pleases the Lord in its personal holiness—a willing personality! Would you take a blank piece of paper right now and write at the top, "Dear Lord, I am willing . . ." Now leave the rest of the paper blank, and sign your name at the bottom. Post that paper over your desk or refrigerator to remind yourself that you have completely committed to *serving* the Lord. That is trust in God. YOUR DIVINE PURPOSE WORK IS IN LOVING SUBMISSION TO HIM, NOT THE WORK THAT YOU WOULD *LIKE* TO DONATE! "You yourselves like living stones are being built up as a spiritual house, to be a holy priesthood, to offer spiritual sacrifices acceptable to God through Jesus Christ" (1 Peter 2:5).

TOMORROW IS TOO LATE!

Ben and Nancy became Christians when their children were school age and like many, found it challenging to leave non-Christian friends behind. Nancy's sharp mind and interest in reading caused an older Christian woman to comment that, "Nancy learned the Bible more quickly than anyone she had ever known." As Ben grew steadily more faithful, Nancy struggled with ties to worldly friends and neighbors and continued to smoke, drink alcohol, and socialize. Ben became a sound leader in their congregation, but Nancy began drifting away into the lure of pop psychology and self-help books. In her mind, she felt that she could worship God on her own terms and so began attending church sporadically. In the last few years, she stopped worshipping completely.

At times, Nancy would accompany Ben on his business trips, and being particularly interested in genealogy, she decided to come along for a trip to Utah and research Ben's roots in the Family History Center. Before they flew out on Sunday afternoon, Ben invited her to attend services with him that morning, but she declined. After catching up on her reading the first few days of the trip, she set out on Thursday to the History Center's Library to look through the microfilms and records. At 10:30 am, a man entered the Library's lobby and began shooting. A 62 year-old security guard and 55 year-old Nancy were killed and several others injured.

After Nancy's death, Ben got a call from a work associate whose daughter knew someone who had been close to that day's events. Ben called him, and as it turned out, he worked at the Family History Center and was the first one to reach Nancy once the shooting stopped. He told Ben that she let out a gasp and then died in his arms. To this day Ben wonders if that gasp was, "O my God, forgive me."

The power of this true story speaks for itself. You have only *this day* to commit yourself to God in passionate dedication to His service. While we know what regret feels like in this life, it is hard for us to fathom what *eternal* Fear and separation will feel like, for those who turn their backs on the Lord. I live to never feel that.

"Then he said to his disciples, 'The harvest is plentiful, but the laborers are few; therefore pray earnestly to the Lord of the harvest to send out laborers into his harvest'" (Matthew 9:37-38).

THE VICTORY GARDEN OF GRATITUDE

In the center of this garden, a flowering tree is planted. As a young plant, this tree sends its "tap root" of Gratitude deep beneath the soil, which stabilizes and strengthens the trunk for life. When great winds come, if tree roots are anchored deeply in the soil, they continue to receive the rejuvenating sustenance of water and nutrients from below, no matter what is happening in the atmosphere above. In your life, branches may break off in the wind and bark may get chipped, but if your *tap root of Gratitude remains steadfastly connected* to the life-giving source through faith, your eternal focus is unharmed. The Weedmaster can encircle you with thorns and bring storms crashing upon you, but if your root system extends far below, you will weather the fury. *Sinking deeply into Gratitude draws up the nutrients of belief that will explode into a faith-blossoming life of service and Joy.* "For you are our glory and joy" (1 Thess. 2:20).

As you awaken your sleeping garden within and *realize that you had forgotten why you are here, your attitude toward Joy changes.* In bringing your mind to focus on the tasks of your body, every act of service becomes *Joyful when it is counted as a blessing.* You can now see that no other flower in the Master's Garden looks exactly like you. You are as distinctive as a hydrangea from a daisy. Discovering your rare talents and uniqueness only deepens your waters of Gratitude that flow back to the Lord. It is a cycle of Joy. The *deeper* your Gratitude to the Lord, the *more passion* you feel for your Divine purpose to glorify Him. "Therefore, as you received Christ Jesus the Lord, so walk in him, *rooted and built up in him* and established in the faith, just as you were taught, abounding in thanksgiving" (Col. 2:6-7). *[Emphasis added]*

Neurobiologists who research Gratitude have shown that we actually re-wire our brains' anxiety centers by learning to *practice* Gratitude. Don't forget!

A negative experience is five times more powerful than a positive one, so we need to celebrate the positive ones!![4] We must actively practice the *beneficial* aspects of an experience in lessons learned, to offset the negativity.[5] Don't underestimate the Weedmaster! He hates Gratitude and wants you to focus on the pain and rejection thorns of life (Gal. 5: 22-24). Reality check: *Weeds grow faster and easier than roses.* Joy-filled gardeners:

- Give thanks in the moment itself—*whatever* is happening.
- Ask, "What do I *get* to learn?" and give thanks they can *grow*.
- Focus on little tiny Joys like a "thank you" or compliment and rehearse them.
- Savor Joy seeping deeply inside—like water hydrating every cell.

In the depths of a Nazi prison camp, Betsie and Corrie Ten Boom gave thanks to God for the warmth of their watery broth soup and the blessing to lie down at night. In seeking to be grateful for all things, they struggled to thank God for the lice and fleas that swarmed throughout their beds and clothing. Until they realized that the vermin infestation allowed them more freedom, by keeping the guards from coming inside the barracks[6] (Eph. 5:20; Col. 3:17; 1 Thess. 5:18).

For three short decades the earth felt the footprints of the greatest servant who has ever walked upon it. *Jesus' Loving sacrificial service to us—does not make any sense.* For even when we hated and turned our backs on Him, He volunteered for the cross to surrender His holy blood to save us, and did not even receive a "Thank you" in return. The pure grace that spilled forth can never be earned or deserved, only grasped onto and *honored*—with Joy-filled service rendered to Him (John 6:27).

Meditating on Jesus' voluntary service to *you* will "bring you to life" in the balance of proactive and patient that every gardener needs to survive storms and infestation. *Jesus' Love, life, teaching, and ultimate sacrifice was the use of His talents.* He was never lazy or made excuses. He came here to *serve us* and we *get* to use our talents to *praise Him*. A Joy-less life rots away His sacrificial gift. "Do not neglect to do good and to share what you have, for such sacrifices are pleasing to God" (Hebrews 13:16).

One Christian with a passion-filled Joyous heart has more "talent" than 100 "Christians" sitting on their abilities. Have you thanked God that you *get* to serve Him today? "Enter his gates with thanksgiving, and his courts with praise! Give thanks to him; bless his name!" (Psalm 100:4).

FEARBREAKER-JOYMAKER JOURNEY

Joyful resilience grows with a wide spectrum view of life. Those seasons that you made paintings of, whether gorgeous or rotting, have great contributions to your gallery exhibit, if you have *interpreted* them with the Joy-filled lessons they provide. If you learned *forbearance* in a difficult season of life, you can explain that on the brass plaque that hangs beneath the painting. If you were *lazy and negative* and wasted a season in decay, inscribing on the plaque how you *matured* from that is a delight to the Master Gardener. Since you alone are responsible for what you make of your earthly life, you may want to paint this moment,

> *"Like the long-forgotten garden that awoke in the spring, this was the moment that I realized why I am here."*

"What shall I render to the LORD for all his benefits to me? I will lift up the cup of salvation and call on the name of the LORD" (Psalm 116:12-13).

As you only control the garden season that you are standing within, how useful are you to the Lord with the same family, same house, same car and clothes, but new ambition in Divine purpose? You can *choose* the abundant life of Joy that using your talent offers you, or the unlived life that the Fear of mistakes provides. Which would you choose, living one day of true Joy or 100 days of half-life? "I am the vine; you are the branches. Whoever abides in me and I in him, he it is that bears much fruit, for apart from me you can do nothing" (John 15:5).

"And I heard the voice of the Lord saying, 'Whom shall I send, and who will go for us?' Then I said, 'Here I am! Send me'" (Isaiah 6:8).

GROWING THROUGH FEAR

1. When my sweet Grandmother turned 89, she told me, "When I get to be an old lady, I am going to learn to knit." Are you surprised that she never learned? What talent could you be using in His Kingdom? What do you need to do to germinate and ripen that talent?

2. Name a Bible character that inspires you to work. What is the deepest power within inspiration and how does it reduce Fear of rejection? Make a list of five Christians whose servant-living inspires you to use your gifts/ talents. What does 1 Corinthians 3:5-11 say about team work?

3. Share with someone that you trust what your greatest weeds and thorns are that keep you from a life of service.

4. How is it that a Heroine-servant never knows boredom? As you think of working for the Lord "one spade of dirt at a time," make a choice to talk to someone new today about the Lord. Just drop it in a conversation: "I was giving thanks to God today and . . ."

5. Memory Verse: "Be strong and courageous. Do not be frightened, and do not be dismayed, for the Lord your God is with you wherever you go" (Joshua 1:9).

Sing: "Count your Blessings"

~ 10 ~
The Desert Crossing of Life
Fears about our health
A woman with an issue of blood (Mark 5:25-34)

From the crest of the sand dune, the Heroine sees only wide open desert with no relief in sight. Only a vast expanse of blowing sand and heat lays ahead, with no visible end to the torture. With her supply pouch empty and leather water bag gone dry, there is no respite from the burning and parching heat. Beyond dehydration, her face and hands are now covered with open burns. She presses on without stopping in the hope that there is relief somewhere. The Map tells of an Oasis lined with lush green plants and clear blue pools. All her life focus is now a quest for water. The Heroine daydreams of a water that quenches, but awakens to the harsh sun and life-robbing heat of Reality. Caravans invite her to join them in a direction that is easy and filled with companionship. Passing clouds and hot winds tease of rain and relief. Every step and footprint in the sand sends a momentary wind-powered blast of dust into the air, relentlessly trying to cover over the evidence that she survives—by fading her every trace into the earth.

And a great crowd followed him and thronged about him. And there was a woman who had had a discharge of blood for twelve years, and who had suffered much under many physicians, and had spent all that she had, and was no better but

187

rather grew worse. She had heard the reports about Jesus and came up behind him in the crowd and touched his garment. For she said, "If I touch even his garments, I will be made well." And immediately the flow of blood dried up, and she felt in her body that she was healed of her disease. And Jesus, perceiving in himself that power had gone out from him, immediately turned about in the crowd and said, "Who touched my garments?" And his disciples said to him, "You see the crowd pressing around you, and yet you say, 'Who touched me?'" And he looked around to see who had done it. But the woman, knowing what had happened to her, came in fear and trembling and fell down before him and told him the whole truth. And he said to her, "Daughter, your faith has made you well; go in peace and be healed of your disease" (Mark 5:25-34).

Have you ever felt true desperation? Have you been so sick and filled with pain, exhaustion, and hurt that you would do anything for relief? Within this huge pressing crowd, we get to see a moment in time for two people:

- A master and a pupil
- A healer and a desperately ailing woman
- The Son of God loving a woman—who was seeking life.

It was a snapshot in time, as if only *they* existed in the midst of the mob chaos. She pursued him anxiously hoping for help as, "She had heard the reports about Jesus." He granted her deliverance *Lovingly,* not grudgingly.

She was a Jewish woman with no other relief in sight. There was no money left for any other treatment—she had tried them all. By Jewish law, her issue of blood excluded her from the companionship of others and from worshipping God. She was an outcast (Leviticus 15:25-27). Her Fear of living this debilitating life for one more day pressed her to reach out and touch the fringes on the cloak of Jesus. Can you feel her Thought storm of Fear? "How much worse can life get? I can be beaten or stoned, but maybe that is better than this misery." Desperation, embarrassment, and Fear had battled within her and she reached out thinking, "If only I can touch the edge of His garment, I know He will heal me." She refused to believe that her *suffering was really all there was to life*.

Fear:
- can motivate us to make change
- can find remedy in Jesus Christ

She quickly found out that her last resort *was* the solution. The Son of God was so powerful that even a faith-filled touch of His clothing healed her. In Jesus, she felt the welcoming arms of Love. "Come to me, all who labor and are heavy laden, and I will give you rest" (Matthew 11:28).

The desert of physical pain coerces people to do desperate things. At one point in life my neck pain was so severe, I wore special magnets taped to my neck and shoulders. The promise was that these would improve circulation and "heal" the injured tissue. I now have areas of my neck and shoulders that are completely numb because the nerves were "burned" by the magnets and will not regenerate. I was frantic for relief, but found none. Nothing will bring those nerves back.

This woman of perseverance refused to give in to the despondency of Fear and just curl up in a corner. Even though she was drained and despairing, she *hoped* and fought through the parched winds of her Fearful embarrassment for healing from the Great Physician (Mark 2:17). Jesus Christ was the luscious Oasis of healing that quenched her thirst in the desert. "They did not thirst when he led them through the deserts; he made water flow for them from the rock; he split the rock and the water gushed out" (Isaiah 48:21).

Jesus saw and Loved her as *one piece.* It was her whole person that He cared for, not just her body, and not just her spirit. *He knew her sadness and Joy were as interconnected as her body and soul.* As if no one else mattered in the midst of this great crowd scene, Jesus focused on her great *faith* in Him, and He Loved her. All else had failed this woman who persevered through Fear—except the Lord (Psalm 31:9).

THE DESERT CROSSING OF LIFE

Every doctor diagnosed something different. Chronic fatigue, perimenopause, fibromyalgia, depression, and a rare syndrome were some of the few. For three years, Lisa dragged herself from doctor to doctor seeking solutions. Nine different medications, napping, and trying to meet the needs of her family consumed her days. While her family tried to help, when an exact diagnosis could not be made, they were concluding that she was mentally ill. A friend sponsored Lisa in a visit to an alternative physician and the answer was found: Lyme disease. In those three years of mysterious symptoms, it had spread throughout her system ravaging her body and spirit.

The desert crossing of life will be filled with overpowering thirst and Fear-filled moments when you think you are crazy and are told that, "You are imagining things." As your mind and body *together* traverse the scorching heat of life's expedition, they are *both* affected by every sensory experience. "Now may the God of peace sanctify you completely, and may your whole *spirit* and *soul* and *body* be kept blameless at the coming of our Lord Jesus Christ" (1 Thessalonians 5:23). *[Emphases added]*

The sandstorm of Fear is as tall as a mountain and is as fast as the wind. Fear-driven worry can give you key information, but uncontrolled, its dust only chokes and damages your spirit and body. Worry does not change the past nor prevent awful things from happening in the future, but it can possess you to the point of exhaustion, where you give in to the *overwhelming wall of sand that things will never, ever, get better* (Matthew 6:25-34).

The woman who persevered through Fear knew that *problem-solving was power.* When one doctor failed to help her, she sought out another, and another. She did not want to be defined by her disease and persisted to find a solution. This incredible woman refused to accept the life of a health exile and kept on searching for an answer. "I stretch out my hands to you; my soul thirsts for you like a parched land" (Psalm 143:6).

Wild blueberries thrive in severe conditions. Extreme temperatures, pests, and disease plague these plants that fight back by releasing protective chemicals. When we eat wild blueberries, these same chemicals protect *us* from cancer.[1] *These fruits' response to harsh growing conditions creates a curative compound.* It is in the scorched Journeys of existence that we most often reveal what we are *made of,* and in *whom we really trust.* When we survive and weather tough times, *we push beyond ourselves* (Psalm 119:143).

Like inescapable scorching heat in the desert, the burden of illness permeates our every cell and cannot be lifted. Yet, in the humility of personal sickness, we have the opportunity to *dry up our Fearful pride* and feel the human Journey of those we are walking beside. God knows that when we grow through pain and frustration, our perspective changes to be more *mature* and *less petty.* Deep physical illness strips us of caring about anything unimportant.

Dehydration kills the spirit of a sojourner across life's desert who loses her way. You must complete the challenge before every cell in your body is drained of the water of life. If you have yet to experience a health crisis that shakes you to your core, *fill your canteen now: there is a desert ahead.*

Job's health was the last area that the Lord allowed Satan to touch, for He knew how deeply sickness affects the spirit (Job 2). Satan, the Saltmaster, is the creator of sickness, decay, and suffering, and will entice you to follow *his caravans* on easy trails. But, each time you join him you will find that the wells he brings you to—have been poisoned with salt. *Be clear about his intent to pollute the waters of the Oasis daily and dry you into despair.* Your physical and spiritual thirst will only be quenched in the living waters of Jesus—the great Oasis. *The desert challenge of your one-way Journey requires far more courage than you could ever imagine.* "Blessed are those who hunger and thirst for righteousness, for they shall be satisfied" (Matthew 5:6).

SPRINGS OF COMPASSION BURST FORTH

> Say to those who have an anxious heart, "Be strong; fear not! Behold, your God will come with vengeance, with the recompense of God He will come and save you." Then the eyes of the blind shall be opened, and the ears of the deaf unstopped; then shall the lame man leap like a deer, and the tongue of the mute sing for joy. For waters break forth in the wilderness, and streams in the desert; the burning sand shall become a pool, and the thirsty ground springs of water; in the haunt of jackals, where they lie down, the grass shall become reeds and rushes (Isaiah 35:4-7).

Isaiah is foretelling Jesus coming! God knows that you are longing for water in this wasteland crossing of life and His Love causes the ground to burst forth with the living water you need. Jesus said, "If anyone thirsts, let him come to me and drink. Whoever believes in me, as the Scripture has said, 'Out of his heart will flow rivers of living water'" (John 7:37-38).

Jesus was the master of empathy and compassion. He could put himself in the place of a woman with a twelve-year issue of blood and *Love* her. In the midst of a crowd, like a movie moment with the camera spinning around them, she had his full Love and attention. *His compassion poured down on her like a torrential rainshower in the desert.*

Many times we share *our* feelings, but do not *give* compassion. "I know *just* how you feel, when my mother died, I felt. . ." is not compassion. It might be *sharing*, but it is not compassion.

Compassion is not:

- talking about yourself when someone else is truly hurting
- comforting yourself as you tell the sorrowful one—*your* feelings
- competing that you had a "more difficult time" than another
- reminiscing your past distress
- about you. . . .

Compassion is:

- the desire to ease the distress of another
- empathy for someone who is hurting
- listening to gain information from a Fear-filled or grieving heart
- a wish to alleviate any suffering within your power
- that extra gesture of patience
- giving

Compassion listens and responds with, "I am just so sorry this is happening to you. . . . What can I do?" *Pure compassion* is the gift of *empowering significance* that says, "You matter to me." You cannot give miraculous healing as Jesus did, but you can Love and comfort each other as Jesus did. When you give pure compassion with the desire to support and connect someone with the tenderness of the Lord, *you are behaving like Jesus.* Jesus radiates an insightful kindness that drips like healing and hydrating waters on the parched hearts of His children. "Gracious words are like a honeycomb, sweetness to the soul and health to the body" (Proverbs 16:24).

In Jesus dwells all the fullness of true Love! His compassionate Love is the anti-Fear that says: "If you believe and trust in me, I will take care of you." It is the deepest truth that He will care and comfort you in *His* way, *if you will not faint in staying close to Him.* His Loving and providing hands are here to cradle you at the moment you feel you are going to crack. It is the deepest truth that He is the Oasis of Joy on your life's Journey. "'For the mountains may depart and the hills be removed, but my steadfast love shall not depart from you, and my covenant of peace shall not be removed,' says the LORD, who has compassion on you" (Isaiah 54:10).

They all shivered on the wing of the plane as it floated in the freezing waters of the Hudson river, but one passenger was soaking wet. "I was obviously very cold, and one of the pilots turned to me and said, 'Please take off your wet shirt, and I'll give you my dry one' . . . He literally gave me the shirt off his back to keep me warmer. I still have it. And I'm never going to give it up."[2]

Compassion says, "I feel for you and want to do something to help." *Compassionate actions can change lives.* "They shall not hunger or thirst, neither scorching wind nor sun shall strike them, for he who has pity on them will lead them, and by springs of water will guide them" (Isaiah 49:10).

Your brain receives a blast of mood-lifting serotonin every time you make a compassionate connection with someone and *respond* to their need. Joan Borysenko calls it "helper's high—an intense feeling of joy—an expansive, enlivening energy that makes you grateful to be alive. It kicks in like a rush of euphoria after a good deed and then mellows into a longer period of calm, contentment, and emotional well-being."[3] When you are the giver, you *receive* this blessing for every empathic response (Isaiah 55:6-13).

The healing waters of compassion and kindness may be difficult to give to someone who is ill and grouchy. While God's understanding forgiveness is ever-present for those who desire it, the boundary of the DO NOT SIN line helps the ailing and the care-giving beware of the edge they are approaching (Eph. 4:26; Psalm 4:4). Enlivening the truth that God *sees* all behavior and *hears* every word spoken can motivate us to exercise maximum self-control and set healthy boundaries (Luke 6:31; John 13:34). We DO NOT enable others to sin with words or actions. Much of the New Testament is devoted to teaching and explaining godly living. Why would God have inspired so much instruction regarding godly/ungodly treatment of each other if it were "ok" to cross the SIN line when frustrated and hurting? (Ch. 2) (Romans 4:8, 6:12; 1 Timothy 5:20; James 4:17; 1 Peter 2:20).

As you seek to understand, and *live pleasing the Lord*, true empathy helps you remember a time that *you* were sick and afraid and search for ways to *share* Love. When you consistently *try to position yourself within the other person*, you will convey the Love you are feeling—the Love that Jesus felt (1 John 4:9-12). *When you offer compassion, you are behaving like Jesus.*

Keep in mind that even when you are at your worst, you still have that SPACE in between stimulus and response (Ch. 8). Frankl saw it in the few men who rose up, served, and cared for others under the most horrible of circumstances. In that split-second SPACE, there is complete freedom to choose your next word or expression. Will your next word/expression be Fear-filled and reactive? Inspire someone? As difficult as thriving in a desert wasteland, *responding to Fear with tender compassion is very, very hard.* Engrave on your heart that it is your *response to Fear* that shows your character (Psalm 51:6).

Purest compassion is:

- a holy gift expressing the Love of the Lord
- a cloud burst of refreshment upon Fear
- the deepest Love and purest empathy
- not forgotten when you have experienced it
- treating someone as *Jesus* would have treated them

Our Lord feels compassion for all who Love Him—especially *you.*

> [A]nd a highway shall be there, and it shall be called the Way of Holiness . . . the redeemed shall walk there. And the ransomed of the Lord shall return and come to Zion with singing; everlasting joy shall be upon their heads; they shall obtain gladness and joy, and sorrow and sighing shall flee away (Isaiah 35:8-10).

As the first grains of dry sand begin to dissolve beneath the Heroine's feet, she must think swiftly. Grabbing onto a withered bush prolongs her life as the dry quicksand filters away underneath her. At some point in a Heroine's life Journey, she must grab hold of Reality.

WEATHER REPORT – *Reality heat wave continues*

Your desire to grow keeps you asking the question, "Who wins in an argument with Reality? Accepting Reality means that you look at yourself knee deep in a sand drift and say, "I am sinking knee deep in a sand drift, what now?" Acceptance does not mean resignation. Acceptance is the launching point for *dealing* with Fear. "If you faint in the day of adversity, your strength is small" (Proverbs 24:10).

With one bound, the mountain lion was off the cliff and onto Debbie's shoulder. It happened so fast that all Amy could do was scream. The big cat had slammed the hiker to the ground and was dragging her up through the brush to finish the kill. Amy ran toward her friend and grabbed her leg and hiking boot, beginning a tug-of-war with a 150-pound cougar. Debbie cried as the cat pulled her with its teeth and tried to drag her away, but Amy dug her heels into the dirt and rock unwilling to let loose of her friend. Within minutes that seemed like hours, their screaming brought other hikers who pelted the cougar with rocks until it retreated. Even as Amy pressed her sweatshirt on the wound, Debbie's mangled arm continued to pump blood. Surgeons tried to restore the limb, but the damage was too extensive to repair. Debbie only lost her arm, instead of losing her life. Amy said afterward, "I am terrified of blood and mountain lions, but I just could not give up." In addition to the loss of her arm, Debbie's leg bore the fingernail markings of a friend who just would not—let—go.

Amy had a defining moment in her life Journey and she chose to "Show up!" That means she could have argued with Reality and run in circles of Fear, but she chose to meet it head on and see the *cause-effect-choice* snapshot of this moment. A mountain lion (cause) is trying to eat my friend (effect) and I must do something (choice). Thought storms of Fear say: "This should not be happening to me. I should not *have* to cross this desert!" *Capture this truth: you can argue, fight, and run from it, but Reality is still there.* Unlike lost sojourners meandering the wastelands, when a child of God *accepts* Reality, the Lord is right there with you to help you *deal with Reality*. The constant, steadfast Love of the Lord is part of your Reality.

The woman who persevered through Fear said, "I have an issue of blood that is limiting my life (effect) there must be a *cause* and there must be some help (choice)." God wants us to use our created brains to find solutions, look for His doors opening and closing, and ask Him, "What can I learn from this?" Even in the most severe and disabling physical ailment, we are always left with a choice of, "How shall I cope?"

- Denial says, "You have got to die from something" and rolls over.
- Cause-effect says, "I am not afraid of *information*."
- Problem-solving says, "I get to act or decide something."
- Accountability says, "I take *responsibility* for what I have power over."

Unlike the woman with an issue of blood who had so few choices, consider these Realities of modern living:

1. In 1960, 13.3% of Americans were overweight.[4]

2. Today, we lead the developed countries of the world with a 74% over-weight population.[5]

3. "Studies show that 70% of obese children will grow up to be obese adults and for the first time in 100 years our young have a shorter life expectancy than their parents."[6]

4. A Harvard Public Health Study showed that "80% of coronary heart disease and 90% of type 2 diabetes is preventable."[7]

Is it right to blame our DNA for the 70% of *all* disease that is preventable?[8] Is it possible that our DNA has "evolved" in the last 50 years to produce an overabundance of "lifestyle-diseased" people? If our DNA is the 30% of our health cards that we are dealt in our birth, our lifestyle is likely the 70% of how we play those cards. We make Fear-driven excuses when we blame our DNA or our family for something that we can control. Cause-effect might ask the question, *"What is the correlation between self-control and fork-control?"* When asked about cholesterol numbers during a visit, a family doctor hung his head and said with despair, "But most people just don't want to hear about it." *If we are ignoring health advice to eat right/exercise and their cause-effect on the body and mind, are we living in Reality?*

Figs, pomegranates, olive oil, grapes, and honey are the Biblical diet of super foods touted by the top health researchers today.[9] We don't read of the Mega-burger in the Bible, nor on medical researchers' "daily foods" list for energetic, abundant, healthy living. The Creator invented cause and effect (Job 37:13).

Co-existing in all of us is cause-effect and denial. We choose which one will power us every moment. Four times, glutton and drunkard are used in tandem in the Bible: Deuteronomy 21:20, Proverbs 23:20-21, Matthew 11:19 and Luke 7:34. Early Christians did not attend the feast banquets of the Roman world for the point was to *overindulge* in delicacies.[10] We see how clearly alcohol damages our bodies and minds, but do we see how food abuse does likewise? God created food to be *pleasurable*, but the *purpose of food is nourishment*, not overindulgence or medicating feelings (Genesis 2:9). Say these words, "I am not afraid of information. I will examine myself."

With so much available about health and wellness, is the Fear of losing food as a comfort or hobby stopping you from grabbing hold of wisdom? A maladaptive behavior like overeating is *easy* for us because it *comforts* our inner Fear instead of *deals* with it. How much more difficult is it to listen to your feelings, ask the Lord for help, share with a friend, study your Bible and take a walk than stand over the sink and eat ice cream? Analyze your Fearful excuse: *What would I be giving up if I kept a balanced approach and did not medicate my feelings with food?*

> The school year was beginning the next day and fourth-grade teacher, Nicole, went to lunch at a friend's house after church. She socialized, but deep inside she was feeling increasingly overwhelmed by a new class and school year. They had brownies and ice cream for dessert and she asked for seconds. On the way home, she stopped to pick up a pie at the bakery and some cookies for her lunches. Passing the ice cream shop, she got two quarts just to "keep in the freezer." Her body and spirit were feeling the stress of her job, but instead of acknowledging the Fear of, "I am afraid I am: not prepared, not capable, overwhelmed," she turned to the maladaptive behavior of overindulgence to comfort herself.

Admit you are frightened or overwhelmed. The acid level in your stomach and tightness of your neck are telling you about it. If your spirit is feeling something, but your body's actions are burying it under the sand, you are in two pieces. *It is the burying of feelings that causes maladaptive coping behaviors.* When you acknowledge, "I am afraid . . ." *the truth of the exposed feeling brings your body and spirit voicing in agreement to face the Fear.* This is a *healthy* "synch" of two Realities. Admit it to yourself and the Lord—out loud. "Lord, I am frightened, stressed, and overwhelmed, please help me deal with this in a spiritually healthy way" (Matthew 5:3).

- Admit: "I am afraid of what lies ahead in life."
- Recognize Thought storms: "You are not good enough. You will fail."
- Face thoughts with evidence: "That is not true, I am the Lord's servant."
- Learn: "What can I influence? What is out of my control?"
- Deal with life in Reality: "You must cross this desert—that is Reality."
- Listen to His Word—how much the Lord Loves and values *you*.

- Find: Joy in knowing that He is completely in charge.
- Believe: "I *get* to glorify Him every day"—that is my Divine Purpose.

"Or do you not know that your body is a temple of the Holy Spirit within you, whom you have from God? You are not your own, for you were bought with a price. So glorify God in your body" (1 Corinthians 6:19-20).

    The bottom-line question to ask ourselves is, "Am I as *useful* as I can possibly be to the Lord making the health choices that I am making? Do I feel Fear of changing? When so much of my life is unpredictable, why not take charge of *any* piece that I can control?" Most of us would not like to admit how much of our low energy, irritability, and short-tempered behavior flows from our low blood sugar, high blood pressure, sleep apnea, and hormones. Worse yet, we keep trying to justify our frustrated attitudes by analyzing how "flawed" everyone else is! Until we are end-stage terminal, it is likely there is always *something* we can be doing better. Only you and the Lord know if your health choices limit your vitality level and usefulness to Him, and it is *only* to Him that you are accountable. "For you formed my inward parts; you knitted me together in my mother's womb. I praise you, for I am fearfully and wonderfully made. Wonderful are your works; my soul knows it very well" (Psalm 139:13-14a).

    God created your body and spirit uniquely for HIS service. If you complete your Journey at the paradise Treasure and are raised into Heaven at judgment, you will receive a spiritual body (Phil. 3:23; 1 Cor. 15:44). Until then, your *spirit is knitted into this physical body to serve together*. Spend a moment and reflect on this question: "Am I pretending that what I do to my physical body does not affect my spirit?" "Do you not know you are God's temple and that God's Spirit dwells in you?" (1 Corinthians 3:16).

Her mind begins hallucinating as she looks out across the desert heat. She sees fountains of water and chilled mugs of exotic juices served under cool tents filled with pillows. After days without water, the mirage turns ugly and she hears roaring tigers in the distance and stampedes of camels coming in around her. In moments of clarity, she thinks, "I am trying so hard to serve the Cause, how does this suffering Journey glorify Him?"

MIRAGE: *Are you all one piece?*

When a body is enduring trial, its traveling companion, the mind/spirit, suffers as well. Job understood that his flesh was created by God and the Father's Love *cared for* his spirit within him. "You clothed me with skin and *flesh,* and knit me together with bones and sinews. You have granted me life and steadfast love, and your care has preserved my *spirit*" (Job 10:11-12). *[Emphases added]*

Paul's *spirit* gave service to God as his *body* traveled and preached the gospel. "First, I thank my God through Jesus Christ for all of you, because your faith is proclaimed in all the world. For God is my witness, whom I serve with my *spirit* in the gospel of his Son" (Romans 1:8-9). *[Emphases added]* He also knew that the body and spirit *glorified or defiled* the Lord together. "Since we have these promises, beloved, let us cleanse ourselves from every defilement of *body* and *spirit,* bringing holiness to completion in the fear of God" (2 Cor. 7:1). *[Emphases added]*

Neither the wisdom of Solomon nor the most advanced technology of today can detect the amazing moment your spirit is joined to your bones as a microscopic embryo. "As you do not know the way the spirit comes to the bones in the womb of a woman with child, so you do not know the work of God who makes everything" (Ecclesiastes 11:5). While we know that our "godliness training" has value in *every* way (1 Timothy 4:8), the body/spirit survive and thrive as life partners separating only in death. "For as the body apart from the spirit is dead, so also faith apart from works is dead" (James 2:26). Pretending that your body's choices do not affect your spirit and your Fear level may be a mirage in your life's desert.

A mirage believer might have her identity intertwined with being a "patient" and be Fearful of losing that distinction. "How are you today?" is her cue to recite her aches and medical chart for you. A mirage believer may think, "If I don't talk about my health, I won't get any attention and no one will care about me." Her "negative" brain continually focuses on her personal suffering. She may control her family by her illness and guard her health hobby, dedicating carefully her "going to the doctor clothes." A mirage believer might be *resentful* of information that points toward personal responsibility for body and spirit. She may be using the body's aches to fill a Love/attention hole of need inside her, and revealing a responsibility connection may feel *threatening.*

The mysterious connection of body/mind is difficult to understand and even scientific research is trying to shed light on the brain's communication between the two. Consider these recent findings:

1. University of Pennsylvania: "Persistent anxiety can kill neurons in brain structures concerned with memory and decision-making and such damage is even visible on brain scans." Your brain actually shows the injury of Fear/worry. "Mental armor" can be developed with stress-fighting techniques and learning to live in the present moment, instead of in the Fear of the future.[11]

2. Princeton University, Northwestern University, and Georgetown University: Neurons in the brain can become stronger and more resilient through *physical* exercise. Research on exercise and its importance in treating depression shows that moving improves well-being and lessens anxiety, ameliorating the symptoms of depression. "Physical exercise changes the level of serotonin in your brain. It increases the feel good hormones, the endorphins . . ."[12]

3. Multiple studies: "Research suggests that people with chronic anxiety have lower-than-normal levels of omega-3 fatty acids. Studies have found that balancing this deficit may help relieve symptoms."[13]

4. How emotions are stored in the body (Fascia Memory Theory) is researched by practitioners of Myofascial Release and studied to understand how our bodies hold onto both physical and mental pain.[14]

5. University College London: Researchers have located the "two brain structures that trigger smiling, good-will and cooperation." These structures produce dopamine, a neurotransmitter, which counteracts negativity and activates laughter and pleasure.[15]

6. University of Chicago: "Clenching any part of your muscles increases will power . . . like a mental metaphor for resisting temptation. Health-conscious people who tightened a muscle (like clenching their fist) while selecting food from a snack bar were more likely to pass up decadent treats and opt for good-for-you fruit. Caveats: You have to be focused on healthy eating, and you have to clench the muscle while facing the dilemma."[16]

7. University of North Carolina: "Light therapy" had comparable effects on depressive disorders as antidepressants. Mood lifting light therapy increases the wonderful serotonin that makes us feel great and raises melatonin levels that helps us sleep better.[17]

How deeply your physical body is networked in with your emotions! Ask yourself this question: "Am I afraid to persevere and embrace change because it might mean that I would have no excuses?" Your attitude determines the whirlwinds of the sand in your desert crossing. Whether in the physical inflammation of disease or emotional damage of Fear, *if you do not "feel and deal" with Fearful emotions, you will use maladaptive behaviors to cope with them.*

In your desert survival parchments, there are warnings to protect your *brain* from the effect of dehydration or you may succumb to mirages. If you are ignoring the cause-effect of nourishing your brain/spirit/body, and believing you are optimally useful to the Lord, you may be believing a mirage. Your body health **is** your brain health. Your brain is the seat of your:

- ability to reason and make decisions
- spiritual values—your faith
- IQ and personality
- emotions—including the feeling of Fear
- goodness and compassion
- compass heart that thirsts for God—is actually in your brain!

Beware of your "negative" brain telling you that change is "useless." When in Reality, you have dropped your cloak of responsibility and it is gradually being buried over with blowing sand.

Novice sojourners on the desert-crossing quickly shed layers of clothing, believing that those layers are making them hotter. Experienced desert dwellers wear layers of cotton gauze to capture body moisture and hold on to it for cooling. The Heroine's cloak of responsibility which seemingly would be a burden, gives the most protection from the blistering heat and freezing cold of night. Its insulation preserves every drop of life-sustaining moisture and the secure silk pocket carries the Map to the Oasis and Treasure.

The Heroine opens the Map to read letters from those who have endured the scorching temperatures and traversed the desert ordeal. The Creator's guidance flows through those ancestral sojourners to her as she studies their character. As the ancient desert-trekkers learned how to listen through the sand for the sound of water, the Map guides her in acquiring the skills and expertise for this Journey. The Map also teaches the Reality that "No magic carpet is coming to fly you away . . . you must walk this desert valley."

THE AMAZING CROSSING

So here in Reality, if you knew that thirty days from now you had to fight your way across the Sahara desert, what would you be doing? How hard would you train, run, weight lift and learn desert survival skills in order to stay alive? What if your **life depended on** your endurance conditioning? Well, you *do* have to make that race across the desert of life and your survival **depends on your vigorous training.** "[H]olding fast to the word of life, so that in the day of Christ I may be proud that I did not run in vain or labor in vain" (Philippians 2:16).

Human muscle is developed in the *tearing* of soft tissue. When you lift weights and strain your muscle, that soreness is actually microscopic tearing. If you continue to lift that amount of weight correctly, that *torn bundle becomes strong muscle tissue.* Athletes subject themselves to high pain thresholds knowing that the only way to build more muscle is through painful tissue-splitting and rebuilding. *Building spiritual muscle and strength is developed by straining and exercise, just as physical muscle is.* IF YOU FIND SPIRITUAL GROWTH TO BE EASY—PERHAPS YOU ARE NOT REQUIRING ENOUGH OF YOURSELF. "Every athlete exercises self-control in all things. They do it to receive a perishable wreath, but we an imperishable" (1 Cor. 9:25).

Tough times can build your strength as you climb the sand dunes of trials or cause you to just lie down and let the sand blow over you. With every step in a sand dune, your calf muscles are stressed and grow stronger. *Pain is the only way to grow strong*! A thriving spiritual athlete develops a *rigorous training* schedule as she studies and applies the Map principles to her daily trials. The muscle of perseverance sees *long-term*

Joy, instead of *instant gratification*. This constantly requires the POWER of self-control. "A man without self-control is like a city broken into and left without walls" (Proverbs 25:28).

Your struggles only have meaning *if* they drive you on to "Show up," for this great event of life. You *choose* which muscles that you develop on your life Journey and build the vigor of your character by dealing with Fear! Living your Divine purpose means, with every muscle-building lift you say, *"I will serve Him no matter what lies ahead"* (Isaiah 50:10).

Desert Survival Training:

- *Think for yourself vs. Follow the caravan:* Research new help for your challenges—instead of following a caravan that beckons, "Take some pills and ignore it."
- *Fearful stubbornness vs. Perseverance:* Stubbornness says, "I have always done it this way!" Perseverance says, "Maybe there is something better!"
- *Cause-effect vs. Denial:* "I am what I repeatedly do. My daily choices show who I really am and I accept accountability for every one of my choices."
- *Training vs. Fear-powered Illusion:* "I will train spiritually through Bible Study and self-discipline of body and spirit." Fear-less = Faith-filled.

Unpredictable aerial bombing raids killed and demoralized the British people throughout WWII. Winston Churchill spoke over the radio to his beloved and terrified people, "Never give up, Never, Never, Never give up." (Galatians 6:9).

You can sit beside a *dried-up* ancient well in the desert and pretend there is refreshing water waiting deep inside, but that will not fill your canteen for the Journey. The Reality is—miles of searing sand still lay ahead. When the snapshots of your desert Journey are collected and the power point begins, what music will play? Will the tremolos of Fear overcome you as you lie in the sand? Or as you stand yourself up one last time and pull your cloak over your nose and mouth to press on through the driving dust and sand, will you hear the chorus of victory sound forth?

> When the poor and needy seek water, and there is none, and their tongue is parched with thirst, I the LORD will answer them; I the God of Israel will not forsake them. I will open rivers on the bare heights, and fountains in the midst of the valleys. I will make the wilderness a pool of water, and the dry land springs of water (Isaiah 41:17-18).

Even the chill of night brings her no relief, for desert ants come from their burrows and bite her feet and hands as she tries to rest. The sky above her glitters like diamonds spilled upon the deepest black velvet and reminds her of the loving-kindness of her Creator. Her compass heart keeps recalling that the Map promised a lush Oasis ahead.

THE LORD'S SATELLITE GPS

From hundreds of miles above the earth, a man-made satellite can read a compass in the hand of a child. Is it possible that the Creator of Heaven and earth is no greater than the technology His children built? Do you think that you need a microchip tracking device implanted inside you for Him to find you? Not one heartbeat of your life is out of range of the Lord's GPS. Whether you are trembling in a hospital bed with IVs in your arms or comforting yourself with a package of cookies at midnight—He is there with you. You are not alone. He sees you and His arms of steadfast Love reach down to envelope you (Isaiah 40:11).

> Jennifer sat in her car in the driveway. Everything in her life had fallen apart and her worst Fears had come true. Her family was a disaster and every inch of her body was being torn apart from the pain of her cancer treatments. With unblocked emotion, she sobbed and prayed out loud in the car, "Lord, I have absolutely no idea what you want me to do with my life. I feel like I am doing everything I can, but I am overwhelmed and terrified of what is ahead. Use me as you see fit, for my breath is yours. I lay everything at your feet, Lord, and I submit to you completely." "My grace is sufficient for you, my power is made perfect in your weakness" (2 Cor. 12:9).

As you lie there helpless in the sand, wracked with unbearable pain and misery, with your feet too badly blistered to walk—Jesus is there next to you. There is nowhere to hide from His presence (Jonah 1:3), nor to be lost from His cool, gentle arms (Luke 19:10). He will never leave you stranded and helpless. He will never turn His back and refuse to help you, consistent with His nature. When you faint at your weakest and your burden is the most oppressive, His tender providing hands will lift you in His arms and lay your blistered body next to the life-giving waters. He is your greatest Hero—not of your dreams, but Reality. No one will ever do for you what He did for you. No one can. He knows your health status already—physical and spiritual. He knows how scared you are that you will never smile again. He knows what *real* pain is—as He stepped in front and took the torment *for you* on the cross. While there may be a food or medicine that will heal your body, His blood sacrifice is the only thing that you can *reach out and receive* to save your soul. "[K]nowing that you were ransomed from the futile ways inherited from your forefathers, not with perishable things such as silver or gold, but with the precious blood of Christ, like that of a lamb without blemish or spot" (1 Peter 1:18-19).

Jesus did not fail the woman with the issue of blood and He will never fail you. Does that mean that He will give you a miraculous healing? No. Does that mean that He will keep your earthly body from being devastated by disease? No. Does that mean that if you train in the Word and take responsibility for your Fears that He will open doors for you to live your one-way Journey filled with Joy? Absolutely!

> They shall hunger no more, neither thirst anymore; the sun shall not strike them, nor any scorching heat. For the Lamb in the midst of the throne will be their shepherd, and he will guide them to springs of living water, and God will wipe away every tear from their eyes (Rev. 7:16-17).

Living inside the Lord's protection means *grabbing onto the help He sends you*. That help will come in your study of the Word, conversations with one who has traversed a similar valley, or it might be a *provided rainstorm in the desert, at just the moment your body could no longer go without water*. He *knows* what you need and never tires of Loving you and holding your hand, if you will only ask and trust in Him. "That times of refreshing may come from the presence of the Lord, and that he may send the Christ appointed for you, Jesus" (Acts 3:20).

As the sun rises, she stumbles once again on the ascent of a large sand dune. The skin of her feet has split open from burns and her hands and lips are covered with blisters. She hears the cries of scavenger birds circling above her and can no longer raise her arms to brush away the sand flies that crust around her eyes and mouth. At the top of the dune, she blinks her swollen eyes at a haze of green in

the distance and her disfigured lips cannot even utter her thought, "Could this be the real Oasis?" As she descends into the luscious tree-lined refuge of thirst-quenching pools, she stops to feel the Joy and pray, "Thank you." The Heroine trusted the Mapmaker's promise of an Oasis if she persevered through her Fear, and as always—He fulfilled it.

OASIS HEALTH SPA

> O God, you are my God; earnestly I seek you; my soul thirsts for you; my flesh faints for you, as in a dry and weary land where there is no water. So I have looked upon you in the sanctuary, beholding your power and glory. Because your stead-fast love is better than life, my lips will praise you. So I will bless you as long as I live; in your name I will lift up my hands . . . My soul clings to you; your right hand upholds me"(Psalm 63:1-4, 8).

In thanksgiving, you submit that your life is a gift of God. Real Gratitude drips from asking the Lord, "What can I learn from this?" when yet another doctor gives you no answers. As I grow older, I realize that *Joyful Gratitude is the by-product of having known despair.* The contrast of "how bad things could be," brings clarity to *look* for ways to praise and thank God. "You make known to me the path of life; in your presence there is fullness of joy; at your right hand are pleasures forevermore" (Psalm 16:1).

Fear-driven anxiety separates body and spirit in its frenzy, so that your mind is "elsewhere." When you *stop* and *feel thankful* for your beating heart or marvel at your eyesight, you pull your mind/spirit to where your body is standing. *Fear of the future runs rampant* within you when you do not stop and feel the *Gratitude* of this very moment. *Thanking God engages your spirit into the awareness of the Lord's Loving and providing hands, and this praise is the companion on a life walk of JOY.* "Therefore, as you received Christ Jesus the Lord, so walk in him, rooted and built up in him and established in the faith, just as you were taught, abounding in thanksgiving" (Col. 2:6-7).

Scientific studies abound on the life-lengthening, health-increasing practice of Gratitude. They all reach the same conclusion: practicing being thankful makes you less stressed, less materialistic, healthier, enjoy a higher quality of life, and live longer! " Rejoice always, pray without ceasing, give thanks in all circumstances; for this is the will of God in Christ Jesus for you" (1 Thessalonians 5:16-18).

"I cried because I had no shoes, until I met a man who had no feet."
—Anonymous

Close this book and begin by thanking Him for your feet. "Thank you, Lord, that I have feet and I *get* to make this Journey serving you." Thank God that you *get* to move about in this vessel He designed, see His world, and sing His praise. *Gratitude as a hobby will bless your life more than any quilting, scrapbooking, or gardening. It has endless resources and the outcome is a more abundant life!!* (John 10:10).

Thanksgiving hydrates your spirit with Joy, even if your body is being ravaged by cancer. The faith that you are nurturing in your spiritual body strengthens your physical body for what they will pass through together. *The sands of time only flow one way through the hour glass of your life. Spend them well.* "For with you is the fountain of life; in your light do we see light" (Psalm 36:9).

FEARBREAKER-JOYMAKER JOURNEY

The cancer had metastasized throughout Brother Tuggle's body. Weakened from pain and treatments that were not succeeding, he would not stay at home when he could possibly come together with Christians and worship God. Until days before his death, his sons would carry him to the back pew where he could listen to the lessons, pray, and sing with us. When he grew too frail to sit, this once robust man would lay down on the pew during worship. I was a fairly new Christian at the time, and almost 30 years later, I am filled with emotion for a man who would not keep his vigorous spirit, nor delicate body, from communing in worship to God. He wore his cloak of responsibility with Joy before the Lord and lived as an example to me (Psalm 33:21).

How much more did the woman who persevered through Fear appreciate the Joy of her health after suffering for twelve years? How much did she value the Lord? How does she inspire you—2,000 years later? What is *your* desert crossing here to teach you? As you cast a shadow every time you walk in the sun, how does that shadow—inspire others? Is it possible that *your* spiritual development and example is *that* important that you are getting the opportunity to cross a great obstacle and show *how* you trust in Him? "My flesh and my heart may fail, but God is the strength of my heart and my portion forever" (Psalm 73:26).

The Joyfully resilient exemplify how deeply God Loves and cares for them! He knows *you* and whether you are suffering physical disease or a Fear-filled sadness of mind, you are His child whose obedient faith *brings Him Joy.* "Let those who delight in my righteousness shout for joy and be glad and say evermore, 'Great is the Lord, who delights in the welfare of his servant!'" (Psalm 35:27).

One day a desert crossing will overcome your body and you will—cease to breathe (2 Peter 1:13-14). Your soul, however, only wanders from the Oasis of Jesus and eternal Joy, if you choose to give up. "And the Lord will guide you continually and satisfy your desire in scorched places and make your bones strong; and you shall be like a watered garden, like a spring of water, whose waters do not fail" (Isaiah 58:11).

GROWING THROUGH FEAR

1. Albert Einstein wrote, "Insanity: doing the same thing over and over again and expecting different results." How does a new cause-effect lifestyle affect someone's attitude and service?

2. As we give thanks for the Lord's gift of life by honoring our bodies, what one habit could you change to become more useful to the Lord?

3. Since your brain receives a surge of dopamine when you "reward" yourself, what would be a healthy "reward" to give yourself after accomplishing a fitness milestone?

4. What does the brain-ravaging disease of Alzheimer's show us about the effect of the physical body's health on the personality?

We met a couple ———✳——— husband and wife. The wife has alzheimers. The husband told Ken she has had this for several years. He said its like being married to a completly different woman!

~ 11 ~
Frozen to this World by Fear
Fearful attachment to things
The rich young man (Mark 10:17-31)

The first flakes of snow float down like a giant pillow spilling its tiny feathers. Each little work of art is visible for only a moment on the Heroine's cloak as she stands on the back of her sled. The beauty of this frozen valley rapidly turns fearsome as the snow begins coming faster and harder upon her. Turning into the gorge ahead, she is walled in on both sides by cliffs of ice and blinding snowdrifts. The Map warns her to pack well for this part of her Journey as she will pass by a large crevasse and cross many frozen lakes. If she plans poorly and packs too lightly, she will freeze or starve. But, if she tries to carry too much, her sleigh will break through in the icy wilderness and she will perish. The Map teaches repeatedly that a balance of provisions is crucial to passage through the glacier world.

Snowy winds blow her onto the frozen lake and her sled glides easily. She rubs her eyes with a frost-laden mitten and opens them to see a red object peeking through drifted snow in the distance. Pulling alongside, she clears the snow away to find a large red velvet bag drawn by a golden cord. As she loosens the cord, out spills gold coins, jewels, and pearls worth a queen's dowry. She looks *across the lake for a royal Sojourner—who might have abandoned his wealth. "Surely my sled can handle the weight of these riches!" she thinks as she drags the large bag and lifts it with all her might onto the sled.*

And as he was setting out on his journey, a man ran up and knelt before him and asked him, "Good Teacher, what must I do to inherit eternal life?" And Jesus said to him, "Why do you call me good? No one is good except God alone. You know the commandments: 'Do not murder, Do not commit adultery, Do not steal, Do not bear false witness, Do not defraud, Honor your father and mother.'" And he said to him, "Teacher, all these I have kept from my youth." And Jesus, looking at him, loved him, and said to him, "You lack one thing: go, sell all that you have and give to the poor, and you will have treasure in heaven; and come, follow me." Disheartened by the saying, he went away sorrowful, for he had great possessions. And Jesus looked around and said to his disciples, "How difficult it will be for those who have wealth to enter the kingdom of God!" And the disciples were amazed at his words. But Jesus said to them again, "Children, how difficult it is to enter the kingdom of God! It is easier for a camel to go through the eye of a needle than for a rich person to enter the kingdom of God." And they were exceedingly astonished, and said to him, "Then who can be saved?" Jesus looked at them and said, "With man it is impossible, but not with God. For all things are possible with God." Peter began to say to him, "See we have left everything and followed you." Jesus said, "Truly, I say to you, there is no one who has left house or brothers or sisters or mother or father or children or lands, for my sake and for the gospel, who will not receive a hundredfold now in this time, houses and brothers and sisters and mothers and children and lands, with persecutions, and in the age to come eternal life. But many who are first will be last, and the last first" (Mark 10:17-31; Matthew 19:16-26; Luke 18:18-30).

The Lord knew that the freezing chill of possessions was this man's weakness, and therefore, asked him to deal with it. Perhaps the young man had checked off a packing list of "obediences" from his life and wanted the Lord's stamp of approval on the bottom. He may have designed a "perfect" life and had an agenda for a "perfect" future. His Fear-controlled comfort zone was warm and filled with delights. Why didn't Jesus just ask him to donate money or help serve bread to the poor? How often an expectation cracks open when Fear tries to *control the outcomes of life!* Giving up his wealth did not fit in his "vision of the future." Imagine the pounding Fear in the rich young man's heart when the Lord *pinpointed the one thing he cherished most*. His Fear-filled Thought storms came with record-setting speed, "Anything but my wealth, I can't give up my money!"

Perhaps he never dreamed that the Lord would ask this of him because he knew that some Christians were noted for their wealth, like Joseph of Arimathea (Matthew 27:57), and others (Acts 4:32-37). But this man had "invented a god" who was pleased with him trusting in riches, and the Jesus knew it. The Lord knew this would be his—one moment in time. "And Jesus, looking at him, loved him" (Mark 10:21). *Mark records the Lord's compassion for a young man who had not used submission as a measurement of success.* "No servant can serve two masters, for either he will hate the one and love the other, or he will be devoted to the one and despise the other. You cannot serve God and money" (Luke 16:13).

SLIDING INTO THE CREVASSE – The lure of possessions

- 1650 – Explorers had mapped the globe in search of wealth and were settling a New World called America.
- 1750 – Colonists coming to the Americas dreamed of fresh air and freedom.
- 1850 – The American Dream traveled in a covered wagon crossing the prairie in search of more land to homestead.
- 1950 – Post WWII America now televised a "keep up with the Joneses" dream house, car, perfect kids, and a dog. We can only wonder what the American Dream will look like in 2050 (1 Timothy 6:6).

The first Pilgrims lived peacefully with the Massasoit tribe who had helped them survive in this New World. While that initial band of settlers came here to live peaceful and quiet lives before God (1 Tim. 2:2), others came pursuing wealth. For many, the "American Dream" had more to do with the *pursuit of greed* than any noble motive or interest in souls. Greed and competition power the history of the American "success" story. Top of the ladder entrepreneurs explain that Darwin was right and they are the proof of "the survival of the fittest" (Psalm 49:6).

Visiting Pompeii, Italy today allows us to step back even further in history and stand next to the ruins of the ancient Temple of Apollo. Its former glory bears witness of a time when people "invented" pagan gods and created businesses around "Apollo"—for profit. As the Roman Empire grew rich, the elite grew in boredom, overabundance, and opulence which spawned the invention of new and more revolting ways to sin. They were spoiled and Godless. Does that sound like any society that we live in?

The "Christian" world would recoil at the idea that we are idol worshippers as people of old, and yet we worship cars, clothes, phones, and every new technology (Isaiah 40:19-20). Our 21st century techno-love, focuses on building skills and relationships with *things* and not real *people*. Are we as a generation more peaceful or Joyful as the result of acquiring new technology? Not possible. Like the Romans, our society is inventing a god that is pleased with our focus on the *things* of this world. "For what does it profit a man to gain the whole world, and forfeit his soul?" (Mark 8:36).

With the wind at her back she glides lightly for a time, but without warning the wind changes direction and tips her to the side as she stops. Breathing hard with excitement, the Heroine's thoughts storm of what this fortune means for her life. "I will not have to focus on this Journey to the Treasure. I can take it easy!" But her delight turns to terror as she hears the sound of a crack at the front of the sled. She releases her grip just as the ice beneath the sled opens up. Terrified, she sprawls flat on the ground as the sled catches on the craggy edge of the hole and freezes to its sides. Frigid waters engulf half the sled, but the red bag is still visible. "If I can just grasp it and drag it away from the opening . . ." she breathlessly whispers. Crawling on the ice, she inches her way over, but as she removes her mitten and reaches out with her warm, moist hand to grab the ice-crusted bag, she is frozen to it. . . .

IS YOUR TONGUE FROZEN TO A LIGHT POLE?

Many of us live under the constant strain of just having enough cash to put food on the table. Every day we wonder, "Will there ever be enough money?" (Luke 12:22-34). Our stress hardens us into thinking that *money will solve all of our problems,* and we dream of being rich. Without spiritual management in little or in much, the burden and tension surrounding money will end up demanding that *we serve it,* instead of money being a useful tool to help *us serve the Lord.* The quest for freedom from financial stress can just as quickly turn to indulgence, once our basic needs are met. A deadly self-centered focus begins a temperature-dropping freeze when our purpose is to—"spoil ourselves." "[B]ut the cares of the world and the deceitfulness of riches and the desires for other things enter in and choke the word, and it proves unfruitful" (Mark 4:19).

- A *magazine* layout shows a beautiful woman whose hot red-sequined dress matches the red paint of the Italian sports car she lies on as the caption reads, "You Deserve Me." Message: If you buy this car—you will get women.
- The *billboard* displays a 10-foot high scoop of vanilla ice cream. You can smell the vanilla beans as the first drip begins to form along the edges. Handwritten across the creamy center is the word "LUV." The caption reads, "You Are Worth It!" Message: The delectable, cold smoothness of this ice cream will—make you feel loved.
- The *TV commercial* plays sensual music as the woman dressed in an evening gown dances slowly on the screen. One by one handsome men are drawn to her perfume, stroking her body and kissing her neck. They caress her and sing, "Can you handle the spoiling?" Message: If you wear this perfume—you will attract handsome men.

Learning to be a "material girl" is not a new problem. Indulgence is a vicious god, for he has no bounds and preys upon your Fears of loneliness and anxiety over not being "good enough." While a pioneer in the Dakota territory may have felt that his horse and sleigh were unequal to his neighbor, our 21st century blizzard of advertising stirs up an ice storm frenzy of Fear that, "I am not as good as you, nor as happy as you, because I do not have . . ." "Better is a little with the fear of the Lord than great treasure and trouble with it" (Proverbs 15:16).

Like ski tracks that are constantly run over in the snow, when our "negative" brains run over and rehearse those advertising-born ideas, they carve Fearful Thought patterns into our neurocircuitry. Fear-filled jealousy and insecurity crystallize and solidify within us as our *perception of life*. As we measure our self-worth by our income, house size, car model, or technogadgetry, we begin the *freeze process* of:

- comparing our success to others
- validating our worth
- motivating ourselves to work—only for external rewards

The "Invented god" of technology tells us the lust for faster and more prestigious toys will bring us *power* and happiness. He says that if we will only put him first and focus our money and time on him, our troubles will melt away. All ages are lured into this lie, as instant gratification fills every pocket of the western world (James 2:5).

Satan is not a cute Jack Frost of legends and stories. He is a barbaric Iceman who wants to **harden permafrost in your heart by attaching you to this world's pleasures.** He preys upon your discontent and anger that, "I don't have the American Dream!" He does not need a storm's fury to holler "CHARGE!" Rather a slow mercury drop and whispering wind of "Charge it, you are worth it!" in your ear. He wants to freeze you to *him*, and separate you, make you feel alone and *numb*—toward God. Block by block, he will help you build an ice house around yourself with *things* to insulate you from the warmth of the Lord (Matt. 4:7-11).

Each item/block pleases your senses of sight, touch, or taste, so on the inside of your ice house you have very appealing views of all of your favorite things. Because your senses are giving you constant "pleasure feedback" off the screens inside the ice house, you do not notice how the blocks are hardening into thick walls of ice—*with you on the inside.* Eventually the deep freeze becomes so cold that you harden like a snowman, with a once warm-blooded person within. Like grabbing hold of a frozen railing with your warm, moist hand, you are stuck fast, as the ice crystals bond you together. *And so it is with love for the things of this world—you will be hard frozen and shackled to this world, when you substitue love of things, for true Love from God.* "Take care, and be on your guard against all covetousness, for one's life does not consist in the abundance of his possessions" (Luke 12:15).

The Iceman offers you a counterfeit life. He advertises the forgery of Fear-driven worldly affections as:

- a cheap frozen substitute for real Love
- a cure for all those difficult human relationships
- "giving" to yourself—as your first priority
- power and control
- your connection to your "shopping buddies"
- "You deserve it, spoil yourself—go for excess!!"
- a "must" if you want to get ahead

- the comfort, affection, and reward for all your frustrations
- "HEAVEN IS NOT THAT GREAT—HOLD ONTO EVERY PLEASURE HERE"

Amazingly, this is the opposite of the Joys we have in our godly relationships, eternal security and God's real Love. "For where your treasure is, there your heart will be also" (Matthew 6:21).

> Now there is great gain in godliness with contentment, for we brought nothing into this world, and we cannot take anything out of the world. But if we have food and clothing, with these we will be content. But those who desire to be rich fall into temptation, into a snare, into many senseless and harmful desires that plunge people into ruin and destruction. For the love of money is a root of all kinds of evils. It is through this craving that some have wandered away from the faith and pierced themselves with many [pains] (1 Timothy 6:6-10).

WATER TURNS TO ICE – Feelings

> The snow princess watched as the queen gently lifted up each jewel and admired it. She smiled with pleasure as she raised an earring up against her face and gazed at herself in the frosty mirror. Every day the queen spent hours choosing just the right crystalline jewels for her outfit, and paraded herself before the court—shimmering and resplendent. The princess was thrilled when each year on her birthday, the queen gave her a piece of the royal jewelry to wear and cherish. Every night, the princess dreamed of the day that she too would look glorious wearing the crown jewels.

As an icy drop of water chills each passerby to slowly form a solid icicle, the freeze within us begins slowly. In the course of enjoying tangibles more and more, the mood-boosting chemicals that temporarily surge in our brains from "frozen pleasures" become a vicarious replacement for Love. If we are frustrated or injured by humans in getting our Love-needs met, we may begin to turn to shopping, pets, food, TV, or crafting. We look for *things that will never leave us or hurt us* and use them *to console and comfort us in our sadness. The delicate icy balance that turns an occasional pleasure into a consoler/comforter is crossed very early in life if we bond with the substance our parents regarded as precious.*

I was raised by a very good and Loving mother who grew up very poor in the Depression. My appetite for hard work, self-discipline, and desire to "do the right thing" are a direct result of my mother's devoted Love and influence. Because of her Depression-era childhood of extreme deprivation, my mother became a bargain shopper. She never met a clearance rack or yard sale that did not need "a few minutes" of her time and obtaining a bargain was always very exciting. As I watched my mother take pleasure in acquiring a "good deal," that pattern became a consoler/comforter for me in Fear-filled times. As fluttering snowflakes can become a blizzard of epic proportions, an innocent diversion can grow to be an obstacle to spiritual trust (Psalm 4:5).

If you watched your mother or father take great delight in preparing and eating rich foods, you may have learned to Fearfully console/comfort yourself with delicacies. Geneen Roth writes in **When Food is Love,** "When food is love, love is hard and lacquer-shiny. Love is outside of you, another thing to acquire and make yours. When love is love, there is nothing standing between you and your breaking heart. Love moves you. And that is good."[1]

Whether we comfort our Fears with clothes, jewelry, retirement funds, nails, shoes, techno-devices, or potato chips, it is all the same: *we are using a material object to manage our feelings.* The aching of Fear-haunted rejection, Fear-filled anxiety and loneliness are submerged deep within us. Building a frozen security barrier with *things* to protect us from hurt is just so much easier than feeling and dealing with those Fears. *Life hurts and is pain-filled.* And while we must understand our parents' influence within us, if you are old enough to read this book, *the statute of limitations on "blaming" them has long expired* (Ezekiel 18:20).

The False warmth of the consolers/comforters says: "Relax, I will make you happy." Whether you are soothing your disappointed spirit with food, or seeking to impress others with your wealth, you are creating an iceberg within yourself. Only a small part of the iceberg is visible, but the feelings deep beneath the surface of "I am of no value" are massive.

- I do not matter and I am all alone.
- I am helpless.
- I will always be disappointed.
- I have a right.
- I am stuck with my life.
- I can control this one thing and it will not leave me.

When you choose to *feel* these iceberg underwater Fears and see how they are weighing you, you may begin to see that there is *frozen* and *warmth* within *you* as in all of us. There is a great discomfort within us being half-frozen and half-warm, for part of us is hard-freeze stuck to the world and the other half—filled with the Love of the heavenly Treasure. All of us contain within, materialistic/frozen and spiritually-minded/warm traits at our deepest core (Romans 7:17-20; 2 Cor. 7:5).

The rich young man's Fear list may only have had one thing on it, "losing my wealth," but that weakness was the one thing that held him back. Take a moment and feel the Fear of what it would be like to give up any substance that you use for comfort/security. If you will be courageous and *feel this Fear of loss*, you will begin to melt your crystallizing heart. If not, you may carry your Fears like great chunks of ice on your hunched back every day of your Journey, until your shoulders are breaking and your heart bursts (James 4:1-4).

ICE STORM – *Breaks the limbs from hobbies to hoarding*
When freezing rain paints the earth with its slippery silver, that ice storm will cause even the mightiest oaks to crack and lose their limbs. Thought storms of Fear bombard that accumulating an *abundance of stuff* will stop the pain of loneliness or rejection. But like heavy ice on branches, we soon break under the burden. As they construct elaborate ice castles for protection, some hoarders feel, "*I have stuff that will never leave me, I will never be lonely.*"

The Iceman's lie hardens: that the false warmth of happiness can be found in things. Fear motivates the hoarding of money, clothes, pets, and food. Any *thing* used for the false warmth of Love can become a maladaptive emotional sustainer for ourselves or in the way we *relate to others*. Any *thing* that we are transferring *our feelings* onto or *bribing* someone else's feelings with—can grow into *hoarding*.

* Twelve year-old Brett got paid by his dad for every homework paper, chore, and cursory obedience. Mom had abandoned them when Brett was young, and dad dealt with his Fear-filled sadness by bribing Brett with money and gifts. "I will buy you those new shoes if you . . ." Believing that everything he did would bring an immediate reward, Brett grew up to have huge credit card debt, be unemployed, and divorced.

* Seven year-old Claire cried, "But I want to go!!" as the older family members were packing for a trip to the beach. Her mother said, "No, I don't want to chase you." She cried even harder until mom said, "Hey, do you want a pop tart?" Moments later, tears dried, Claire munched contentedly on a warm, sugary pop tart as the older family members drove off to spend the day together. She learned a lesson in bribing away her Fearful sadness and perhaps felt, "I am not valuable to spend time with. Sugary treats comfort my senses and they will never leave me." Claire grew up to be obese.

Of course everyone enjoys beautiful gifts on their birthday and a scrumptious cake for celebration. A thoughtfully made dinner (mine is lasagna), or a quilt lovingly made by a friend are *pleasures that God allows*, and the Love that powered them is to be deeply appreciated. Buying a new sweater or baking a pan of cookies are wonderful, occasional activities. But remember, the problem with the *infatuation with things* is—the *imbalance* in your sleigh can crack the ice below and *freeze you to THIS world*. When Reality says, "You must limit your consoler," there is *terror within you* to break that icy bond. Many would rather *die* than leave their red velvet bag of valuables behind. It may feel like *losing a limb* as you grieve the loss of a consoler. Actually, your frostbite may be thawing and you are just now beginning to feel painful Reality (Romans 14:17).

If we do not thaw by feeling and dealing with our Fear-filled emotions, we can become a frozen wasteland of greed and obsessions. As *we substitute different elements of this world for what is hurting inside,* we never admit, "Oh Lord, I am hungry for you," and accept *His Love!* The choice to build ice walls is always yours, but igloos built of Fear blocks end up hardening everyone who dwells within. Summon up in your mind that when you are frustrated at your inability to make lasting change: *Deal with your Fears*. Only you and the Lord know what amount of overshopping, overeating, oversaving, or overspending reflect your Love of this world. Do you Love the things you can see and feel, or a God who must be *believed*? "Do not love the world or the things in the world. If anyone loves the world, the love of the Father is not in him" (1 John 2:15).

AVALANCHE – *Turned him into an ice sculpture*

The hills of the frozen valley were heavy with winter's snow. He spoke quietly, but as the young man lowered his head and turned to walk away, the sound of his heavy footsteps began the first rumble of the avalanche. Within seconds, the winter's snowfall from the mountain above tumbled down to bury him. [Jesus said] "'Go, sell what you possess and give to the poor, and you will have treasure in heaven; and come, follow me.' When the young man heard this he went away sorrowful, for he had great possessions" (Matthew 19:21-22).

At the moment the rich young man turned away, he transformed his life forever. His feet were frozen into his labyrinth world of his riches. Instead of warming his compass heart to thaw toward the Lord, he let himself be consumed and hardened into an ice sculpture beneath an avalanche of snow. *Ice sculptures only remain perfect if they are kept in deep freeze*. He wanted a cloak of honor, but found the cloak of responsibility too heavy to bear. When asked to examine himself, he *made the fatal choice quickly* and could not part from the tactile objects that were freezing him to this world (Acts 17:16).

Had the rich young man thought of himself as a worshipper of money when he checked off the commandment, "You shall have no other gods before me?" (Ex. 20:3). I wonder if he thought about Isaiah 44 and how we build idols. "He plants a cedar and the rain nourishes it. Then it becomes fuel for a man. He takes a part of it and warms himself; he kindles a fire and bakes bread. Also he makes a god and worships it; he makes it an idol and falls down before it" (Isaiah 44:14b-15).

The rich young man, just like you and I, did not connect the love of *things* with idolatry, and serving an "Invented god" of pleasure, power, and control. Even as the Lord looked on him with tender Love and made him choose, He allowed his *free will to make the choice*. I have often wondered how long it took him to regret his decision, especially when I hear people making excuses for not obeying the Lord such as, "I am just in a winter of sin right now, I will check in with God when I am finished . . ." You have regrets when you "do or not do," in each micro-choice, *what pleases the Lord* (Psalm 104:34; Eph. 5:10; Col. 1:10). Take a moment and look at yourself against the teachings of the Lord:

- Galatians 5:16-26 "idolatry"
- Ephesians 5:5 "impure or who is covetous (that is, an idolater)"
- Colossians 3:5 "covetousness which is idolatry"
- Romans 1:29-31 "covetous"
- 2 Tim. 3:1-5 "lovers of money . . . lovers of pleasure"

Is your consoler your best friend? *Are you bribing others to love you with some thing?* What is the value of your soul in dollars? Can you list something that keeps you from being a Heroine-servant? _____ Just as He knew the rich young man, the Lord knows the depth of your weakness and *there is no piece of your life that He is not after, to sculpt in holiness.* "Are not two sparrows sold for a penny? And not one of them will fall to the ground apart from your Father. But even the hairs of your head are all numbered. Fear not, therefore; you are of more value than many sparrows" (Matt. 10:29-31).

THE SKI JUMPER – *Identity*

The gold medal hopes of his nation rest on this last jump. At the signal, the ski jumper begins his glide down the ramp and pushes off in perfect form, coasting gently downward to land in the snow below. His country's hopes are resting on these few seconds in time. How will this be his defining moment? Will he be identified as the ski jumper who won the gold, or the loser who fell on his face and tumbled?

Success and its accompanying consolers can become crystallized into our identity. It was the rich young man's very *identity* that was threatened if he gave up his fortune. What threatens your identity? "If I do not *have* my jewelry, hairstyle, phone, car, TV, or kitchen, I will be nothing—powerless. If I can no longer bake or quilt, then I am nothing. I would rather die than be without my . . ." The Fear that "without my _____ I am nothing" is a "wealth" of information about yourself (Job 4:6).

"Oh, are you the shoe lady?" the new boss asked, as she met the accountant. "Your reputation precedes you. I have heard that you have the most amazing collection of shoes on the planet!"

Is your identity connected to something that you can touch? Will the Joys of Heaven really be *that* much better than your key lime pie? *The harder you freeze to the world, the higher the price becomes to thaw and warm your heart in obedience to the Lord.* The Lord showed the young man—the core of his Fear-filled ego, but it was *his* option to *raise his personal holiness* to the Lord's standard. When you examine your Fears/anxieties/consolers, you see what is *keeping your hands frozen to the earth and not held in the warm, tender-loving hand of the Lord* (Psalm 31:5). Imprint in your mind that no human is all good or all bad—all materialistic (frozen) or all spiritually-minded (warm). Are you? Me neither. Just like the rich young man, we have complete *free choice to allow the de-icing of our hearts or not*. Our lives must be *freely given* to the Lord! (Colossians 3:1-4).

Notice that Jesus did not chase after and negotiate a lesser "sacrifice" in order to save this young man! "Ok, how about give up—half your wealth." The Lord asked the rich young man to give up what he LOVED the most because *that identity* was freezing him to this world. Have you ever bargained with the Lord like that? "No Lord, I don't want that trial—not poverty, Lord!" "No Lord, not cancer, ok, I will take poverty instead!"

Reality check: you don't get to *choose* all of your future and YOU DON'T GET TO HAVE EVERYTHING THAT YOU WANT! But, when you feel Fear of the future, notice how much you *can* control by your hard work and spiritual growth. You *choose* to be the "shoe lady!" Isn't it wonderful that God keeps giving you chances to grow in the areas that you *need* the most (Proverbs 20:27).

God knows what you are *substituting for His Love*. He knows what you need to *give up* in order to wholly *depend* on Him. He will not expect anything from you that you are helpless to give (John 15). God understands financial transactions and prices that are paid!! He does not ask anything from you that He has not *given Himself*. Jesus' blood transaction of redemption was paid for *you*! Your bill is paid in full. *Your Love for Him must be stronger than your attachment for this world in order to conquer the glacier that you are frozen to!* Do you really want to be sanctified/set apart for His service, or will someone else serve His Cause? (1 Peter 1:15).

Do you remember psychiatrist Viktor Frankl digging ditches alongside men who had been wealthy and "honored" and were now known by the numbers on their arm? It is a Reality that when two men's bodies lie side by side in the morgue, no one knows how much money they made, or what car they drove. Your Journey from conception through life and on to eternity goes only one way. When all of your stuff is gone to yard sales and charities, your Divine purpose will live on in the investment you have made in souls; it cannot be stopped. Your life movie has ended, but the sled tracks that you leave on the hearts of others—endure. When you strip down your outer identity, you are now able to see that your Divine purpose is—to *live* glorifying God with your life!! (Psalm 86:12).

If you smash down the ice walls you have built, your identity as a Heroine-servant glorifies God! Your *devotion* to Him is the legacy of your Divine purpose which shows, "The reason I draw breath is to serve Jesus Christ."

God looks beyond your *face*, your clothes, shoes, or your phone. *He sees you under your skin layer where your soft and tender heart Loves Him in sincere humility.* There will be moments that you have one chance to prove yourself, like a ski jumper in the Olympic finals. But you will fall from Fear, or land beautifully, depending on how you train yourself in *this* moment right now. "But the Lord is faithful. He will establish you and guard you against the evil one. And we have confidence in the Lord about you, that you are doing and will do the things that we command. May the Lord direct your hearts to the love of God and to the steadfastness of Christ" (2 Thess. 3:3-5).

God allows us "I" statements about ourselves:

- I am God's child.
- I am Loved.
- My life is a gift from Him.
- I will be courageous and confident.
- My Divine purpose matters.
- I can grow and make a difference.
- I am vital to the Cause.
- I am valuable because Jesus died for me—Ephesians 1.

What warm, loving days am I missing out on, by not completely trusting in the God who Loves me? *My life is a devotion to Him, not a donation to Him* (Daniel 9:4).

The Heroine lies there on the ice as the snow blows over her body. Her mind goes to the Map and the eternal Treasure that it promises. Great warmth begins to fill her tender, compass heart and surges like a fiery shooting star within her as she whispers, "I choose life with Him." Slowly her hand warms, and as her frozen grip melts, she peels her fingers away, leaving large pieces of skin behind.

THE GREAT SLED RACE – *A compass heart*

One sign read: "He who dies with the most toys wins!" Another sign read, "He who dies with the most toys, leaves a lot of toys for someone else to play with." Who took the red velvet bag of gold out of their sleigh and had the courage to leave it on the ice where the Heroine found it? Whoever has the most stuff in their sleigh breaks through the ice and freezes. . . . "Two things I ask of you [God]; deny them not to me before I die: Remove far from me falsehood and lying; give me neither poverty nor riches; feed me with the food that is needful for me, lest I be full and deny you and say, 'Who is the LORD?' or lest I be poor and steal and profane the name of my God" (Proverbs 30:7-9).

Do you hope for what the Proverb writer prayed for? Just the right balance—not rich, not poor, not overindulged, but not hungry? The Reality of life in the 21st century is that we must plan and pay for health and home insurance, retirement, and savings. As we have so many choices, worries, and pleasures, our Fears tell us that *"planning" will control our destiny*. How *easy* it is to reach out and freeze to the world! The Heroine's sleigh ride is Joyful when she is in balance, gliding through this beautiful world that God created. But, that balance happens daily when she is depending on **HIS steadfast Love**, not consolers and insurance for this world. *A lighter load increases the Joy of the trek!*

I have been privileged to see many of the great works that men have designed on this planet. I have seen pure gold tiaras worn by Greek royalty 2,500 years ago, the crowns and jewelry worn by the kings and queens of Europe containing precious jewels the size of my fist, the Mona Lisa of Leonardo da Vinci, statues carved by the hand of Michelangelo, and even the precious letters that Jane Austen wrote to her beloved sister. At the day the Lord appoints, these riches will all be reduced to ash and He, the one whom we only now see through the eyes of faith, will be in full view.

> Since all these things are thus to be dissolved, what sort of people ought you to be in lives of holiness and godliness, waiting for and hastening the coming of the day of God, because of which the heavens will be set on fire and dissolved, and the heavenly bodies will melt as they burn! But according to his promise we are waiting for new heavens and a new earth in which righteousness dwells (2 Peter 3:11-13).

So how shall we live knowing that *all things* are impermanent? How will you glide along your Journey with the right balance in your sled? "Keep your life free from love of money, and be content with what you have, for he has said, 'I will never leave you nor forsake you.' So we can confidently say, 'The Lord is my helper; I will not fear; what can man do to me?'" (Hebrews 13:5-6).

1. *ADMIT IT!* Confess your weakness out loud, "I am using _____ as a consoler. Instead of facing my Fears and having confidence in God, I am out of balance and this consoler is freezing me to this world." In exposing your consoler, your pain may be intensified as the numbness thaws away. For now you take responsibility for your Fear's work within. Thank the Lord for this information about yourself and tell Him you are sorry that you have relied on some *thing created* instead of *the Creator* for Love/comfort (Ecclesiastes 5:15).

2. *WATCH YOUR INTERNAL WEATHER FORECAST:* As you walk in your favorite store or bakery, stop and listen to your Thought storms. *Feel* the Fear weather temperature inside you. Your "negative" brain can take you on a downhill luge run of denial—crashing straight into the arms of your consoler. Since your consolers have sustained you emotionally, it will require months/years to change your focus. *Naming* your inner Fear gives your internal weather forecast information to manage that emotion. You must deal with the Fear in order to glide well across the ice. As you stop and are peaceful for a moment, you can quiet your mind and make a conscious choice by asking, "Why am I acquiring this?" I have learned to sit in the car and pray before entering certain stores that are tempting for me (Proverbs 16:32b).

3. *SHARE YOUR STRUGGLE WITH A SUPPORTIVE CHRISTIAN:* Tell them about your Fears and ask them to help you develop a system for dealing with your consoler. You don't need to skate the ice alone! Listen to others' feedback about crossing the line between a pleasure and a maladaptive consoler (Gal. 6:2). My closest friends (and now all my readers) know that I make myself get rid of something anytime I acquire something. It works! Get help developing a new "currency" system of adaptive behaviors instead of your consoler. Feeling compelled to shop may be a signal to call someone who needs encouragement (James 1:26-27). Planning to take a walk after dinner may help deter you from eating "seconds" (Ezekiel

16:49). The Lord offered the rich young man a new life *where the currency was Love*. He offers that to *you* (1 Thessalonians 1:3).

4. *CONNECT YOUR HEART TO GOD'S WORD:* Spiritual growth happens in the quiet moment that the fiery warmth of His Word melts through your frozen heart. When you read God's Word and feel, "Oh no Lord, I have not been doing what is right," the first warmth of change is kindled. Your *power of discernment* (Heb. 5:14) grows as you read about the Divine purpose of all those gone before you and ask, "What *am* I living for?" *Look for the pathways His providing hand is leading you,* through the crevasses and frozen lakes, and follow those trails. With all *humility and passion*, fall in Love with the Word *each* day! Quote it when the Iceman lures you to add blocks of ice to your sled! (Hebrews 4:12).

5. *TRAIN YOUR HEART/BRAIN FOR SACRIFICE—NOT INDULGENCE:* Focus on a balanced sleigh with sufficient insurance and savings, but abundant giving!!! Use the vocabulary of "necessity, pleasure, and indulgence" to train your *discernment*. Practice saying, "This is not mine, this is not mine," when you look around at your abundance. This habit helps train your brain that all things are the Lord's! We *get* to teach Bible class and we *get* to help at the building and we *get* to give our money to the contribution for the Lord's work (Mal. 3:10). Giving away our stuff piece by piece would mean that we eventually would have no more stuff. Giving away Love makes it grow even more and more. In fact, that is how we increase Love within us, *by giving Love to others.* If we want to live a life serving the Lord, our Divine purpose is to share His Love, NOT to amass money to *retire*! (Luke 12:33).

6. *REALITY:* "You are what you repeatedly do." While no one is all frozen or all warm, you become a giver, by giving; a taker, by taking; an indulger, by indulging; and a hoarder, by hoarding. You become Heaven focused by daily being *Heaven focused—it is how you build a Christian life.* Stop pretending that the Lord does not see you! Come off cruise control of TV values and take the reins of your own sled. Credit card living is fantasy and the love of money is the Iceman's forgery for true warm Love. God's steadfast Love is pure providential goodness (James 1:22-25).

7. *PRIORITIES:* If your little daughter and your home were consumed in a landslide, for what would you mourn? Would you mourn the loss of

your furniture or the lost wages she would have earned over her lifetime? Or, would you mourn the absence of her Joy-filled smile and life—lived for the Lord? Show those priorities right now and invest your time and money in Loving experiences that turn your heart and the hearts of others to the Lord. Do you really believe that "This world is not your home," and you are "just passing through"—on your sleigh?[2] Do you believe that Heaven is really that great? *Do you believe God is telling the truth about where your reward lies?* You may have said, "Put your money where your mouth is." Decide if you are doing that and "Put your energy where your priorities are." "But if anyone has the world's goods and sees his brother in need, yet closes his heart against him, how does God's love abide in him?" (1 John 3:17).

8. *MEASURE YOUR SUCCESS BY GOD'S STANDARDS:* Show that you care about God's opinion of your success!! Yes, it is scary and risky to have the *courage to be different* from the frozen ice sculpture-people around you!! Ask yourself these questions, "Did I live my Divine purpose today? Am I learning the lessons that He is providing for me? Am I warmer toward Him or more frozen to the world today than yesterday?" *A successful sleigh Journey through the frozen valley of life is a Journey of character building, not igloo building.* If you measure success by the world's standard of money, ego, and power, your life movie will always be controlled by Fearful anxiety. *If you really want someone else to be in control of your life, allow them to measure your worth.* The Lord's business is salvation. *The battleground is the permafrost of your will.* Will you de-ice your stubborn will and surrender to Him? (Matthew 6:33).

9. *KEEP IN THE FRONT OF YOUR MEMORY:* that Jesus was *never* in style. He owned nothing but some sandals, a tunic, and robe. He never had the "right" clothes for the occasion. He did not carry luggage from town to town as He taught about God's saving Love. Mary and the others who followed Him likely slept on the floor in brethren's homes and ate whatever was given to them. They lived to *serve* and tell the truth about God. *God knows your needs and wants you to peel your freezing hand away and trust Him.* Make the decision that you are going to live *your* life—the Lord's way and ask every choice, "Is this pleasing to the Lord?" (Ephesians 5:10). *Remember that God's standards are really high* (Isaiah 55:8; Philippians 4:19).

If I choose to serve the Cause, I must with passionate Love—melt toward God. *It is God's responsibility to provide for me and He takes it seriously.* Believe Him.

> Do not lay up for yourselves treasures on earth, where moth and rust destroy and where thieves break in and steal, but lay up for yourselves treasures in heaven, where neither moth nor rust destroys and where thieves do not break in and steal. For where your *treasure* is, there your heart will be also. The eye is the lamp of the body. So, if your eye is healthy your whole body will be full of light, but if your eye is bad, your whole body will be full of darkness. If then the light in you is darkness, how great is the darkness! No one can serve two masters, for either he will hate the one and love the other, or he will be devoted to the one and despise the other. *You cannot serve God and money.* Therefore I tell you, do not be *anxious* about your life, what you will eat or what you will drink, nor about your body, what you will put on. Is not life more than food, and the body more than clothing? Look at the birds of the air: they neither sow nor reap nor gather into barns, and yet your heavenly Father feeds them. *Are you not of more value than they?* And which of you by being *anxious* can add a single hour to his span of life? And why are you *anxious* about clothing? Consider the lilies of the field, how they grow: they neither toil nor spin, yet I tell you, even Solomon in all his glory was not arrayed like one of these. But if God so clothes the grass of the field, which today is alive and tomorrow is thrown into the oven, will he not much more clothe you, O you of little faith? Therefore do not be *anxious*, saying, "What shall we eat?" or "What shall we drink?" or "What shall we wear?" For the Gentiles seek after all these things, and *your heavenly Father knows that you need them all.* But seek first the kingdom of God and his righteousness, and all these things will be added to you. Therefore do not be *anxious* about tomorrow, for tomorrow will be *anxious* for itself. Sufficient for the day is its own trouble. (Matt. 6:19-34) *[Emphases added]*

With her sleigh frozen into the ice, the Heroine now walks the ice field. She encounters an ancient stone fountain where once flowing waters are frozen solid. As she smiles and offers thanks for every breath, the frozen stream begins to drip with life. Like a snowball that liquefies in a warm hand, a great thaw begins to melt the ice away and soon the fountain begins trickling water. From this memorial fountain flow the precious waters of Gratitude. As she looks at her world with new courage and openness, all around her seems to come alive with color and Joy... Joy of a new way of walking the Journey. A way of Gratitude.

FEARBREAKER-JOYMAKER JOURNEY

> They lined up for watermelon. Men, women, and children lined up after our outdoor gospel meeting in Venezuela for watermelon. Some of them had walked many miles to come to services. Brother Jack had made countless trips with a rented van filled to capacity to pick people up, for they wanted to come hear a lesson from the Word of God. As we had walked door to door during the day sharing the Bible, we visited in some of the brethrens' homes. Many families lived in just one room built of corrugated tin siding and roof with a dirt floor. I kept wondering what happened during the torrential rainy season, as there was no place for the rain to drain away. What would it be like to watch the water and mud gurgle inside under your walls? But tonight, sixty of us held hands and thanked God for being together, hearing His Word, and for a piece of watermelon.

When you increase your appreciation of the Lord's goodness, you will see how your Divine purpose and *resources* inside and outside you, can be used to bring Him glory.

Joyfully resilient people kindle the warmth of Gratitude as they:

1. *REJOICE IN IMPERMANENCE!* Will you step through your Fear and thank God that every *thing* is transient? My favorite pink cashmere sweater (bought at a thrift store for only five dollars) will one day be dust. The savor of that cupcake you just ate will only remain with you for minutes, and it is gone. There are no taste buds in your stomach! Accepting impermanence is vital to scraping down into your core of thanksgiving, and finding Joy. *Only the permanence of your deeds and your soul will transcend your earthly life* (2 Peter 3:12).

2. *LET THE SIGHT OF YOUR FROSTY BREATH BRING YOU JOY!* Every inhale and exhale is given from the Lord. *Awareness of His grace in every breath fuels the inner Gratitude that powers true Joy.* We can talk and pray to the Lord in a manner that shows that we *live in His presence* and He is the *source* of all delight. When life expectancy was short, the pain of losing children to death, and homes to fire, was Reality. With so many "health and safety controls" available to us, we must remind ourselves who is ultimately in control of all. As we face our mortality, we find the exceptional Joy for daily moments that we undervalue. Try saying this

every day, "I know that I live by Your grace." Showing appreciation for this life gift is pleasing to Him (Psalm 107:1-2).

3. *WALLET DEVOTIONALS!* It was during a period of unemployment in our home that I taught myself to thank God every time I opened my wallet. "Every penny and dollar belongs to you Lord, and I take nothing for granted." I pay cash for 90% of my transactions and on a day that I am running errands, I might give thanks 8 or 9 times. With all sincerity, I acknowledge that every bill and coin that I have is given to me by Him, to be used for Him (James 1:17).

4. *MORSEL DEVOTIONALS!* As you pray before a meal, thank God for, "every morsel of food." Embrace that a bowl of cereal or beans is a pure blessing from His outstretched hand to you. Thank Him for your warm bed, roof over your home, tires on your car, and shoes on your feet. *Nurture your inner singing voice of contentment and shun the yearning for more.* (Ch. 5) Look around you—there are as many things to be thankful for as snowflakes in the sky. Your Joy for life will explode as you stop and give thanks for His Love (Luke 11:3; Job 1:20-22).

5. GIVE! King David prayed before his death, "For all things come from you, and of your own have we given you" (1 Chronicles 29:14). Live with the clarity—that *everything is HIS*. He sees how you are using and honoring Him with your money contribution to His work in your local congregation. You *get* to give back what is already His (2 Cor. 9:1-15; Mal. 3:10; Proverbs 3:9-10).

6. PRACTICE BEING GRATEFUL! That Jesus gave His life in service and sacrifice *just for you* (Eph. 5:2). Warming up your positive thoughts trains your cold "negative" brain to run better on Joy! Practice being grateful! He values you so much that He paid your sin debt in full. Practice being grateful! You are very expensive and were purchased by His pure sinless blood (Hebrews 10:10). Practice being grateful! (Psalm 7:17). "[F]or you were bought with a price. So glorify God in your body" (1 Cor. 6:20).

My grandmother used to say this old proverb, "Use your money wisely, do not keep it to be proud. For you cannot take it with you, there are no pockets in a shroud." Will you die serving the Lord or stuff?

GROWING THROUGH FEAR

1. Even the Lord's physical presence could not unfreeze the rich young man's heart. He alone had the power to do that. What is your plan for warming?

2. Pioneer women owned one dress for daily work, one dress for church and prepared a pie for Sunday dinner—what happened to us? How does TV teach us Fear-powered worldliness?

3. As a snowball picks up size and speed as it rolls downhill, how does regularly indulging in your consoler create more troubles? Brainstorm with someone 100 ways to comfort and celebrate without a maladaptive consoler.

4. How does Fear of failure and Fear of rejection pressure us to live as those around us? What does the "balance in our sleigh" require between successful and faithful?

5. When the scrapbook of your life is reviewed by your great-grandchildren, what will they list as your consoler? Is there anything you need to change now so that those memories of you are more "pleasing to the Lord?" What will matter 100 years from now?

6. How is the irresponsible use of credit cards a Fear leap? How does it "steal" from your future?

~ 12 ~
All the World is a Stage for Fear
Fear that pushes us to lie
Ananias and Sapphira (Acts 4:32-5:11)

"Surely the audience can hear my heart beating," the Heroine thinks as they draw back the long brocade curtains. The glow of hundreds of candles rimming the stage illumine her golden dress as she comes into view. The audience applauds enthusiastically as the lute and drum begin her intro. "What is my cue? Oh no! What is my cue?" her mind surges. The leading man takes her by the arm and she follows across the stage as the music stops—awaiting her line—"Welcome, welcome, one and all! The world is a stage for this costume ball!"

Now the full number of those who believed were of one heart and soul, and no one said that any of the things that belonged to him was his own, but they had everything in common. And with great power the apostles were giving their testimony to the resurrection of the Lord Jesus, and great grace was upon them all. There was not a needy person among them, for as many as were owners of lands or houses sold them and brought the proceeds of what was sold and laid it at the apostles' feet, and it was distributed to each as any had need. Thus Joseph, who was also called by the apostles Barnabas (which means son of encouragement), a Levite, a native of Cyprus, sold a field that belonged to him and brought the money and laid it at the apostles' feet. But a man named Ananias, with his wife

Sapphira, sold a piece of property, and with his wife's knowledge he kept back for himself some of the proceeds and brought only a part of it and laid it at the apostles' feet. But Peter said, "Ananias, why has Satan filled your heart to lie to the Holy Spirit and to keep back for yourself part of the proceeds of the land? While it remained unsold, did it not remain your own? And after it was sold, was it not at your disposal? Why is it that you have contrived this deed in your heart? You have not lied to men but to God." When Ananias heard these words, he fell down and breathed his last. And great fear came upon all who heard of it, the young men rose and wrapped him up and carried him out and buried him.

After an interval of about three hours his wife came in, not knowing what had happened. And Peter said to her, "Tell me whether you sold the land for so much." And she said, "Yes, for so much." But Peter said to her, "How is it that you have agreed together to test the Spirit of the Lord? Behold, the feet of those who have buried your husband are at the door, and they will carry you out." Immediately she fell down at his feet and breathed her last. When the young men came in they found her dead, and they carried her out and buried her beside her husband. And great fear came upon the whole church and upon all who heard of these things (Acts 4:32-5:11).

ALL THE WORLD IS A STAGE

Ananias and Sapphira thought they were writing a glorious scene within the play of their lives that would bring them acclaim and applause. The earthly performance came to an end, but surely not as the grand finale they had hoped for. The Holy Spirit's message was crystal clear: wearing the name Christian is not for liars. Reading this true story gives us all a chance to reflect! As you read this true-life drama do *you* think, "Serves them right, they knew better . . ." or do you think, "I am so thankful the Lord has not struck *me* dead, all the times that I have lied." Your response gives you vast information about yourself (Proverbs 24:17).

Perhaps Ananias and Sapphira had struggled with Fear-driven insecurity/ jealousy their entire lives, and felt, "We are not important." Something about the generosity of Barnabas and the others swirled their Thought storm of Fear into a plot for action. "Maybe we will get attention and respect if we *do* something big and generous, but let's lie that we are giving *all* the money we made." No one coerced or even suggested to them that they should donate this land/money, but Thought storms become sinful actions when they move our hands or mouths (Proverbs 17:20). "For nothing is hidden that will not be made manifest, nor is anything secret that will not be known and come to light" (Luke 8:17).

Peter exposes *Satan as the author of this plot.* "Peter said, 'Ananias, why has Satan filled your heart to lie to the Holy Spirit and to keep back for yourself part of the proceeds of the land?'" (Acts 5:3). Satan, the great Liar, saw an open door to their hearts in their Fearful Thought storms and capitalized on it! He is a special effects expert, costume designer, and advertising agent for the theater of deception. At the beginning, he preyed on Eve's Fear and lied to her that she would not die, but she did (Genesis 3:4). Never forget that Satan is the father of lies. "When he lies, he speaks out of his own character, for he is a liar and the father of lies" (John 8:44).

Ancient theatre stages were built sloping downward toward the audience in order to project the sound. Fear-driven Thought storms, like sound in a theatre, will push you downhill to your lowest edge and land you in the pit. The great Liar will help you perfect your lying by training your stage technique in lighting, smoke machines, and other special effects. He encourages you to manipulate situations and people—through deception. He knows that LYING IS A WAY OF CONTROLLING THE FEELINGS OF OTHERS. It is the opposite of the Reality of accepting your *power* and *limits.* The great Liar can only provide *temptations.* He cannot *make* you lie or take your soul—without your consent (2 Corinthians 2:11).

In the heart of every lie is a denial of a Reality. Stop and think about that. I do not want to admit a Reality, so I invent a lie to change or control it. Stretch—pretend—cheat—steal—manipulate—exaggerate are other words for *lie* meaning—I deny Reality.

- I deny Reality about my finances. I want that designer purse, so I charge it and tell my husband that it was a gift.
- I deny Reality about relationships. I "exaggerate" my wife's behavior to gain pity from my co-workers and friends.
- I deny Reality about my Integrity and do just *enough* at work. I lie to the boss about how long it takes to get those reports done.

Lies help you change Reality's "image." "Whoever hates disguises himself with his lips and harbors deceit in his heart" (Proverbs 26:24).

Modern day actors and politicians who behave badly often hire "image" consultants to promote their charitable and sincere "acts." It is a very costly venture that creates more lies in order to cover up Fear-driven sin. Ananias and Sapphira were early do-it-yourself image consultants pretending to be honest and gauging the "audience response." "Will the audience be impressed with A . . . how about B?" What they never learned was—pretending will *never* bring true Joy. True Joy is always in Reality. They wanted a cloak of honor in front of the church, but without a cloak of responsibility. "The fear of the Lord is instruction in wisdom, and humility comes before honor" (Proverbs 15:33).

ACTING SCHOOL – Build a character and role

You are a graduate of an acting school. How do I know that? Because you were raised by humans and we are masterful actors. You learned to act from your parents, siblings, teachers, peers, and brethren. You learned how to get attention, "stretch" the truth, and "enhance" the details of events. While childhood is a small part of life, it is where your richest acting lessons are learned. *You inhaled what the role models in your life exhaled* as they lied, "exaggerated," or told the truth in their interactions. The subtle ways of deception that come along with faking, lying, and cheating must be observed and practiced to be learned. Dorothy Law Nolte, Ph.D. wrote, "Children learn what they live."

In Reality, children learn to act like adults, but adults often choose to act like children. Irish statesman, Edmund Burke, wrote in 1756, "Example is the school of mankind, and they will learn at no other." He also wisely wrote, "Those who do not learn the lessons of history are destined to repeat them." A quote we should all recall when replaying the tragedy of Ananias and Sapphira. "Blessed is the man who makes the LORD his trust, who does not turn to the proud, to those who go astray after a lie!" (Psalm 40:4).

Paul worked hard to be a good example and let the brethren know that he was not acting or lying:

- "I am speaking the truth in Christ—I am not *lying;* my conscience bears me witness in the Holy Spirit" (Romans 9:1).
- "The God and Father of the Lord Jesus, he who is blessed forever, knows that I am not *lying*" (2 Corinthians 11:31).
- "[I]n what I am writing to you, before God, I do not *lie!*" (Galatians 1:20).

- "For this I was appointed a preacher and an apostle (I am telling the truth, I am not *lying*), a teacher of the Gentiles in faith and truth" (1 Timothy 2:7). *[Emphases added]*

We know that "acting out" in children and adults comes from deep inner Fears of, "I need attention. I do not feel Loved/valued." Fear powers all the lies and pretense we use to disguise our innermost hurt. Fear-driven insecurity and denial of Reality is at the core of every lie. *Lying is an attempt to control our Fear of the future.*

In acting school children learn:
- Life is a stage for gaining attention, giving put-downs, and manipulating the feelings of others.
- Be careful to rehearse deceit and deliver your lines/lies at the right time.
- Follow the popular script that pleases people. Never say what you feel.
- Special effects of facial expression and tone of voice can manipulate the feelings of your audience.
- "Exaggeration" is just fine.
- Withhold the "whole story."
- Sunday acting is very different than "home acting."
- Deflect unwanted questions with a question. When mom asks dad about his credit card debt, he asks, "What's for dinner?"
- Even "negative" attention is better than being ignored.
- Playing games is not just for children. It is the way of gaining power among adults.
- The Acting school graduation song begins, "Oh yes, I'm the great pretender . . ."[1]

Your acting school had different classes for different grades. When did you learn comedy, drama, adventure, and tragedy? What was the great conflict that you watched, rehearsed, and performed in the spotlight every day? Did you feel as if you were a stage puppet with few choices?

Pinocchio's growth from a naughty wooden puppet to a truth-telling sincere boy is legendary. Every time he told a lie, his nose grew long! While he would not have admitted it at the time, he had been given a great gift to be able to see that immediate nose growth (effect) from the lie (cause). Just like all of us, he had to grow up and learn to deal with his Thought storms of Fearful selfishness before they **resulted** in lies. We too get feedback on our lies. But like Pinocchio, the Fear-driven dishonesty is still there, **until we decide to give up acting and become Real.** "But the hour is coming, and is now here, when the true worshipers will worship the Father in spirit and truth, for the Father is seeking such people to worship him" (John 4:23).

"[A]s long as my breath is in me, and the spirit of God is in my nostrils, my lips will not speak falsehood, and my tongue will not utter deceit. Far be it from me to say that you are right; till I die I will not put away my integrity from me" (Job 27:3-5).

She dashes backstage and quickly pulls off her ball gown. The cat costume for the next act has a long tail which twists between her feet as she tries to pull it on. "Ok, change posture from diva to cat," she mumbles as she adds on the whiskers. "Feel the new character . . . must shine . . . I must be the best . . . the show needs me . . ." She scurries back onto the candlelit stage.

A COSTUME OF FEAR

In theatre productions, the moment a show is cast, actors immediately begin to fantasize about what lavish costumes they will wear to portray their character. They think, "What will I be dressed in to depict the hero, villain, brave rescuer, older wise woman, or drama queen?" In real life, we design costumes depending upon what roles we accept on the life stage. Some popular costumes:

VICTIM – I dress to gain attention and sympathy from others. I want people to feel sorry for me and pity me (Proverbs 19:22).

IMAGE MAKER – I wear the latest style and have a fast put down for anyone who does not. Image is everything (Proverbs 17:4).

SCHEMER – I can manipulate and control your feelings. I want you to think I am _____ and I have the power to do it (Proverbs 24:8).

PROJECTOR – I keep the spotlight on the lies and flaws of others. Here in the shadows, I look better in comparison to them (Matt. 7:3).

TECHNICIAN – I technically tell the truth—when asked, "No, I was not with James at 7:30." I lie by omission that I was there from 7:45-11 (1 Jn. 2:4).

SPECIAL EFFECTS – I use fog machines and strobe lighting to keep everything fuzzy. I am not sure about what was said or done (Proverbs 13:15).

RELIGIOSITY – In public, I am charming and never lose control. I am in the pew at all times, but scream at my family, blame them and lie to cover up my weakness (1 Jn. 4:20).

EXCUSES – I forget, "have to" be late, and always have things "happening to me." I really think only of me and feel everyone else can just wait (Proverbs 20:4).

SCENERY CAMOUFLAGE – I wear lots of disguises to keep from being found out. You won't recognize me as I don't even recognize myself (Psalm 26:4).

PERFECTIONIST – I have the perfect costume for every occasion and I want life to be clean and tidy. If I am in control, everything will be fine (Rom. 10:3).

"A false witness will not go unpunished, and he who breathes out lies will perish (Proverbs 19:9).

The great Liar will help you design a costume for any occasion or relationship. This pageantry can feel very daring and exciting. As long as you are in costume, you will be *protected* from anyone seeing who you really are and rejecting you. But every day that *you zip into a Fear costume*, you will also never *heal* or *grow*. Costumes help you *deny a Reality that you do not want to admit.* The purpose of costumes is to dress up as a character on the outside and *cover the hurt person on the inside.* Costumes, make-up, wigs, and scenery keep people from seeing exactly who you are—*one who is terrified of being "found out" and exposed* (Proverbs 9:6).

Angie and Tammy had worked all morning at the church building. They had scrubbed and laughed and had gotten to know each other better. When Angie's husband arrived around midday, he asked, "How is it going?" Angie's tone suddenly went dark, "Oh, we have worked *so* hard and it was *so* hot and now I am *so* exhausted." Tammy scratched her head and thought,

"Her ploy for attention is really—lying." *When we see someone else put on a costume—dishonesty is easy to spot.*

Lying disguises the truth to others, but worse yet, to ourselves. Some actors change their birth names to stage names, and then assume a character name for their role in the evening's play. No sacrifice is too great to ensure that *the desired image is created* in the mind of the audience. The danger is in living a real-life image that believes lying is ok in order to justify any outcome. "A lying tongue hates its victims, and a flattering mouth works ruin" (Proverbs 26:28).

Fear pressures us to lie in order to:
- protect ourselves from consequences
- benefit ourselves through "enhancing" bits of Reality
- gain sympathy by exaggerating Reality
- manipulate feelings by turning one person against another
- damage another to make ourselves look better
- control the outcomes because we think we know best

Lies tend to connect like scenes in a play. Lies are about control and underneath all control is Fear. The motive is usually the same, "I want you to *think* that I am better than I am because if you *knew* the Real me, you would not Love/respect/care about me." Once a life plot changes with a lie, it must be followed through and *managed*. Remember, *adults lie to control how they are viewed by others*. We lie to be more accepted, impress others, and elevate our image. WE WANT TO BE BETTER PEOPLE THAN WE ARE, BUT THAT IS TOO MUCH WORK. Lying is so much easier! "If we say we have no sin, we deceive ourselves, and the truth is not in us" (1 John 1:8).

A single lie has changed the course of many people's lives and human history. Take a moment and think about that. Whether it is a lie of omission (leaving out some facts) or a bold-faced lie, there is a consequence in every relationship/situation when lies are told. *Lying closes the thick stage curtains between people as it prevents trust and intimacy*—the major bonding cements of the family and the church. More importantly, there are *consequences deep within the liar every time we get away with dishonesty*. "A dishonest man spreads strife, and a whisperer separates close friends" (Proverbs 16:28).

Deep within all of us, there exists a struggle between a liar/ truth teller, fake/authentic, costumer/genuine person. Each time we "get away with" a lie, our Fear-filled *liar grows more powerful.* Instead of the lie comforting our Fear, it grows to *constantly seek control*, greater thrill, and applause for the lying action. Lies created to soothe, now inflame an itch for more lies. Lies are very powerful and *plans begun in deceit, do not succeed.* Second marriages that begin from adulterous relationships (lies) have miniscule chances of survival[2] (Psalm 21:11).

Most of us lie at work because we want our employers to think that we are busier or more industrious than we are. Personally, people lie about how much money they spend, how they use their time, and how many calories they eat. *Rehearse the fact that adults lie to control how they are viewed by others* (Psalm 140:2-3).

The *Journal of Basic and Applied Social Psychology* recently published a study that found "60 percent of people lied at least once during a 10-minute conversation and told an average of two or three lies." Even the researchers were surprised at how easily the average person lied![3]

Lawyers, investigators, and jury selection companies are very interested in the science of lying and body language. God designed us as all one piece and our bodies show our feelings (Ch. 6). However, no amount of special effects or change of outfits can clean out our hearts. Acknowledging our *costumes as obstacles to honesty,* is the first step in growing through them and living a constructive and peaceful life in Reality. *What would happen if we realized that every lie—was a lie before the Lord* (Acts 5:4). Would we stop rehearsing scripts and live genuine lives if we realized that He knows *everything* we say and do? (1 Timothy 2:3; Eph. 5:10).

GOD KNOWS EXACTLY WHAT HE IS DOING

Ananias and Sapphira came to understand God's authority in a split-second of time. This life is not a rehearsal for a play and scenes that are performed cannot be rewound or "taken back." *Words spoken will never return* (Proverbs 10:19).

God knows:

- *the real you*—every inch of your heart, body, and soul. He knows your thoughts, your intimate weaknesses and your goodness (1 Samuel 16:7).
- *your costumes*—as you prepare and design them to fulfill *your* agenda (Romans 16:18).
- *what was said/done and what you meant.* He knows your intentions and what you were *really feeling* when you made that comment (Mark 4:22).
- *who really wants to please Him* with their humble life, and who wants acclaim before an audience (2 Corinthians 7:1).
- *the standard for wearing the name Christian* is clear as are the limits of His forbearance (Rom. 2:3-5). He is fair and just. As you embrace that your reward is in Heaven, wrap you mind around this: God will exact his revenge on whom He judges (1 Pet. 4:5). This is not *your* job! Always remember, God cannot lie. "[I]t is impossible for God to lie" (Hebrews 6:18).

"For we must all appear before the judgment seat of Christ, so that each may receive what is due for what he has done in the body, whether good or evil" (2 Corinthians 5:10).

He delivered the line with just the right pause so that the audience erupted with laughter. The laughter fed his immense ego, and he flipped out his wrist with perfect timing. The Heroine waited for him to deliver her cue, but instead turned around to see him poised to make her trip and fall. Uproarious laughter from the crowd encouraged him to keep up the ad lib. The handmaiden poked her head through the set window to watch the scene, as the minstrel retreated across the stage. . . .

ENSEMBLE CAST – Cooperation vs. competition

An ensemble casts' goal is to work together. When one person takes the spotlight, the goal must still be for the *show* to succeed and have a great run. If an actor, through Fear-driven selfishness, looks to his own success instead of cooperation within the theater troupe—disaster is the end result for that evening's show.

God designed the church (His body—Eph. 1:22-23) to be a cooperative ensemble with a common Love, purpose to serve, and focus on the heavenly Treasure. The spiritual growth of each member ideally *fuels* the group's synergy. If all are submitting to Him and the Word, the teamwork is win-win against the great Liar. Barnabas and the others who gave of their money *inspired people* with their Love of the church (Acts 4:34-37). This same act of cooperation, however, aroused Fear-powered jealousy and competition within Ananias and Sapphira, who looked at their church family like warring siblings fighting for attention. (Do you remember those attitude lenses from Chapter 8?) "Wrath is cruel, anger is overwhelming, but who can stand before jealousy?" (Proverbs 27:4).

Fear-driven jealousy feels:

- I have no value and feel scared.
- I feel threatened by your goodness and honesty.
- I confirm this danger by comparing myself to everyone.

Reality check:

- The Lord gave His life for You.
- You are priceless and He Loves you.
- He compares you to *no one.*
- You are missing a lot of Joy by living life as a competition.

When you look at all humans as your enemies, you pour your energy into deceptive costume design. If I *feel* cast as the impoverished loser and *you* as the overpowering hero, I must compete with *you.* *In this Fear-filled competition, you will never know the synergy of Joy.* Organizations implode because the individual members do not recognize their own Fear-driven jealousy/dishonesty and grow to cooperate.

- Athletic teams lose because Fearful individuals cannot work together.
- Companies fold because slack workers do less work and want more pay.
- Congregations do not thrive because Fear causes division.
- Once faithful Christians invent new "faith groups" because they cannot submit their egos to the Lord, to His Word, or to each other in righteousness.

"If we live by the Spirit, let us also keep in step with the Spirit. Let us not become conceited, provoking one another, envying one another" (Gal. 5:25-26).

Becoming irritated by fellow humans in the church gives *you* a chance to grow! But too often, Fear-driven jealousy reigns and the great Liar smiles because we are *divided*. We should be an ensemble of sincere truth-lovers working *for* the Cause and *against* him! Yet he slithers among us and we speak *his lines* on stage. He pushes us to grab the credit and step into the center spotlight. Refresh your memory that our *actions* are our *thoughts* on the *outside*! If "attitude is everything," our Fear attitudes in: *playing games, petty irritations, and holding onto grudges keep us from growing closer to God by focusing on the weaknesses of others.* "A fool's lips walk into a fight, and his mouth invites a beating" (Proverbs 18:6).

The Lord designed the church to be team-builders just like those Philippians! (Ch. 4) It is disconcerting when Christians do not bond in Love/friendship with other Christians. Some slide into the pew on the Lord's day, grab some juice and bread, shake a few hands, and are itching to go, so they can "get on with their day" and meet their "friends" for barbecue (Proverbs 24:12).

Do you prefer the company of non-Christians? Can you "let your hair down" with them, and be "yourself?" Since the Lord observed your worship to Him, does He not see your afternoon "activities" with your "friends?" (1 Cor. 15:33). Are you remembering His ever-presence? Are you schooling yourself to enjoy the company of Christians? As you loosen your costumes, you may find others who are struggling with their Fears, flaws, and feelings of unworthiness, but are seeking to grow in obedience—just like you are (Psalm 26:3).

Barnabas' name appears 28 times in the New Testament, including in this Acts 4:34-37 story, where he exemplifies sacrificial giving. He is the beloved companion of Paul, Acts 11; leader for truth, Acts 13; and shines forth with the meaning of his nickname, "son of encouragement," Acts 15. But, even Barnabas had a "dark" moment recorded, when he succumbed to pressure and stepped back from the fellowship of Gentile Christians, in presence of the Jewish Christians. "And the rest of the Jews acted hypocritically along with him, so that even Barnabas was led astray by their hypocrisy" (Galatians 2:13).

Remember that one of the many proofs for divine inspiration of the Bible is that human *mistakes are recorded*! (Ch. 4) When you look at yourself and your brothers and sisters in Christ, as flawed, struggling humans who *make mistakes one day and do better the next*, you will criticize less and encourage more. This is living in Reality. "Not that we dare to classify or compare ourselves with some of those who are commending themselves. But when they measure themselves by one another and compare themselves with one another, they are without understanding" (2 Corinthians 10:12).

Bear in mind that the *passage of time does nothing to mature you.* Your character is being formed in your every response to Fear. If you do not grow through your rivalries and Fears, you will compete through your children's accomplishments and press them to become Broadway actors because of *your* failure in the third-grade play. You may spend your entire life pressured to fulfill some grandiose dream because deep inside you feel, "I will only be good enough if I am the star." Fear-powered insecurity will control you to be reactive and have a win-lose attitude, until you *admit your faults and see yourself and others as fellow sojourners on a one-way Journey.* "Therefore, confess your sins to one another and pray for one another, that you may be healed" (James 5:16).

The curtain rises on Tragedy when those who are supposed to "build each other up" are the cause of lose-lose warring within the body of the Lord (1 Thess. 5:11). *Are you lying because you are competitive and want to be the best?* If you are "doing good" in order to get star stickers on the Lord's chart, you are not in Love with the Lord. *It is your job to uplift your brothers and sisters, not be their rivals!* Think about it—GOD DID NOT CALL YOU TO GO SIT ALONE ON AN ABANDONED STAGE. ANYONE CAN CONTROL THEMSELVES—IF THEY NEVER INTERACT WITH OTHERS!! (John 13:34).

> As a 13 year-old boy, Muzafer Sherif watched soldiers enter his Turkish village and kill every adult male. He lived through Nazi imprisonment, escaped to America, and devoted his life to studying group aggression and leadership.[4] His 1954 study using healthy, middle-class, boy scouts at summer camp still stands as classic research. He found that boys who had never met, *bonded together when needing to accomplish challenging tasks.* They overcame physical and mental challenges and insecurities when having to *work together.* His classic research has been the foundation for team-building cooperation studies used for decades.[5]

Determine that you will not *compete* with other Christians, but rather *complete* them as we work together. God asks us imperfect humans to Love each other, teach each other, and care for each other. He created a team/ensemble that *gets* to grow by dealing with frustration! How else have you learned patience and compassion except by *having to exercise those virtues when working with others? Who do you think is going to be in Heaven with you?* (Acts 9:31).

Every lane was full at the Special Olympics celebration on that hot Saturday. Twelve special-needs runners waved to their families in the stand as their "coaches" stood by. The "pop" of the starting pistol sent them sprinting down the track as they had practiced numerous times before. After the curve, Alicia tripped and sprawled out, scraping her palms and knees. Just as her friend Elizabeth was about to step over the finish line, she swung her head back and saw Alicia starting to rise up off the track. With the loving heart of a young woman with Down's syndrome, she turned around without hesitation before crossing the line and ran back to her friend, lifting Alicia's arm over her own shoulder. "We win together," Elizabeth said, as they trotted toward the finish line to the shouts of the ecstatic crowd.

Pure-hearted Alicia and Elizabeth were true champions that day. The seemingly insurmountable obstacles of your labyrinth Journey are not meant to be faced alone. Reaching out to others with your transparent, flawed, struggling, inner self is the way of Joy. We hold hands at the final curtain and bow together! "Beloved, if God so loved us, we also ought to love one another. No one has ever seen God; if we love one another, God abides in us and his love is perfected in us" (1 John 4:11-12).

She races back to the dressing room, digging through the depths of her costume closet, "Where is it? Where is it?!" she screams as she digs through dozens of evening gowns hurling them to the ground. "I cannot believe this. I know that I gave it to you, and I am on in five minutes! How can this be happening to me!" Her assistant stands by, tearful, helpless, and cringing from her tirade. "I must have that shawl for the next scene or it will be a disaster. Where did you put it?" The Heroine opens her tapestry satchel at the bottom of the wardrobe to find the shawl that she put inside after dinner last night. As she rises up, she spots a small embroidered sign hung in the back of the wardrobe that she stitched decades ago as a young girl.

> *"But You Have Upheld Me Because Of My Integrity,*
> *And Set Me In Your Presence Forever" (Psalm 41:12).*

CLEANING YOUR COSTUME CLOSET

How scary would it be to throw your costumes away and stand in the presence of the Lord? If you cut all your old costumes into pieces, you would be left with a pile that would never be the same. What if you could start fresh, how would you dress yourself to interact with people? (Revelation 19:8).

After a live theater performance, the director sits down with the cast and gives them "notes" on what needs improvement. "The tempo was too slow, the butler was late with his entrance, and the Hero messed up the timing of his first line." It is great feedback for cast members who *want* to perform at their best.

Christians have several ways of accessing "notes" on their life performance. Interactions with other faithful Christians, studying the Word, and developing a large clear mirror to look at yourself are great tools. It may be in a backstage moment when you see yourself clearly, piled with costumes and wigs and make-up, that you realize, "I don't want to do this anymore. I want to be free." This is the first terrifying step on a Journey of Integrity and Joy. *Removing your wig, wiping off your stage make-up, and dropping your costume to the ground is the only way to let your spirit grow.* "[A]s he who called you is holy, you also be holy in all your conduct, since it is written, 'You shall be holy, for I am holy'" (1 Peter 1:15-16).

A married drama professor frequently used the term "integrity" with his college theater troupe. Each Sunday, he sat with his wife in the front row of the college church congregation. He used the term "integrity" as he coached his young actors about their study habits and learning their lines. He spoke of "integrity" regarding their timeliness in arriving for rehearsal and their grades. He had numerous adulterous affairs with young college girls. His credibility for teaching "integrity" was zero. If you *are* "what you repeatedly do," he was a man of low Integrity and a liar. Integrity is:

- speaking and behaving the truth
- being one piece—body and soul
- giving up costumes or image changes to control outcomes
- accepting Reality *even when it hurts*

- admitting your faults (All mentally solid people do this!)
- who you are, not who you *want* people to think you are

"Vindicate me, O LORD, for I have walked in my integrity, and I have trusted in the LORD without wavering" (Psalm 26:1).

"He stores up sound wisdom for the upright; he is a shield to those who walk in integrity" Proverbs 2:7.

Opening up your closet of costumes and facing them is one of the most powerful actions that you will ever take in your Christian life. Admitting that Psalm 41:12 is the truth, takes tremendous courage. Do you really want to be in God's presence forever? *Find your Integrity where you left it in the back of your closet.* Live before Him with Integrity. *Believe that lying will ruin your life.* Are you ready to shed the costumes that are your obstacles to intimacy with the Lord and the strongest tools of the great Liar? "Whoever gives an honest answer kisses the lips" (Proverbs 24:26).

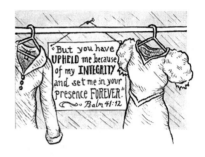

When you decide to clean your costume closet and bring your life into symmetry, expect an intense battle with the great Liar. "Show yourself in all respects to be a model of good works, and in your teaching show integrity, dignity, and sound speech that cannot be condemned, so that an opponent may be put to shame, having nothing evil to say about us" (Titus 2:7-8).

Rehearse these truths:

1. *JESUS WORE NO COSTUMES, PLAYED NO GAMES AND MANIPULATED NO ONE* – He was never "Il Divo" craving the spotlight. He had the true words of life and people followed Him to their deaths because of it (Acts 4:20). Jesus knew who He was. Even when He was rejected and spit on and beaten, He accepted that Reality. *If no one on the earth respected Him, He was not threatened.* He put one foot in front of the other fulfilling His Divine purpose. Jesus had respect in the eyes of His Father. How about you? (Hebrews 1:5).

2. *GET REAL ABOUT THE LIFE-CHANGING CONSEQUENCES OF DENYING* REALITY – Grasp how lies have powered wars/slavery/greed/

theft/adultery. Someone hated Reality and would *not* accept it. They taught that lie to others to get what *they* wanted. *Lying and acting change the course of lives and bring death* (Romans 1:25).

3. *GIVE UP THE BLAME SPOTLIGHT THAT YOU POINT ON OTHERS* – Life behind the spotlight in the dark backstage wings may feel safe, but there are no delights! Transcend your childhood "victim and blame" scenery that you keep repainting and repairing—that keeps reliving your pain (Matthew 7:3-5).

4. *REALIZE THAT YOUR BODY AND SPIRIT SIN TOGETHER* – We clearly see that the body/spirit sin in fornication, but your body bears the effects of lies. Like an actor that lives in two pieces, there are enduring results when you are not saying—doing—being who you really are. You are all one piece; and glorify or sin as such. Notice the ensemble of sinners that will accompany liars at the last judgment. "But as for the cowardly, the faithless, the detestable, as for murderers, the sexually immoral, sorcerers, idolaters, and all liars, their portion will be in the lake that burns with fire and sulfur which is the second death" (Revelation 21:8; 1 Timothy 1:8-11).

5. *ACCEPTANCE AND LOVE HEALS FEAR AND COMPETITION* – Like all of us, Barnabas grew up in acting school and had to learn how to take off his costumes and clothe himself in righteousness. Surely, he did not do that at the *same rate* Peter or Paul did. *Everyone has Fear-filled and selfish feelings*, and struggles with costumes! Admit that you are a fellow-struggler, not a superman or superwoman, and determine to *Love* your brethren. "As for that in the good soil, they are those who, hearing the word, hold it fast in an honest and good heart, and bear fruit with patience" (Luke 8:15).

6. *GOD COMPARES YOU TO NO ONE* – Your spirit and body were joined at conception for a one-way Journey and endowed with exquisite gifts of character. God never says, "Why aren't you like her?" Your Divine purpose—glorifying God manifests differently because *you are unparalleled.* You are not a mannequin to be dressed and painted nor a marionette being controlled by strings. You have complete *freedom* to serve!! (John 15:12-17). *The Joyful life of a Heroine-servant is not about astounding others with*

your greatness. It is about cleaning off that servant's tunic beneath your cloak of responsibility and being ready to serve Him. (Matthew 16:24).

> Vocal musician Bobby McFerrin regularly joins with a small group of singers to experiment using sounds and harmonics. A promoter approached him with an offer to go on a performing tour with this group of vocalists. He reasoned with the promoter that it might not be that entertaining for an audience to *watch* the singers experiment because they were building songs and improvising together. As they toured, the small group sat on the floor of the large stage weaving beautiful sounds together, but McFerrin was right, audiences were drowsy and irritated at the lack of "showmanship."

Honest lives are not as entertaining as acted and costumed ones. What if all the readers of this book got together, sat on the floor in our jeans, and shared our deepest Fears? Not very theatrical to watch—but very, very, Real.

"Do not lie to one another, seeing that you have put off the old self with its practices and have put on the new self, which is being renewed in knowledge after the image of its creator" (Colossians 3:9-10).

FEARBREAKER-JOYMAKER – *Conquer your inner actor*

> When a famous Hollywood actress found out her teenage son was on drugs, she cancelled her hit TV series and broke a contract for a movie she was to film that summer. She picked him up after school one day and drove straight to the airport, where they boarded a plane for Ireland. In an ancient stone cottage in rural Ireland, she spent the next six months alone with her son. There were no pretenses, distractions, excuses, or lies, just the two of them together—talking. The actress gave up everything to be Real with a child who was hurting, and it worked.

Do you ever clean out your closet and think, "Ok, I am never going to mess this up again!" Like any closet that we shove things into, life requires constant cleaning and maintenance. Maturity and honesty are with us one moment and gone the next, but the more regularly and deeply you clean, the easier it gets. Do you want to be less Fearful/jealous/insecure and more Joyfully resilient? Be more honest about what is going on inside you and your appetite for costumes will fade. "Create in me a clean heart, O God, and renew a right spirit within me" (Psalm 51:10).

When you fuse your outer person's actions with increased purity in your inner character, you gain freedom and lose desire to control Realities. Will you be the one to be honest and give up the lie—that there is Joy in anything but serving the Lord? *Stop playing the Heroine and be one*! Notice how fundamental giving up lying is to our godliness.

> [T]o put off your old self, which belongs to your former manner of life and is corrupt through deceitful desires, and to be renewed in the spirit of your minds, and to put on the new self, created after the likeness of God in true righteousness and holiness. Therefore, having put away falsehood, let each one of your speak the truth with his neighbor, for we are members one of another. Be angry and do not sin; do not let the sun go down on your anger, and give no opportunity to the devil (Ephesians 4:22-27).

Rehearse these strategies:

1. *MIRRORS SHOW TRUTH* – Look into your big, clean, spiritual mirror each day and examine the divided truth-teller/liar inside. Look deep with compassion at the Fear reason *why* you lied and take responsibility: "I want him to think that I am better than I am." Genuine repentance before the Lord is liberating! As you learn to use your "space" preceding the "acting," you can stop the lie before it comes out. "Seek the Lord and his strength and; seek his presence continually!" (Psalm 105:4).

2. *FALLING IN LOVE WITH THE MAP WILL CHANGE YOUR LIFE* – Honestly search for a Bible example for any Fear/weakness you are facing. After the death of Ananias and Sapphira, the church *grew* from this lesson about the consequences of deceit (Acts 5:11-14). "I have stored up your word in my heart, that I might not sin against you" (Psalm 119:11).

3. *KNOW YOUR ANTAGONIST* – When you hear special effects Thought storms rustling in your "negative" brain, speak aloud, "These are *my* thoughts and I will not be filled with Fear." Now fill your Thoughts with powerfully *positive* scriptures—instead of the criticisms you are ruminating about others or the lie that you are hatching. *Remember that every lie is a lie before God* (Acts 5:4). The great Liar cannot force you to live for earthly applause in lieu of eternal glory. Stop reading Satan's teleprompter and speak the Word of God (2 Corinthians 11:14).

4. *WHO ARE YOU HONORED TO STAND BESIDE IN THE SERVICE OF THE LORD?* Who is honored to stand beside *you*? Paul wrote, "Be imitators

of me as I am of Christ" (1 Cor. 11:1). Could you be a close friend to the apostle Paul? Barnabas? Authentic relationships are constructed "sitting on the floor in your jeans"—speaking the truth. Ball gowns, wigs, and long white gloves can be fun for a moment, but they are heavy, hot, and make you trip and fall. When you honestly share your Fears without judgment, you realize that we all "put our pants on one leg at a time" (Ephesians 5:1).

Continually pray for the dishonest people in your life as Jesus taught, "Love your enemies and pray for those who persecute you" (Matthew 5:44). *BE the kind of person you want THEM to be.* Sapphira was not killed for her husband's lie. She was killed for hers. "[S]peaking the truth in love, we are to grow up in every way into him who is the head, into Christ (Eph. 4:15).

5. *STOP DENYING REALITY—LIVE IT!* Right now today, accept your life. If beneath your lies is a hatred of Reality, then accepting Reality will drain the desire to lie! Write on your bathroom mirror: IN EVERY MOMENT YOU MAKE A CHOICE BETWEEN WHAT IS EASY AND WHAT IS RIGHT. "And you will know the truth and the truth will set you free" (John 8:32).

Great actors train to evoke scripted emotion in their audience. Are you Reality training to be more genuine and honest by asking tough questions? (1 Timothy 4:6-8).

- Is this pleasing to the Lord? (Psalm 104:34; Eph. 5:10; Col. 1:10)
- Want respect? Be respectable. (1 Peter 3:15)

Abraham Lincoln wrote, "Character is like a tree and reputation like a shadow. The shadow is what we think of it; the tree is the real thing." Be a beautiful truthful tree!

6. *"POSITIVE" BRAINS ARE NURTURED IN GRATITUDE FOR REALITY –* When you rehearse the times that you tell the truth, those neural pathways get stronger. "Good job, you told the *whole* truth about that." "Surely the righteous shall give thanks to your name; the upright shall dwell in your presence" (Psalm 140:13).

In the dark backstage wings of the theatre, the only glow is the EXIT sign over the door. Follow that glow and exit the theatre and step out into the sunlight of Reality. Your life was designed to be a Journey of Integrity and Love and *not until the Treasure will there be genuine applause and a happy ending.*

GROWING THROUGH FEAR

1. Think of a lie that changed the course of history. How did someone hate their Reality and sought to manipulate/change it? When have you told a lie that changed the course of events?

2. As you learn that every lie is a lie before the Lord, how would a morning prayer meditation about God's presence help you in the temptation to lie?

3. How can you better use your "space" (Ch. 8) to pause and pray—checking that you do not lie/exaggerate? (Hint: rehearse the positives)

4. Remember that Ananias and Sapphira agreed together to do this lie and while that may be cooperation, it was Fear-driven sin. What relationship do you have that encourages you to lie? To be a faithful Christian?

~ 13 ~
The Heroine's Rescue
The Fear of death
Paul's last words to Timothy (2 Timothy 1:3-14)

*M*edieval castles were built with towers of refuge called castle keeps. This chamber was the stronghold sanctuary for the nobility if an adversary should overtake the castle. Because of the importance to protection, the keep's fortification, design, and construction were integral to a castle's prestige and security. It was the desperation vault: the safest place on earth, the historical panic room.

Her time within the castle has been filled with sorrows and Joys. There has always been much to explore and learn and many interesting people. Invaders and barbarians have tried to battle their way into the fortress at times in the past, but the Heroine has been safe inside the castle. This latest siege is intense and she awakens to the sound of shouting. Grabbing her cloak, she runs through the passageway and climbs the spiral staircase into the castle keep. Bolting the door behind her, she slumps to the ground and whispers, "Is this the end?"

I thank God whom I serve, as did my ancestors, with a clear conscience, as I remember you constantly in my prayers night and day. As I remember your tears, I long to see you, that I may be filled with joy. I am reminded of your sincere faith, a faith that dwelt first in your grandmother Lois and your mother Eunice and now, I am sure, dwells in you as well. For this reason I remind you to fan into flame the gift of God, which is in you through the laying on of my hands, *for God gave us a spirit not of fear but of power and love and self-control.*

Therefore do not be ashamed of the testimony about our Lord, nor of me his prisoner, but share in suffering for the gospel by the power of God, who saved us and called us to a holy calling, not because of our works but because of his own purpose and grace, which he gave us *in Christ Jesus* before the ages began, and which now has been manifested through the appearing of our Savior Christ Jesus, who abolished death and brought life and immortality to light through the gospel, for which I was appointed a preacher and apostle and teacher, which is *why I suffer* as I do. *But I am not ashamed, for I know whom I have believed, and I am convinced that he is able to guard until that Day what has been entrusted to me.* Follow the pattern of the sound words that you have heard from me, in the faith and love that are in Christ Jesus. By the Holy Spirit who dwells within us, guard the good deposit entrusted to you (2 Timothy 1:3-14). *[Emphases added]*

PAUL'S EARTHLY JOURNEY COMES TO AN END

It was a hot afternoon in Rome when Renee and I sat down on the walkway above the Mamertine prison and read 2 Timothy quietly aloud together. No one was around as we sat atop the air vents and could feel the cold, mildewy air coming from the cistern-turned-prison cell where it is likely that Paul spent his last few days. Tears filled our eyes as we read, "[F]or God gave us a spirit not of fear, but of power and love and self-control" (2 Timothy 1:7).

Paul would have walked the few yards from the Senate Curia to the Mamertine prison in chains, after his sentence was pronounced before Caesar and the senators. High profile "criminals," such as Paul and later Peter, awaited their executions in the Mamertine's damp cells. Prisoners were lowered on a rope through an opening in the floor of the upper chamber down into the lower cistern cell, 12 feet below ground level. Conditions were so brutal and unsanitary that most died long before execution (Acts 18:9; Acts 27:24).

Paul was familiar with prisons, having been incarcerated many times from Judea to Philippi, and now for a second time in Rome. The letters of Ephesians, Philippians, Colossians, Philemon, and now 2 Timothy were all written from confinements. He had chosen a servant's life as one of the most thoroughly Christ-focused workers of the early church. And in teaching the gospel, he suffered beatings, stonings, shipwrecks, hunger, and rejection (2 Corinthians 6:3-5, 11:23-28). Paul knew the *truth* and he had to share the gospel of Jesus. *Whatever resulted from doing that—was not in his hands.*

His heart bore constant concern that faithful Christians would turn away. "For this reason, when I could bear it no longer, I sent to learn about your faith, for fear that somehow the tempter had tempted you and our labor would be in vain" (1 Thessalonians 3:5). In Philippi Paul had watched the prison doors swing open (Acts 16:26), but many other times known the Lord's Loving presence comforting him—when his cell remained locked for a purpose (Acts 23:11; 2 Tim. 4:17; Col. 4:18; Eph. 6:20). Knowing the executioners block awaited him shortly, *he did not write with self-pity*, but of courage and steadfast hope, to a young Timothy—who was ready to hear it.

To whom would you send the last message of your life? As the flames and smoke of the World Trade Center choked him from below, a young man called home to leave a message on his mother's answering machine, "Mom, I love you, no matter what else, remember the love."

Paul wanted Timothy to focus on developing endurance for the Journey ahead, and forewarns him against a "spirit of fear" that would besiege his courage. The valorous traits of "power and love and self-control" will be required to *generate this great durability for Christian living and dying* (2 Timothy 1:7). God provides for us:

- power/strength to rise to the occasion and meet suffering head on (Rom. 5:3).
- Love from Jesus Christ who stepped in and sacrificed Himself for you (1 Jn. 4:18).
- self-control to be master of our Fears as we allow ourselves to be mastered by the Lord (Rom. 8:31-39).

As Paul's one-way Journey to the Treasure was about to transition, he knew his last investment was to Lovingly empower his beloved brother-in-Christ. Paul's final words to young Timothy were to point him to the strength within Jesus and arm him for the attacks to come, so that he would not be afraid. Paul knew *who* he believed in and that Jesus' eternal promises *could not fail*. "But I am not ashamed, for I know whom I have believed, and I am convinced that he is able to guard until that Day what has been entrusted to me" (2 Timothy 1:12).

JESUS – A death with meaning

The ultimate Fear of the unknown resides in our Fear of death. Jesus knew that Fear and explained, "Let not your hearts be troubled. Believe in God; believe also in me. In my Father's house are many rooms. If it were not so, would I have told you that I go to prepare a place for you? And if I go and prepare a place for you, I will come again and will take you to myself, that where I am you may be also" (John 14:1-3).

In Christ's dying sacrifice:

- His pure, sinless blood made our salvation possible (Eph. 1:7; 1 Peter 1:18-19)
- He was rejected by the very people He came to save (Luke 9:22; Acts 4:11)
- He accepted every filth and sin ever committed (1 Pet. 2:24)
- He could have lifted himself off the cross, but He chose to endure (Gal. 1:4)
- He brought us to God—by taking our punishment (1 Peter 3:18)
- He gave himself for His Cause—His eternal kingdom—His body—His church (Colossians 1:15-20)

When you feel the Fear of death, ask yourself this question: If Jesus' death was foretold, timed, and executed at the exact moment the Godhead planned for *your* salvation, do you think they are unconcerned with *your* dying? (Galatians 2:20).

Reading the story of Elijah being taken up to Heaven in a chariot of fire, we might think, "Oh yes, that would be a great way to go!" (2 Kings 2:11). Elijah's departure was a miracle designed for *God's* purpose. But all of *us* will die. Some will die quickly, and some very slowly. Often, we question God and beg Him to keep us from suffering. God's Loving compassion pours freely on His children when we suffer in righteousness, but we all must face the Reality that suffering is the result of sin (1 Peter 3:14).

Satan, the great Tormentor, brought *suffering* into this world when Adam and Eve fell to sin (Rom. 5:12; 2 Cor. 11:3). Summon up in your mind that he lied to Eve that disobeying would *cause death*. "But the serpent said to the woman, 'You will not surely die'" (Gen. 3:4). Jesus' *agonizing* death and redemption were necessary because of that human sin. Satan hates Jesus. Satan hates humans and wants us to join him in *eternal torture—a place devoid of Love or Joy* (John 8:44).

Suffering can have great purpose. Jesus' death in anguish and torment, paid Adam's and *your* sentence and *purchased your eternal freedom with that high price*. God knows how hard it is for us to suffer, as it was hard for Jesus to face what was ahead. "My Father, if it be possible, let this cup pass from me; nevertheless, not as I will, but as you will" (Matt. 26:39).

Meditate on this: If a pain free death (or life) is *the* evidence of God's Love, why did Jesus have to suffer so terribly? (Hebrews 2:9, 5:8).

THERE ARE ALWAYS CHOICES

Abbie's mom died on a Tuesday morning. She stood in the doorway of her mother's bedroom as the funeral director opened the huge white shroud on the bed. She had used the word "shroud" in her adult life, but had never seen one, until now. The man rolled her mother's tall, slender body onto the pure white cotton and wrapped her round and round like a swaddled newborn baby.

Abbie loved her mother very much. Her mother had taught her to quilt and sew at a very young age and that bond had always been their greatest happiness together. A decade earlier, Abbie's mom had watched her beloved husband "waste away" from a painful cancer that ravaged his body and mind. The strain had taken its toll on her mom, Abbie, and her brothers. Her brothers argued bitterly over their dad's care and spoke deeply hurtful words to each other, causing wounds that festered to the present day.

Fearing pain and abhorring becoming dependent on others. Abbie's mom determined that she would not be debilitated and suffer in death. Exercising her right to control, she pre-planned a "death with dignity" pact in accordance with Montana's state law. Years earlier, she had quizzed her family doctor to make sure that he would be willing to prescribe the legal, lethal dosage, "when the time came."

Knowing Abbie's feelings about the Lord's right to choose our time of death, her mom enlisted the help of her niece for the paperwork and support, "when the time came." Her mother always reminded Abbie and her brothers that, "God would not want anyone to suffer."

When her mother's cancer diagnosis was confirmed, Abbie took an extended leave from her secretarial job and reassured her mother that she would "be there every moment to take care of her." But, after a wonderful evening with the family, her mom took the legal, massive dose of phenobarbitol at bedtime, and ended her life. She saw no purpose in a dying process and chose to control it. Trying to protect Abbie's feelings, her cousin lied about giving her mom the pill and said, "She must have just decided to stop living." But, overhearing a conversation, Abbie learned the truth.

At the graveside service a few days later, Abbie almost bit a hole through her lip as person after person commented how her mom had "died so suddenly" and they "wished they could have said good-bye." Abbie put on her smiling face and comforted others, but kept thinking, "If this is supposed to be 'death with dignity,' why are there so many lies?"

Weeks later, while cooking dinner one night, Abbie's thoughts were storming as she tried to process her mother's death and decisions. As tears streamed down her face, she knelt down on the kitchen floor and said, "Lord, I surrender to you the exact moment of my death. I trust you who are in charge of the universe, to be in charge of the moment that I die. If the Lord Jesus' voluntary saving of me was accomplished in His suffering and dying, then He will hold my hand when it comes my turn to do so." "Then Jesus, calling out with a loud voice, said, 'Father, into your hands I commit my spirit'" (Luke 23:46).

A HOME PREPARED FOR YOU
"Paul, an apostle of Christ Jesus by the will of God according to the *promise* of the life that is in Christ Jesus" (2 Timothy 1:1). *[Emphasis added]*

> The mini-bus had travelled six hours from the far region of Hunan province. On board, were fifteen precious Chinese baby girls and their nannies. The toddler orphans had never known life outside of the orphanage nursery. They had been shown photos of their new mommies, daddies, and houses, but could not conceive of what a beautiful home filled with toys might be like. "What would the loving arms of a mother reading stories feel like? What does a cheerful grandfather's voice tenderly teaching me to water tomatoes or gather eggs from a chicken sound like?" Their minds could not conceive of this world that awaited them, for they had only been *promised it*.

The baby girl orphans did not know or comprehend it, but they were going to a home that had been *prepared just for them*. We read the promises and can paint pictures from the scriptures, but like the orphan babies, we have no point of reference for the glories that lie ahead. Filled with Fear of the unknown, the baby girls cry to leave their nannies and cribs. Yet we can see from the outside how much better their lives will be. If they could envision the future Joys, they would gladly leave that orphanage.

Would you want to live in an orphanage forever? Ask yourself this question, "Would you really want to live forever on this earth?" What if everyone else passed through life's seasons and grew old and died and you remained here forever? Worse yet, imagine if new people were born, but no one ever died! Think of what it would be like to have Julius Caesar, Napoleon, and Adolf Hitler living at the same time. Even if all the good people remained alive, *it would not make sense*. What if Moses, Isaiah, and John the Baptist were all delivering their messages simultaneously? What would be the point of it all? This earthly section is just part of the one-way Journey where we "take turns" being here, learning, and making choices for our eternity. It is not a permanent home.

The Tormentor, who hates you, wants your soul for his side. He does not want you to go to your Treasure home and will relentlessly pursue you, as long as you dwell on this planet. Like the woman in a movie who is pursued down every corridor by a murderer, but whichever way she chooses—he appears in that doorway. *On this earthly side, you are Satan's prey, and you will never be free of him in this world.*

Spend a moment in your "negative" brain and list all the ways Satan torments you *every day*. Thought storms, self-centeredness, dishonesty, using "consolers," and constantly having to be on the defensive to his temptation invaders start the list (1 Chron. 21:1; Job 1:6-12, 2:1-10). In eternal terror with Satan, he never allows a split-second of Love or peace (Matt. 25:46; 2 Thess. 1:9). Stop for a moment, and give thanks to God that you can choose a life Journey toward Paradise and then into Heaven, where *the Tormentor will have no power or influence*!!! Eternal life with the Lord means eternal life *away* from Satan. "The God of peace will soon crush Satan under your feet. The grace of our Lord Jesus Christ be with you" (Romans 16:20). "[S]o that we would not be outwitted by Satan; for we are not ignorant of his designs" (2 Cor. 2:11).

"But as it is, they desire a better country, that is, a heavenly one. Therefore God is not ashamed to be called their God, for he has prepared for them a city" (Hebrews 11:16).

The spirit that the Lord created in you at conception dwells in your physical vessel for the earthly Journey. But when your earthly heart pumps its last, and your physical body begins its decay, your spirit will step across the veil into eternity. The touch of the heavenly Father's hand will still any Fear or loneliness within you. In the resurrection moment when you are united with your new spiritual body, *your belonging will be complete. Immortal spirit united within spiritual body dwelling at home.* The oneness of your sprit with its spiritual body is a Joy that you cannot fathom as you exist now (1 Cor. 15:44). You will be perfectly Loved and perfectly cared for, with no more aches or trials, in the arms of your Father forever. In the Treasure of Heaven you will:

- receive a glorious spiritual body (Philippians 3:20-21)
- live where God's will reigns (Matthew 6:10)
- have an end to all suffering (2 Thessalonians 1:5-12)
- know the end of earthly labor (Revelation 14:13)
- get to serve the Lord (Revelation 7:15)
- dwell with the faithful (Matthew 8:11)
- stand before God's throne (Acts 7:49)
- be perfectly Joy-filled in His presence (Revelation 7:17, 21:4)
- see the glorious Heaven—prepared for you (John 14:3)

Do you *want* to live forever in Heaven? Do you think that God is *lying* about how wonderful your new home is? Are you willing to *live* obediently to receive this reward? (Acts 2:38). Do you *believe* God will raise you up immortal?

> For we know that if the tent that is our earthly home is destroyed, we have a building from God, a house not made with hands, eternal in the heavens. For in this tent we groan, longing to put on our heavenly dwelling, if indeed by putting it on we may not be found naked. For while we are still in this tent, we groan, being burdened—not that we would be unclothed, but that we would be further clothed, so that what is mortal may be swallowed up by life. He who has prepared us for this very thing is God, who has given us the Spirit as a guarantee. So we are always of good courage. We know that while we are at home in the body we are away from the Lord, for we walk by faith, not by sight. Yes, we are of good courage, and we would rather be away from the body and at home with the Lord. So whether we are at home or away, we make it our aim to please him. For we must all appear before the judgment seat of Christ, so that each one may receive what is due for what he has done in the body, whether good or evil (2 Corinthians 5:1-10).

"How could there be anything better than life within the castle?" she wonders as she gazes out of the small window in the keep. Her life inside is surrounded by lovely tapestries, beautiful pillows, and cheerful music. The castle has delicious food and warm beds, and all of her friends dwell here. She thinks, "There is such peace and security within the manor and the towers. What could be better than being a castle-dweller?"

STAY THE COURSE

You are the daughter of humans by your natural birth, but the Lord's daughter-servant by choice, by oath, and by wearing the cloak of responsibility. A Heroine-servant labors under the protection of a King who has no equal in the Universe. If the *Epic Movie of the World-Part II* were shown *without* your life in it, what would be different? Would the movie have less courage and less honor given to the Cause without you? "But God's firm foundation stands, bearing this seal: 'The Lord knows those who are his,' and, 'Let everyone who names the name of the Lord depart from iniquity'" (2 Timothy 2:19).

Medieval knights wore a tightly woven tunic of pure silk, underneath their heavy armor. The silk fabric was so strong that it held up to the harsh, abrasive metal, but was soft against their skin. It is the dual nature of *courage* and *humility*, like silk, that gives Heroine-servants the Joyful resilience for the Journey. Heroine's have two feet and two hands but only one—one-way life to live. *A Heroine-servant is formed, when her willing spirit puts on the cloak of responsibility and picks up the banner of Christ.*

At times your Journey feels like a constant battle and you stamp your foot and say, "This is too hard, I don't want to do this!" and drag your cloak in the mud. Understanding that there is Courage and Fear in each of us, the merciful Sovereign forgives your weakness, and says, "Even when you have dragged your cloak of responsibility, I will throw mine over you as we walk, and keep you safe, right here by my side." He gently reminds, *"You are not alone. You are not lost. I am beside you in every breath and movement."*

In tearful humility, the Heroine-servant submits and bows down to give thanks for her role in the fight for the Cause. With an obedient heart, she says, "I will stay the course of this Journey and prepare myself for what is to come." "For I am sure that neither death nor life, nor angels nor rulers, nor things present nor things to come, nor powers, nor height nor depth, nor anything else in all creation, will be able to separate us from the love of God in Christ Jesus our Lord" (Romans 8:38-39).

"Indeed, all who desire to live a godly life in Christ Jesus will be persecuted" (2 Timothy 3:12).

"Perhaps I can find a trapdoor for escape," she thinks, *as she pries at the stone flooring. For many days she has watched the guards march and drill throughout the courtyards, preparing for siege. The Heroine daydreams legions of rescuing forces appearing on the horizon. She imagines the guards dropping ropes from above and rappelling down to rescue her, or an alliance storming the castle and overpowering the barbarians. But as the sun begins to set, all she sees in the distance are fires.*

PREPARE – The passage is temporary—the destination eternal

Of the many things you prepare for in life such as holiday occasions, vacations, and retirement, "prepare for the moment of death" is not likely to be listed. Fear of death is lessened, if you will Joyfully anticipate your one-way Journey into the next world. The Reality is, *you are terminal*. Stand at the moment of your death and imagine it. With new enlightenment, begin preparing yourself *now* for letting go of life in this castle (Psalm 91:2).

Prepare for:

- where you are *going* in the next phase of this one-way Journey. Are you qualified for entrance into the heavenly Kingdom?
- what you will *leave behind*. Is your breath spent leaving a legacy within others that points them to that Treasure?

I will leave behind a rocking chair that traveled with my great, great grandmother, Mary Chesebro, on a covered wagon to homestead in Michigan after the Civil War. Deep within my cedar chest, I keep intricately-pieced quilts, stitched by my great, great aunts in the 19th century. While I treasure these heirlooms, they will one day burn up with fervent heat (2 Peter 3:12).

Paul leaves behind him—a letter to Timothy. Tapestry threads of a relationship woven through decades of loving effort. Paul's last, tender, pen strokes implore Timothy to prepare himself to serve the Lord with all passion and fidelity, after Paul has stepped through the window into the arms of Jesus.

1. *PREPARE TO SUFFER:* Admit that you are afraid of pain, weakness, and the oppressive Fear of death. Tell the Lord your Fears, but realize that

suffering is part of your one-way Journey. If you have used Fear-driven control to *calm* your life's anxieties, accepting that you are *powerless in the moment of death* may be a difficult passageway for you.

Accepting that pain is part of, godly life and death—is Reality. Fighting this truth breeds Fear. *Humbly surrendering to suffering is a huge challenge.* He knows exactly how much you can take and His tender-loving, compassionate arms are with you, in every gasp and cough and struggle. *When your Fear of the unknown is the heaviest, embrace that you are intimately known by the God who created you.* Your deepest character is formed in your attitude, as you respond to suffering (2 Timothy 1:7; Romans 5:3).

Remind yourself that if a painless death, timed for convenience and no suffering were a yardstick of God's Love—how is it that Jesus suffered the loneliest, most painful and rejected death that has ever occurred? His great Love and great suffering had great purpose! As you are hurting, remember: There is only one Sovereign Lord who rules the world and He gave His life just for you (Psalm 103:19).

"[W]hich is why I *suffer* as I do. But I am not ashamed, for I know whom I have believed, and I am convinced that he is able to guard until that Day what has been entrusted to me" (2 Timothy 1:12).

"Therefore do not be ashamed of the testimony about our Lord, nor of me his prisoner, but share in *suffering* for the gospel by the power of God" (2 Timothy 1:8).

"Share in *suffering* as a good soldier of Christ Jesus" (2 Timothy 2:3).

"[F]or which I am *suffering*, bound with chains as a criminal, but the word of God is not bound!" (2 Timothy 2:9).

"[M]y persecutions and *sufferings* that happened to me at Antioch, at Iconium, and at Lystra—which persecutions I endured; yet from them all the Lord rescued me" (2 Timothy 3:11).

"As for you, always be sober-minded, endure *suffering*, do the work of an evangelist, fulfill your ministry" (2 Timothy 4:5). *[Emphases added]*

2. *PREPARE BY KNOWING HIS WORD:* Every weapon is made from materials mined from the earth, *except* the sword of the spirit—the Word of God (Eph. 6:17; Heb. 4:12). After every piece of paper is burned, the Word and the kingdom it reflects—will live on. The Bible Map has every answer for what lies ahead and a detailed autobiography of our Sovereign King who *has no equal, and can never be conquered.* The true Lord cradles *you* for the safe crossing into Paradise.

> During the 9/11 disaster, in seeking to make the best decision, some groups of office workers voted together whether to go to the roof or take the stairs below. Would you trust your eternal destiny to someone else's judgment or a vote? If you do not know what His Word says, you might follow anyone. While it is a Fearsome thing to leave this castle world, as you open the wisdom vaults within the Word of God, the explanations of His Loving sacrifice, one baptism and one church are revealed (Eph. 1:22; 4:4-5). He drops *His Loving hands* down to you and says, "trust in me and I will always care for you."

"[B]ut the *word* of God is not bound!" (2 Timothy 2:9)

"[H]ow from childhood you have been acquainted with the *sacred writings*, which are able to make you wise for salvation through faith in Christ Jesus. All *Scripture* is breathed out by God and profitable for teaching, for reproof, for correction, and for training in righteousness, that the man of God may be competent, equipped for every good work" (2 Timothy 3:15-17).

"I charge you in the presence of God and of Christ Jesus, who is to judge the living and the dead, and by his appearing and his kingdom: *preach the word*; be ready in season and out of season; reprove, rebuke and exhort, with complete patience and teaching" (2 Timothy 4:1-2). *[Emphases added]*

3. *PREPARE TO BE A WORKER:* When you wrap your mind around *your* Divine purpose being vital to the Cause of Christ, your living and dying will flow into one. Paul shared his feelings with the Philippians: "[A]s it is my eager expectation and hope that I will not be at all ashamed, but that with full courage now as always Christ will be honored in my body,

whether by life or by death. For to me to live is Christ, and to die is gain" (Phil. 1:20-21).

If your unique precious heart beats in order to serve the Lord, and He needs you to serve Him tomorrow with your dying, are you ready? If in the dying process, there is Divine purpose in your gradually unlearning the skills of childhood, and becoming helpless as if you were newly born, are you willing? Jesus' *death* served *us* by providing the sinless blood sacrifice. Have you thought how *your dying* could serve the Cause?

In desiring to lessen your Fear and give meaning to your death, look now to oxygenate every cell of your precious *life* with meaning, and spend your breath on things eternal. *Connect your life's work—with where you want to be at life's end*. When He leaves a door ajar for you, are you grasping the handle and confidently walking through it? Is your life a Joyful Journey in His presence? What if you die as you work for the Sovereign? Bow down and say, "Lord you know *who I am* and *where I am* in life, show me how to *live* and *die* for you."

"Do your best to present yourself to God as one approved, a *worker* who has no need to be ashamed, rightly handling the word of truth" (2 Timothy 2:15).

"[T]hat the man of God may be competent, equipped for every good *work*" (2 Timothy 3:17).

"As for you, always be sober-minded, endure suffering, do the *work* of an evangelist, fulfill your ministry" (2 Timothy 4:5). *[Emphases added]*

4. *PREPARE YOURSELF TO BE COURAGEOUS:* If you were lost in the woods, how hard would you fight to get home? Would you walk all night and climb mountains and cross rivers? Whose face would you keep in your mind to motivate you? When your feet were cut open and bleeding, would you then crawl on your hands and knees to get there? You will need that level of courage to surmount the bridge that is ahead. Trace back to the insight that endurance is built by small muscle tears that get strengthened through exercise. *You will not become a Heroine at the last moment if you have not trained yourself in valor and tenacity.*

    When you look into a Thought storm of Fear and say, "I will NOT be controlled by you," you have grown in courage. *Courage is the summit of*

devotion, purpose, tenacity, and Love in action. Moral and spiritual cour-
age is only developed because of an unyielding and relentless focus on the
goal of "Is this pleasing to the Lord?" (Eph. 5:10).

"[B]e *strengthened* by the grace that is in Christ Jesus" (2 Timothy 2:1).

" If we *endure,* we will also reign with him; if we deny him, he also will deny
us" (2 Tim. 2:12).

"But the Lord stood by me and *strengthened* me, so that through me the message might be fully proclaimed and all the Gentiles might hear it" (2 Timothy
4:17). *[Emphases added]*

5. *PREPARE BY KEEPING YOUR PASSIONS UNDER CONTROL*: As Fear
    powers you to reach out for some *thing* as a consoler, you must protect
    yourself from these arrows of the Tormentor. Worldliness, Fear-filled
    ego, and unforgiveness are like barbarians beating down your doors. If
    you are to withstand the Tormentor, you cannot be innocent of his ways
    (2 Cor. 2:11).

    As you deal with predators and consolers, look for the lessons the
    Lord is offering. *Live in Reality about what weakens and strengthens you*
    as a Christian. Your personal holiness is *that* important to the Cause!

"So flee *youthful passions* and pursue righteousness, faith, love, and peace,
along with those who call on the Lord from a pure heart" (2 Timothy 2:22).

"But God's firm foundation stands, bearing this seal: 'The Lord knows those
who are his,' and, 'Let everyone who names the name of the Lord depart from
iniquity'" (2 Timothy 2:19).

"For people will be *lovers of self, lovers of money, proud, arrogant*, abusive,
disobedient to their parents, ungrateful, unholy, heartless, unappeasable,
slanderous, without self-control, brutal, not loving good, treacherous, reckless, swollen with conceit, lovers of pleasure rather than lovers of God, having the appearance of godliness, but denying its power. Avoid such people"
(2 Timothy 3:2-5).

"For the time is coming when people will not endure sound teaching, but having itching ears they will accumulate for themselves teachers to suit their own *passions*" (2 Timothy 4:3). *[Emphases added]*

6. *PREPARE BY BUILDING AN EXCITEMENT ABOUT HEAVEN:* Read, learn, and recite what you know about the Treasure! You will lessen your Fear of dying as you learn the truth, and *yearn for Heaven*. Your Fear-filled anxiety heightens when you do not know *where* your eternal spirit is going on this next leg of the Journey. Say this every day, "My eternal spirit *gets* to go to Heaven!" Heaven is a sanctuary of God's presence and we will dwell in His eternal glory (Romans 8:11).

Loving energy is recharged within you as you give thanks for God's incredible blessings here and in the great Treasure! The earthly Joys of godly friendships, beauty, encouragement, and worship remind us of what Joys await us in Heaven. When you hold His providing hand of Love, the security of knowing that He is in charge—brings peace. *Even when the siege is at its worst and your death is imminent, focus on His goodness in allowing you to come over into eternal glory.* He has prepared this place for *you and His great Love is the only motive for this gift.*

"[W]hich now has been manifested through the appearing of our Savior Christ Jesus, who abolished death and brought life and immortality to light through the gospel" (2 Timothy 1:10).

"Therefore I endure everything for the sake of the elect, that they also may obtain the salvation that is in Christ Jesus with *eternal glory*" (2 Timothy 2:10). *[Emphases added]*

THE SIEGE OF DEATH – *Safe crossing*
"And this is the testimony, that God gave us eternal life, and this life is in his Son. Whoever has the Son has life; whoever does not have the Son of God does not have life" (1 John 5:11-12).

"Precious in the sight of the LORD is the death of his saints" (Psalm 116:15).

She awakens to the sound of hatchets below, but the iron door to the keep remains firm. She looks out her tower window for rescuers to come, but all she sees is fire ablaze in the citadel below. No more screams or noises come from the passageway, but a strange roar thunders in the distance. The smell of smoke grows stronger as her eyes begin to burn. The stone walls warm and the room fills with haze. Suddenly, a burst of flame shoots across the ceiling like a bolt of lightning out of the wood. The heat of the flames makes the air unbearable, and she runs to the window—fighting with the smoke for air to consume. Fiery boards from the ceiling begin to fall as she slumps down below the window. As she gasps and closes her eyes, beautiful divine arms appear and a gentle voice whispers, "Keep your eyes on me." She sobs through her choking, "But I can't do this, I'm frightened." "Focus on me and I will carry you across," the voice says. As soon as she jumps into the arms, she opens her eyes into Paradise.

As Paul waited in that foul, lowest, underground cell, no rescue came for him. There was no earthquake, or door swinging open for escape. But, even in the deepest, darkest cistern, the Sovereign King of the universe was *there* with him. Riding in the back of the cart to the Appian way, with his hands and feet bound, the Good Shepherd's arms were around Paul. Stepping up to the executioner's block knowing his physical life was about to be stopped, the Resurrection and the Life was *there* with Paul. In the instant of death, the Lord of Heaven and earth received Paul's spirit with the greatest Joy, and angels carried him to Paradise (Luke 16:22; John 10:11,11:25; Acts 20:24).

> But the Lord stood by me and strengthened me, so that through me the message might be fully proclaimed and all the Gentiles might hear it. So I was rescued from the lion's mouth. The Lord will rescue me from every evil deed and bring me safely into his heavenly kingdom. To him be the glory forever and ever. Amen (2 Timothy 4:17-18).

Why did the Lord not send a chariot of fire for Paul? Why not an angel with a rescue rope? Why did Paul get his head chopped off for teaching the gospel of Jesus Christ? Why? The answer is not your business. Paul was not executed one moment earlier than the Lord allowed, and *the time of Paul's death is not your business.*

The time of your death is not your business.

When in all humility you surrender your Fears to the Sovereign King of the universe, you are saying, "I trust you completely with the time of my death." Can you use your brain, problem solve, study the Word, look for doors to open, and still let *Him* decide the outcomes? Paul did.

Your surrender in death is as a beloved daughter leaping fearlessly into the arms of a completely adoring Father, who whispers in your ear, "You bring me so much Joy!" Because He has always cared for you, your faith in Him is resolute. As He breathed life into you at conception, He is there to receive it when you are translated. He will not only grasp you securely, but carry you safely and Joyfully to your new home. "Fear not, I am the first and the last, and the living one" (Rev. 1:17b-18a).

When you were a child, you had to step back and let your parents handle things beyond your capabilities. As God's children, you must step back and let Him handle your dying Journey. Can you imagine what the embrace of the Lord will feel like? As Jesus' triumph over the grave was the most glorious moment of His life, *can the moment of your translation in death be the most glorious moment of all your living?* Can you give up control of your *passage* to the Father that you know? Can you give up control of your *living* to the Father that you know?

Making this passage without Jesus, to a place of eternal separation from Him is the worst thing that can happen to you (John 11:25). Leaving your pride behind and placing your soul into His arms, humbly says, "I have no will, but your will." *Paul voluntarily surrendered his spirit to the Lord*, not to *Caesar.* Remember, history accounts that every one of the apostles was killed as a martyr except John.[1] Perhaps you will die defending the Cause as they did, or perhaps frail and elderly having lived a long and faithful life. Whatever brings you to the moment of death, God will provide you *His strength* for the safe passage over. "[B]lessed are the dead who die in the Lord" (Rev. 14:13).

If you were the only human on this planet, Jesus would have suffered and died for you, so that you *get* to be with Him in *eternal glory.* He cradles you in life and in death in His world-encompassing hands of Love.

> For I am already being poured out as a drink offering, and the time of my departure has come. I have fought the good fight, I have finished the race, I have kept the faith. Henceforth there is laid up for me the *crown of righteousness*, which the Lord, the righteous judge, will award to me on that Day, and not only to me but also to all who have loved his appearing (2 Timothy 4:6-8). *[Emphases added]*

A CROWN OF LIFE

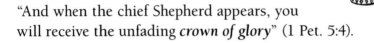

"Be faithful unto death, and I will give you the *crown of life*" (Rev. 2:10b).

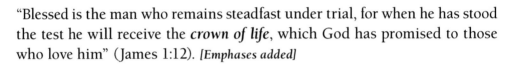

"And when the chief Shepherd appears, you will receive the unfading *crown of glory*" (1 Pet. 5:4).

"Blessed is the man who remains steadfast under trial, for when he has stood the test he will receive the *crown of life*, which God has promised to those who love him" (James 1:12). *[Emphases added]*

Will you walk slowly as a chorus of angels sings praise to the Lamb? Will the heavenly aisle be lined with all the smiling faithful who have come before you? Will the sanctuary presence of the Lord be so beautiful it will be the essence of overwhelming Joy? Will your tattered cloak of responsibility now be of the lightest spun silk? For your whole life, you have been preparing for this moment to kneel before the Sovereign King. Will He place a crown of glory on your head and say, "Rise daughter of the Lord, enter in!" Will His Joyful arms then embrace you as the angels rejoice? (Eph. 1:12-14; Matt. 25:21).

A real crown is made of solid gold and precious jewels. It barely resembles the plastic tiara of childhood. It is weighty and filled with responsibility and you must stand straight and tall to balance it on your head. Your spiritual crown will be glorious and fit for the heavenly work you will do—praising the Lamb! On earth or in the heavenly realm, your Divine purpose remains: to live as a Heroine-servant, at the feet of the King of Kings and Lord of Lords (Psalm 24).

In all humility, I hope to see the true scene one day, as now I can only imagine it. I know that a crown awaits you if you will keep from Fear and walk in Joy!

> [K]nowing that he who raised the Lord Jesus will raise us also with Jesus and bring us with you into his presence. For it is all for your sake, so that as grace extends to more and more people it may increase thanksgiving, to the glory of God. So we do not lose heart. Though our outer self is wasting away, our inner self is being renewed day by day. For this light momentary affliction is preparing for us an eternal weight of glory beyond all comparison, as we look not to the things that are seen but to the things that are unseen. For the things that are seen are transient, but the things that are unseen are eternal (2 Corinthians 4:14-18).

FEARBREAKER-JOYMAKER JOURNEY

As a young girl, Victoria's life was dominated by the controlling, political ambitions of others. Amidst the turbulence, she records in her diary a very simple vow, "I will be good."[2] During her life as the longest reigning monarch of the British Empire, Queen Victoria took that vow seriously and brought a level of morality and social reform never before experienced, into English society.

Envision the detonation within the world if every blood-bought Christian made the vow—"I will be useful to the Lord. I will not be bound by a life of Fear" (Psalm 61:5). If the Cause of Christ became your priority, your Divine purpose in glorifying Him would change your world. As a devoted Queen puts the needs of her people ahead of her own, raise up within yourself the desire to live in *honor* before the Lord.

- Know that you must deal with your Fears or they control you.
- Remember how important you are to the Cause.
- Fall in Love with the Word of God and its power to change lives.
- Embrace Reality by learning your power and limits.
- Build your courage by making small good choices.
- Live each day as a *worker* for the Lord.
- Believe the Lord rejoices in your Integrity.
- Train your spirit to be filled with Love and Joy, knowing that *this part of you is eternal and goes on to live forever.*
- Be thankful in everything. Live in Gratitude for every moment, trial, morsel, and blessing, knowing that *He is completely in charge.*

In earthly knighthood ceremonies, the one being honored is given a surname of their qualifications such as, "Phillip the Just," or "Catherine the Good." What will you be known for? _____ daughter of the Lord and servant? As every spirit lives eternally ever after, where will you spend it? How will this part of your life story end? "And she lived Joyfully ever after . . ."

"Now to him who is able to keep you from stumbling and to present you blameless before the presence of his glory with great joy, to the only God, our Savior, through Jesus Christ our Lord, be glory, majesty, dominion and authority, before all time and now and forever. Amen" (Jude 24-25).

GROWING THROUGH FEAR

1. Our culture is afraid of being old, sick, and useless. How can you prepare to be useful to the Lord in every season of your life?

2. We feel Fear when we do not understand how important we are to the Lord. If Jesus is preparing Heaven for you, how valuable are you? (John 14:1-3).

3. As you became a saint when you obeyed the Lord, what area of your life do you need to grow in, to reflect your status? (1 Tim. 5:10; Jude 1:3; Gal. 3:27).

4. Discuss this: On this one-way Journey, in the dying process and in glory, I am the breathing child of Jesus Christ.

5. Take a moment and write your own obituary.

6. At the moment of your last breath, will you jump with your arms wide open? Will you live today with your arms wide open?

Notes

Chapter One

[1] http://www.cyberhymnal.org/htm/a/m/a/amazing_grace.htm

[2] http://www.seekfind.net/Bible_Dictionary_Define_phobeo_Definition_
of_phobeo.html

[3] Daniel Goleman, *Emotional Intelligence* (New York: Bantam Books, 1994) pg. 16

[4] http://blogs.psychcentral.com/mindfulness/2010/03/neuroplasticity-the-
good-the-bad-and-the-ugly/

[5] http://www.psychologytoday.com/articles/200306/our-brains-negative-
bias

[6] Gerald G. Jampolsky, *Love is Letting Go of Fear* (Berkeley: Celestial Arts, 1979) pg. 18

Chapter Two

[1] http://www.christiancourier.com/articles/939-why-do-natural-
disasters-happen

[2] http://www.christiancourier.com/articles/258-our-universe-a-
great-machine

[3] http://www.christiancourier.com/articles/105-a-study-of-divine-
providence

[4] Letter to Joseph C. Cabell, January 22, 1820

[5] http://www.withagratefulheart.com/2009/02/master-tempest-is-
raging.html

Chapter Three

[1] William Barclay, *Acts of the Apostles The New Daily Bible Series* (Louisville: Westminster John Knox Press, 1975) pg. 82

[2] http://www.christiancourier.com/articles/623-nero-caesar-and-the-christian-faith

[3] Viktor E. Frankl, *Man's Search for Meaning* (New York: Pocket Books, 1946) pg. 25

[4] http://www.christiancourier.com/articles/1540-a-history-of-the-baptism-apostasy

Chapter Four

[1] http://poptop.hypermart.net/howdied.html

[2] http://www.christiancourier.com/articles/1000-a-subtle-argument-for-bible-inspiration

[3] http://en.wikipedia.org/wiki/Bible_translations_by_language foot http://simple.wikipedia.org/wiki/Bible

[4] http://www.preteristarchive.com/Books/1976_robinson_redating-testament.html

[5] http://www.christiancourier.com/articles/575-bible-accuracy

[6] http://www.esvbible.org/search/brothers/Philippians

[7] http://www.squidoo.com/corrie-ten-boom

Chapter Five

[1] Steve Farrar, *How to Ruin Your Life by 40* (Chicago: Moody Publishers, 2006) pg. 107

[2] http://www.cyberhymnal.org/htm/j/u/justasam.html

Chapter Six

[1] http://www.history.com/videos/secrets-of-body-language-part-1#secrets-of-body-language-part-1

[2] http://www.ehow.com/how_5311172_detect-micro-expressions.html

[3] Jim Collins, *Good to Great* (New York: Harper Collins, 2001) pg. 39

Chapter Seven

[1] http://www.ehow.com/about_5525742_negative-effects-alcoholism-american-society.html

[2] http://www.alcoholism-and-drug-addiction-help.com/statistics-on-alcoholism.html

[3] http://www.cnn.com/2010/HEALTH/11/01/alcohol.harm/index.html

[4] http://www.christiancourier.com/articles/308-what-about-moderate-social-drinking

[5] http://www.familysafemedia.com

[6] http://en.wikipedia.org/wiki/Sex_in_the_American_Civil_War

[7] David Bercot, *Will the Real Heretics Please Stand Up* (Anderson, PA: Scroll Publishing 1989) pg. 29

[8] http://earlychurch.com/ModestDress.php

[9] Bercot 31

Chapter Eight

[1] http://www.swartzentrover.com/cotor/Bible/Doctrines/ Holiness/ Drugs%20&%20Alcohol/Wine-Drinking%20in%20New%20 Testament%20Times.html

[2] http://www.christiancourier.com/articles/220-what-about-social-drinking-and-the-old-testament

[3] Artwork by Lin Na Lau-Kan

[4] Frankl 86

[5] Joan Borysenko, *It's not the End of the World* (New York City: Hay House, Inc., 2009) 58

[6] Borysenko 56

[7] Frankl 126

[8] Frankl 97

[9] Borysenko 25–26

[10] http://www.vision.org/visionmedia/depression-trauma-resilience/ 5816.aspx

[11] Frankl 75–76

[12] Frankl 63–64

Chapter Nine

[1] Frankl 42

[2] Frankl 93

[3] http://www.suntimes.com/business/5979189-420/americans-watching-more-tv-thanks-to-mobile-devices-internet.html

[4] http://www.psychologytoday.com/articles/200306/our-brains-negative-bias

[5] http://greatergood.berkeley.edu/article/item/the_neuroscience_of_ happiness/

[6] http://shorterdesigns.com/prayercoach/2009/11/29/thank-you-for-the-fleas-about-corrie-ten-boom/

Chapter Ten

[1] http://healthybodydaily.com/dr-oz/healthy-eating/dr-oz-wild-blueberries-black-currants-muscadine-grapes-cancer-fighting-foods

[2] http://citizensagainstproobamamediabias.wordpress.com/2009/01/26/us-air-flight-1549-flight-crew/

[3] Borysenko 53

[4] http://www.livestrong.com/article/359624-obesity-history-in-america/

[5] http://www.forbes.com/2007/02/07/worlds-fattest-countries-forbeslife-cx_ls_0208worldfat_2.html

[6] http://bigfatindustries.com/scary.html

[7] http://www.lifeclinic.com/fullpage.aspx?prid=529099&type=1

[8] http://www.voanews.com/english/news/usa/Study-Says-Preventable-Diseases-Reduce-US-Life-Expectancy--90233817.html

[9] http://www.beliefnet.com/Health/2009/05/Super-Foods-of-the-Bible.aspx

[10] Bercot 31

[11] Amishi Jha, PhD, American Psychological Association *Emotion* 2010, Vol. 20. No. 1: pp. 54–64

[12] http://well.blogs.nytimes.com/210/07/07/your-brain-on-exercise/ Unstuck: Your Guide to the Seven Stage Journey out of Depression

[13] http://www.lipidworld.com/content/3/1/25

[14] http://www.chalicebridge.com/FasciaMem-Pg6-Theory.html

[15] Article Source: http://EzineArticles.com/3242213http://ezinearticles.com/?How-Can-a-Fake-Smile-Produce-Health-and-Avoid-Stress?&id=3242213

[16] Aparna Labroo, PHd , Iris W. Hung, PhD, *Journal of Consumer Research* 2011, Vol. 37 April 2011: 1046

[17] http://www.unc.edu/news/archives/apr05/lighttherapy040405

Chapter Eleven

[1] Geneen Roth, *When Food is Love* (New York: Dutton Books, 1989) pg. 205

[2] http://www.hymnary.org/hymn/HHOF1980/311

Chapter Twelve

[1] http://www.metrolyrics.com/the-great-pretender-lyrics-the-platters.html
[2] http://www.menstuff.org/issues/byissue/infidelitystats.html
[3] www.sciencedaily.com/releases/2002/06/020611070813.htm
[4] http://guweb2.gonzaga.edu/againsthate/journal3/GHS110.pdf p. 52
[5] http://en.wikipedia.org/wiki/Robber%27s_Cave_study

Chapter Thirteen

[1] http://poptop.hypermart.net/howdied.html
[2] http://www.fullbooks.com/Queen-Victoria1.html

Bibliography

Barclay, William. *The New Daily Study Bible: The Acts of the Apostles.*
  Louisville: Westminster John Knox Press, 1975 .

Barclay, William. *The New Daily Study Bible: The Gospel of John* Vol. 2.
  Louisville: Westminster John Knox Press, 1975.

Barclay, William. *The New Daily Study Bible: The Gospel of Luke.* Louisville:
  Westminster John Knox Press, 1975.

Barclay, William. *The New Daily Study Bible: The Gospel of Mark.*
  Louisville: Westminster John Knox Press, 1975.

Barclay, William. *The Daily Study Bible Series: The Letters to the Philippians,
  Colossians, and Thessalonians.* Philadelphia: The Westminster Press,
  1975.

Barclay, William. *The Daily Study Bible Series: The Letters to Timothy, Titus
  and Philemon.* Philadelphia: The Westminster Press, 1975.

Bercot, David W. *Will the Real Heretics Please Stand Up.* Anderson, PA:
  Scroll , 1989.

Bingham, John P. *Inner Treasure.* Pecos, NM: Dove, 1989.

Borysenko, Joan. *It's not the End of the World.* New York City: Hay House,
  Inc., 2009.

Bunyan, John. *Pilgrim's Progress.* Lansing: Matthew Bookstore, 1678.

Cloud, Henry and John Townsend. *How People Grow*. Grand Rapids: Zondervan, 2001.

Frankl, Viktor E. *Man's Search for Meaning*. New York: Pocket Books, 1946.

Goleman, Daniel. *Emotional Intelligence*. New York: Bantam Books, 1994.

Jackson, Wayne. *A New Testament Commentary*. Stockton: Christian Courier Publications, 2011.

Jackson, Wayne. *Rejoice With Me*. Stockton: Christian Courier Publications, 2007.

Jackson, Wayne. *The Acts of the Apostles*. Stockton: Christian Courier Publications, 2005.

Jampolsky, Gerald G. *Love is Letting Go of Fear*. Berkeley: Celestial Arts, 1979.

Spain, Carl. *The Letters of Paul to Timothy and Titus*. Austin: Sweet, 1970.

Roth, Geneen. *When Food is Love*. New York: Dutton Books, 1989.

The Holy Bible. English Standard Version, Wheaton: Good News, 2001.

Winkler, Wendell. *Heart Diseases and Their Cure*. Hurst, TX: Winkler, 1972.

CPSIA information can be obtained at www.ICGtesting.com
Printed in the USA
LVOW070718140512

281589LV00001B/4/P